EXECUTIVE'S PORTFOLIO
OF
BUSINESS LETTERS

EXECUTIVE'S PORTFOLIO
OF
BUSINESS LETTERS

Bernardine Bermingham Cahill

PRENTICE-HALL, INC.
ENGLEWOOD CLIFFS, NEW JERSEY

Prentice-Hall International, Inc., *London*
Prentice-Hall of Australia, Pty, Ltd., *Sydney*
Prentice-Hall Canada, Inc., *Toronto*
Prentice-Hall of India Private, Ltd., *New Delhi*
Prentice-Hall of Japan, Inc., *Tokyo*
Prentice-Hall of Southeast Asia Pte., Ltd., *Singapore*
Whitehall Books, Ltd., Wellington, *New Zealand*
Editora Prentice-Hall do Brazil Ltda., *Rio de Janeiro*

© 1985 *by*

Prentice-Hall, Inc.

Library of Congress Cataloging in Publication Data

Cahill, Bernardine, B.
  Executive's portfolio of business letters.

  Includes index.
  1. Commercial correspondence.   I. Title.
HF5726.C14   1985   658.4'53   85-9485

ISBN 0-13-294232-1

Printed in the United States of America

Dedication

Executive's Portfolio of Business Letters is dedicated to my husband, Jim, to my family and to the Dominicans of Sinsinawa, Wisconsin.

About the Author

Bernardine Bermingham Cahill heads CAHILL ASSOCIATES, Wordwrights. For several years, she has been researching ways to improve communications in the workplace. The next project is planned to address oral communication skills.

Mrs. Cahill brings to the EXECUTIVE'S PORTFOLIO OF BUSINESS LETTERS a gifted style of informal writing. Her handling of words and her understanding of the need for a book of instant letters with word processor application are the results of her experience in the world of business. In addition to the text of this book, Mrs. Cahill has written, *How to Tighten Your Credit and Collection Methods* and *Model Collection Letters,* published by Prentice-Hall, Inc. Other writing includes user information for computer ordering systems, product information and marketing/sales letters.

CAHILL ASSOCIATES, Wordwrights includes: Dianne Cahill Morr, Mary Denise Cahill O'Hale, James J. Cahill, Jr., Thomas B. Cahill and Steven M. Jefferson.

Acknowledgments

It would not have been possible to prepare a text of the length and scope of *Executive's Portfolio of Business Letters* without the help of many generous persons who believed in my ability. I want to acknowledge each contributor and express my gratitude to members of the business firms and to the individuals listed below.

Business Firms:

The Ambassador East Hotel, Chicago Convention and Tourism Bureau, The Coca-Cola Company, Commonwealth Edison Company, Executive Resumes, Fine Arts Engraving Company, Group One Associates, IDA Ireland, Jewel Stores, Management Consultants, M.C.I., National Community Services, Natural Gas Pipeline of America, The Palmer House, R. J. Reynolds Industries, Salt Delivery Service, Security Pacific National Bank, T. Rowe Price Funds, Trans World Airlines, Wang Laboratories, Inc., Western Energy Company

Individuals:

Gloria Brennan, Rosemary Coughlin, Rita Joyce Downs, Catherine Jacobs, Steve Jefferson, Paul Lazar, La Vergne Novak, Barbara Pinsof, Eileen O'Hara, Robert D. Schalk, Rosemary Schoenberger, Garrett P. Walters

Twenty-Five Ways the
Executive's Portfolio of Business Letters
Will Help You

The *Executive's Portfolio of Business Letters* is unique. The portfolio is designed to enable you to pinpoint, with a minimum of searching, the sample letters that address your need. This comprehensive portfolio provides broad coverage to serve as a handy resource to all the business letters the executive must write.

Here are the many ways the *Executive's Portfolio of Business* Letters will help you:

- Are you preparing a bid for submission? Section 1, Letter 2, will show you how.

- If you are trying to explain your pride in your product and your service to a customer who is being wooed by a competitor, use Section 1, Letter 5, for a guide. It is forceful and honest. Every entrepreneur should study this letter to learn how to sell his/her product or service with pride.

- The Letters of Direction in Section 3, Letters 14 and 15, will save you hours of work. They are well written, legally sound.

- When you ask for credit information, use Section 3, Letter 3. To respond to a request for credit information, use Letter 4.

- Do not work half the night trying to write a land trust agreement. Refer to Section 3, Letter 13. It has been written for you.

- Residential mortgage loan letters? Of course; they are in Section 4.

- Whether you are hiring, firing, managing, or promoting, you will find a letter answering your personnel needs in Sections 12 through 23.

- Do you want to establish a job performance policy? Use the letters in Section 12. They will set it up for you.

- Termination letters are hard to write. Use Section 17. The letters have been written for you.

- How to handle an unfair accusation of discrimination is illustrated for you in Section 13. You will see how to answer such charges and exactly how detailed your response must be to prove you are in compliance.

- When you are ready to improve communications within your company to increase production or improve morale, turn to Section 20. The letters are exactly what you are looking for.

- Do some employees wander in late and leave early? Use Section 20, Letter 10, and Section 21, Letter 1. They will solve this problem.

- Read Section 25, Letter 2. You can use this for an answer when someone tries to shave your fees.

- Has one of your employees been approached by a sharpie who suggests working without a contract? Section 25, Letter 3, has the answer.

- When you want to devote time to the care and feeding of your sales representatives, the letters in Section 25 will help you do this expediently.

- Have you been agonizing over how to reassign territories? Turn to Section 26. It handles this task for you.

- Section 31, Letter 1, is a purchasing policy statement that will show you how to set guidelines to protect your company against unauthorized buying. This will cut your losses if you now find improper use of company buying privileges.

- If your computer service company is not fulfilling your needs, write a letter. Use Section 32, Letter 1.

- When things go wrong, write. Section 32 has letters of complaint for you and letters of response if you receive complaints.

- Letters of request for information are ready for you to use in Section 34. You also will find letters to reply to those who ask you for information.

- Merchandise late or damaged in delivery? Use the letter in Section 35 to handle the delivery problems you encounter every day.

- Collection, collection, collection. If this is keeping you awake at night, turn to Section 38. You will find letters designed to collect your money and keep your customers.

- Send a letter to tell your preferred customers of a special discount. Use Section 41, Letter 6.

- Are you planning a sales meeting, company seminar, or trade show? Use the letters in Section 44 through 48. Things will go more smoothly if you use the preplanning letters to avoid problems.

- Do you want to give power of attorney to someone when you plan to be away on a trip? Section 49, Letter 12, will set it up.

Bernardine B. Cahill

How to Use This Book

To facilitate finding a letter quickly, the Letter Locator is provided in the front of the book. The Letter Locator is a cross-index file arranged by subject to allow you to zero in on the material you want without turning pages.

The section of the book and the number of the letter within the section are given. You only need to locate your area of interest, find your topic, and turn directly to the page. The sample letter is there for you to use as presented or to serve as a base that you adapt to your circumstance.

Another unique feature of the *Executive's Portfolio of Business Letters* is the use of a code name for each letter. The codes are provided to identify the letters for entry and retrieval of material when using a word processor. The codes in this text consist of only four characters to enable the user to personalize each letter or document with initials, date or department designation. Use of a word processor and instant letters for correspondence saves you time and assures you of the same quality of communication whether you or a member of your company writes a letter. This standardization of your correspondence will enhance your company image and give you control of your company policy no matter whose signature is on the letter.

CONTENTS

Contents

BOOK 2: PERSONNEL LETTERS GUARANTEED TO MAKE YOUR JOB EASIER

BOOK 3: LETTERS TO HELP
IN THE CARE AND FEEDING OF YOUR SALES FORCE

LETTER LOCATOR

| B | O | O | K | | 1 |

PROVEN LETTERS TO PROTECT YOUR INTERESTS IN CONTRACTS, REAL ESTATE, AND FINANCIAL MATTERS

SECTION 1:   PUT IT IN WRITING

"Put it in writing." This has always been good advice, today it is even more necessary than before. Whenever you are having a discussion, there are at least three conversations taking place: what is said, what is heard, and what is meant. In addition, since business is carried on today on an international basis and you may be trading across continents and across cultures, you should clarify every detail of a business transaction in which there is a possibility of misunderstanding or misinterpretation.

All contracts for goods that amount to more than $500.00 should be confirmed in writing according to Article II of the Uniform Commercial Code. If later there is a legal dispute as a result of an oral contract, it is your word against your adversary's. For this reason alone, you should lock in all of the details regarding price, performance, dates, rates of interest, delivery, discount, guarantee, warranty, or whatever makes your agreement work for your protection.

A brief, clearly written letter of agreement, outlining the terms of sale or performance, including all points bargained for during the conversation of an oral contract, is binding in a legal dispute.

Points to Remember

- Always protect your interests.
- Whether you are the buyer or the seller, confirm the terms of sale.
- When you are selling a service or hiring a service company, verify the terms of performance.
- If you do not know the name of the individual to whom you can address a letter, write to the president of the firm. A letter will always find its way down. It seldom finds its way up.

2

LETTER OF AGREEMENT
LOA1

Dear Ms. Christopher:

This is to confirm that you have been hired to write a six- to twelve-page, doubled-spaced article on Tess Pet Food's use and application of Wang systems. You will be paid $550.00 upon my receipt of the following: the article, photos of the equipment in use at the company and the insignia or name of the company on a building or sign, and a completed photo release form and captions for the pictures. In addition, you should submit verifying receipts when billing for related expenses incurred while on the assignment. Any extraordinary out-of-pocket expenses related to the article should be discussed with me and approved prior to incurring them. The article should be submitted no later than thirty days after the interview has taken place.

You will be paid another $100 upon my receipt of a copy of the article containing the signature of an authorized representative of the company indicating that he or she has reviewed the article and agrees that the information presented is accurate and reflects the material covered in the interview.

All stories will be considered works for hire. Once I receive the story, it becomes the sole property of Wang Laboratories and its disposition from that point on will be left to the discretion of Wang Laboratories.

Please call if I can be of assistance to you on any phase of the assignment.

Sincerely,

Dick Gauthier
Publicity/Public Relations
Specialist

DG 0621A

BID INFORMATION
BINF

Dear Mr. Longo:

This letter is to confirm our telephone conversation during which you expressed interest in submitting a quote for a die to be used by our company in the performance of a multimillion-dollar subcontract for the Federal Government.

In order to conform with General Widget's required bid procedure and to ensure that sufficient technical information is supplied to you, we request that the following outline, which you and I discussed, be followed precisely:

1. All questions and requests for additional information are to be submitted, in writing to my attention, by March 8, 198—. Your questions will be answered, in writing, by March 25, 198—.

2. Your firm bid must be received in my office at General Widget, in a sealed envelope, by noon on April 5, 198—. No verbal quotations will be accepted at any time.

3. Include with your firm quotation the following information:

    a. A short description of your company and its capability.
    b. Previous experience in machining this type of high-temperature die.
    c. At least one company reference for whom you have machined this type of die in the past.
    d. Suggested material(s) of construction.
    e. A brief list of the major manufacturing steps involved.
    f. Whether any portion of the production operation will be farmed out to another shop.
    g. The number of weeks required to produce this die.

Thank you for your cooperation.

LETTER OF AGREEMENT—CONFIRMATION
LAC1

Dear Mr. Wallace:

It was a pleasure to talk to you today, and I am happy to know that you have decided to accept our bid of $7,550.00 for the cleaning and decorating of your offices. Mr. Steve Jefferson will be crew manager on the job site, and I invite you to call him if you have any questions regarding the work to be done. He is available at 000–0000 after 4:00 P.M..

This letter will confirm our conversation about some of the logistics of the decorating and how it will affect the operation of your business during our work.

We plan to have our crew start to work in the offices of the senior partners after 5 P.M. on Friday, May 13, 198—, and be out before Monday, May 16, 198—, at 8 A.M. This will have the offices ready for the occupants to begin work at 9 A.M. without any disruption.

The work will include:

1. Painting all walls, ceilings, doors, and woodwork with one coat of Dover white latex paint.

2. Steam cleaning all office carpeting and washing all floor tile in outer office.

3. Cleaning and polishing all office furniture and cabinets.

4. Moving and replacing office furniture and cabinets.

5. Clean-up and removal of all debris; leaving the offices ready for business.

6. All work to be of professional quality and done in a neat, orderly fashion.

Our work crews, including clean-up personnel, are bonded. However, we expect that your office personnel will remove anything of value and carry typewriters, adding machines, and other portable office equipment to the office vault as they are accustomed to doing when they leave on Friday evening. If they follow this ordinary procedure, our crew will not be delayed by handling personal property nor will they inadvertently misplace office equipment.

We look forward to serving you and know that you will enjoy the freshness and beauty of your offices when our work is complete.

If I can be of assistance, please do not hesitate to call again.

Sincerely,

LETTER OF AGREEMENT—CONFIRMATION
LAC2

Dear Dianne:

We are glad to learn that you will be available to work on our new brochure. As a follow-up to the conversation you had yesterday with Charmaine, I would like to confirm some of the facets of the material we want to include.

You will be paid $200.00 a page for the copy, which should not be more than six pages. In addition, you will be paid $200.00 per day for approximately two days during which you will interview selected members of our staff and tour our company. If the interviews run into a third day because members of our staff are not available as scheduled, you will be paid for a full day at the $200.00 rate even if you do not put in a full day.

The copy for the brochure will include: a short history of our company, highlights of our manufacturing process, research and development, automated order filling, new products, and customer service policy. You will not be responsible for the photography. Charmaine will work with your copy and submit photos based on the material.

As always, we will appreciate your ideas and suggestions. Welcome aboard.

Sincerely,

LETTER OF CLARIFICATION
LOC1

Dear Mr. Blank:

I am pleased that we had the chance last week to talk about your engraving requirements. Certainly none of your concerns should go unanswered. Any time a problem arises concerning the relationship between your firm and ours, it is advisable to put it all on the table and let the two of us deal with it.

There were several subjects raised in our conversation that I feel warrant clarification. I feel strongly about them, and I want no misunderstandings to arise regarding them.

You mentioned that you can purchase the "exact same letterhead and related items, business cards, envelopes, etc." from another vendor, an all-purpose supply company (with whom I am familiar) and that this company could supply these requirements at a lower price while using a design and format that you feel is superior. Also, you mentioned that this company, although not "yet" in Chicago, has some sort of clever way, through volume possibly, of keeping cost down—hinting that the major reason we have been successful is that we have some sort of specialty in this market.

Unless someone has been misled, or is misleading you, your office cannot possibly purchase that "exact same letterhead" with regard to paper, service, or quality. There are several reasons for this. The first reason is the paper. It is 24# Antique White Wove Crane's Distaff Linen with a private watermark that matches exactly with the typography engraved on the heading of the letterhead. In addition, the watermark is placed in a specific position on each 8½ × 11 sheet, at an extra cost. That paper, made this way, is available in 10,000 lb. quantities. This means that 600,000 sheets of 8½ × 11 and 200,000 #10 size envelopes per year with a 5,000 lb. minimum order thereafter must be purchased. Surely you can see that these requirements far exceed your office's needs for several years.

In addition to these stiff paper purchasing requirements, a dandy roll that is used to custom watermark the paper had to be purchased at an initial cost of $1,000.00. That dandy roll is not available for indiscriminate use, since it is the property of Chicago Paper Company, a major Chicago-based distributor of Crane papers in the Midwest. The three of us jointly paid for it in order to spread the cost out among the three people most involved. Anyone who leads you to believe that they can sell you the exact same paper in lesser quantities, with the same watermark, at the same price, is completely wrong. This paper situation is only a minor part of the overall picture, but I feel that it is a relevant one.

The second reason is our service. Our program for servicing the needs of your firm was carefully established in total harmony with management and there are no accidents or secrets involved. Our quality, attention, performance, and service have proved to be a valuable part in the overall plan for excellence, professionalism, and prestige that we feel befits a firm of your stature.

The engraving plates used are artistically prepared from finished, approved artwork to the firm's exact type specification, then photomechanically etched to avoid hand-cut "versions" of the type on metal dies. They are then hard-chromed for protection and lasting quality.

We are a premium quality house, have been for sixty years, and our reputation rests with each of the millions of items shipped yearly. When your firm's items are engraved, they are carefully checked for quality, position (each item must match its corresponding item—page 1 letterhead with page 1 copy letterhead), and ink color. We are not interested in production to the exclusion of quality.

Each and every item is hand-inspected prior to shipping or putting into inventory. We make mistakes—all engravers and pressmen do—but our mistakes end up in the garbage bins, not on your clients' desks. We have in storage a three-month supply of already engraved stationery items your firm needs to operate. These items are insured and stored in a perfect humidity-controlled and air-conditioned environment that is as secure from theft or fire as humanly possible. They can be delivered to your storerooms within twenty-four hours of an order being placed.

Members of your office staff appreciate this program. They do not have to store these items. They can order any quantity they need, when they need it, and get it for the same price as if they ordered larger amounts. They know the value of not having to order these items three to four weeks in advance, the administrative time saved, and the ability to always have a perfect product, although custom made, delivered the next day. It takes twelve weeks to have the paper made!

The third reason is our quality. Compare closely the quality of our engraving to your previous letterhead. Our quality is far superior to what you have been getting. Make this comparison. Note the sharpness, clarity, and depth of each character . . . that's no small point. We really have a better way not only to make our plates, but to run our presses.

These many important reasons are why we were selected to be your firm's engraver many years ago. I can't tell you how proud we always have been of this relationship. Your firm's reputation for performance, leadership, knowledge, professionalism, dignity, and prestige is really unmatched in your profession. All of our employees react to your needs with enthusiasm and a genuine desire to please.

The design of your items has become your firm's trademark. Easily recognized as one of the finest letterhead, envelope, and business card designs in the country, these items have become the standard by which other firms' stationery is judged. This design was selected by your firm's management because it really reflects the dynamic, modern, and professional image for which your names stands. It <u>frames</u> your correspondence; it is your packaging. This package and this program are simply the finest I have ever seen.

I encourage you to take time to visit our company the next time you are in Chicago. What you will see is the cleanest, best equipped, best staffed, and best managed company in our field. Our apprentice training program is second to none, no small item in a craft such as ours. Meet our people; inspect our facilities and procedures. Only then will my words really mean something.

Engraving to us is not a loss leader to get in the front door in order to sell office supplies. Engraving is our profession and our life.

We want to continue to supply you with the finest products, reflecting your prestige, at the lowest possible cost. We sincerely hope that upon reflection, you will agree that we always have done so. And we look forward to continuing our valuable relationship for many years to come.

Very truly yours,
FINE ARTS ENGRAVING COMPANY

Joseph L. Fontana
President

LETTER OF REVIEW AND PROPOSAL
LORP

Dear Sirs:

We at Fine Arts want you to know that we appreciate, value, and are grateful for your fine engraving business. A trusting and mutually satisfying relationship has grown over the past several months between your firm and our company.

Toward keeping that fine relationship, we would like to review your account for the upcoming year and make some suggestions that we feel could possibly facilitate your ordering system for engraving.

1. We feel that the initiation of a semiannual order/run system is important. The system would begin in October incorporating changes on your full name letterhead and your city letterhead.

    All other items do not change during the year, so this would be an ideal opportunity to run all items.

    By using the semiannual order/run system, we will be able to offer you a better cost per thousand and assure you of never running short on any item at any time.

2. With the necessary lead time for the ordering of paper now at about ten weeks, the above system also gives us the opportunity to chart increases in paper requirements more easily.

    We know from experience that most paper companies raise prices in September. We propose to order your paper at the end of July, which will allow plenty of time to receive the paper and also take advantage of the lower price. Our price to you includes the storage, handling, and taxes of your private watermarked paper throughout the year.

3. It's important for you to be aware of where your firm's account stands at all times. For this reason, we will continue to send you a monthly statement of your use through Natalie's inventory cards.

    If the proposed semiannual order/run system is adopted, we will send you a letter stating quantities and the items that we plan to run for the next six months, as well as when and how much paper we are ordering for the next year.

    Also, a physical inventory will be taken by us every six months and the inventory cards updated. We would like you to come out, at least once a year, for an on-hand inspection of your items.

We are striving to give you the finest products at an equitable cost. We feel that these proposals will be mutually beneficial.

Sincerely,

EXPLAINING FREELANCE OFFER
EFLO

Dear Mr. Zentz:

Judith Dennen tells me you may be interested in our creating a feature article/press release on your organization's use of a Wang system.

The normal procedure in this case is for us to send one of our professional freelance writers to interview the appropriate personnel in your organization to gather sufficient background information to write the story. In addition, he or she may take a few photographs of our equipment in operation at your site.

You will, of course, have full editing privileges; we would not use the document for any purpose until you have reviewed it, made any necessary changes, and given us your written authorization to distribute it. Once we have your OK—and only then—we will attempt to place the story in computer-related publications and/or a few magazines or newspapers relevant to your own industry (perhaps you have some suggestions). Regardless of whether or not our placement efforts are successful, we also would use your story to produce a brochure that would be used by our sales force as a selling tool.

Please let me know whether this idea meets with your approval, and if so, when you might like to be contacted by the writer we would assign to the project. Thanks in advance for your consideration.

Yours truly,

Dick Gauthier
Publicity/Public Relations
Specialist

DG 1578D

SECTION 2: FINE ARTS ENGRAVING
SAMPLE LETTERS

1.	Letter Accompanying Quote—1	ACQ1
2.	Letter Accompanying Quote—2	ACQ2
3.	Letter Accompanying Samples—1	SAM1
4.	Letter Accompanying Samples—2	SAM2
5.	Sales Promotion Letter	SPRO

You cannot look at these exceptional samples of business letters without feeling the pride that the writer takes in his work. It is not coincidence that he sells engraved stationery. He wants his customers to know the special treatment that goes into every detail of producing a quality product.

Points to Remember

- Take care in each step of the preparation of your correspondence and use the finest materials available to you.

- Show your enthusiasm and your pride in your work.

- Let your client know that you want the order and that you will execute it to the best of your ability.

LETTER ACCOMPANYING QUOTE—1
ACQ1

Fine Arts Engraving Company

Dear Miss Anderson:

Thank you for the opportunity to quote on your firm's stationery and business cards. I agree that your design is especially suited to blind-embossing and the intaglio photoengraving process. It will not only compliment the design, it will make for a handsome stationery program.

The engraved plates that we produce are from presensitized copper, which enables us to duplicate exactly the artwork and type matter from which we start. The plates are then chromed for the durability that is needed to withstand the heat and pressure necessary in producing a quality final product. There is a one-time-only charge for plates with no copy changes.

A prestigious firm such as yours knows and appreciates superior quality and appearance. We at Fine Arts Engraving have established our name with a reputation of consistent service, quality, and personal attention, and hope you will give us the opportunity to establish a mutually beneficial working relationship.

Cordially,
FINE ARTS ENGRAVING COMPANY

Joseph L. Fontana
President

JLF/dld
Enclosures

LETTER ACCOMPANYING QUOTE—2
ACQ2

Dear Bill:

Again I wish to thank you for your hospitality and for allowing us to quote on your firm's engraving requirements.

As you know, we are currently the engravers on a national basis of similar programs for several major prestigious public accounting firms. We also are privileged to supply a virtual "Who's Who" of Midwest-based corporations, law firms, financial institutions, and professional organizations with their engraved stationery programs.

The reasons for our success in this field are that we give quality far superior to other engravers, and our procedures and service are extremely helpful. In addition, these organizations find that our location in the direct center of America's trucking network saves them money and time on freight shipments.

If, after considering our enclosed quotation, you feel as we do that Fine Arts could be a valuable supplier to your firm, please allow us to submit finished proofs of our quality on these items. All we would need is a few reams of your private watermarked paper sent from your stockroom.

Bill, we believe that a favorable decision on our proposal will prove to be a popular one. I sincerely hope to establish a mutually beneficial relationship.

If you have any questions on this quotation, please feel free to call me personally.

Very truly yours,
FINE ARTS ENGRAVING COMPANY

Joseph L. Fontana
President

JLF/dld
Enclosures

LETTER ACCOMPANYING SAMPLES—1
SAM1

Dear Mrs. Hickman:

We truly appreciate the circumstances that brought your inquiry to us at Fine Arts Engraving Company.

The implementation of your firm's new stationery program, completely following the guidelines set forth by your firm's management committee, will greatly enhance the appearance of these items.

We have the expertise, equipment, and personnel to be the ideal supplier of your firm's stationery. We know precisely how to accomplish the fine products your designer has visualized. We will not have to "go to school" at your expense. That would be the situation if a less experienced company were handling this program.

Please carefully examine the enclosed samples. The quality you see, the quality we will deliver to you, is unmatched in our industry.

Mrs. Hickman, after you have carefully read our quotation, would you be kind enough to pass on to me personally any questions you have? We are eager to please you because we sincerely want to receive your order.

Very truly yours,
FINE ARTS ENGRAVING COMPANY

Joseph L. Fontana
President

JLF/dld
Enclosures

LETTER ACCOMPANYING SAMPLES—2
SAM2

Dear Mr. Corcoran:

Thank you for this fine opportunity. We are certain that those executives who will receive the engraved stationery package will appreciate its superior quality. Engraving will improve your firm's image and add much prestige to your executive correspondence.

Our quotation is based on the use of two types of paper: (1) 70# Starwhite Text, which is now being used; and (2) 24# Fluorescent White Wove Crane's Crest, a 100% cotton-fiber bond paper, widely considered among the finest stationery paper that can be used.

On the business cards, we are quoting on two papers also: (1) 100# Vicksburg Solid Bristol, a bright white paper similar to Starwhite except slightly thinner and a better engraving sheet; and (2) Winsted Glo Brite Thin Plate, an 82½# business-card bristol with a 50% rag content for more snap.

We are quoting on quantities for seven (7) people, twenty-five (25) people, and forty (40) people—supplying 1,000 letterheads/envelopes and 500 business cards for each. Our quotation is on the next page.

If you have any questions regarding these prices, please don't hesitate to give me a call. We are most hopeful of receiving your business and of developing a long-term mutually satisfying relationship with your company.

Very truly yours,
FINE ARTS ENGRAVING COMPANY

Joseph L. Fontana
President

JLF/dld
Enclosure

**SALES PROMOTION LETTER
SPRO**

TO: THE MEMBERS OF THE ASSOCIATION OF LEGAL ADMINISTRATORS

THANK YOU FOR STOPPING BY OUR BOOTH

I know you're busy, so I'll be very brief!

Our company, Fine Arts Engraving, is the largest engraver in Chicago. We have the privilege of serving a virtual "Who's Who" of major law firms, public accounting firms, corporations, professional service organizations, and financial institutions. The reason for our unprecedented success is quite simple . . . far superior quality and service!

A careful inspection of the samples of our work will tell you more about us than all the fancy sales tools in the world could convey. These samples do not represent an endorsement or recommendation by the firms they represent but are displayed here to demonstrate our quality. We would encourage you to check with your peers at any of these organizations regarding our reputation and performance.

If you or your firm is currently receiving this type of quality from your engraver, we would encourage you to continue that relationship. If, on the other hand, you are not receiving this type of quality or are dissatisfied with the performance or attention your account is receiving, I would welcome the opportunity to speak with you about the many unique programs we have created to serve large and growing law firms.

Please contact me either here at the ALA Convention or at my office. I hope to be able to talk directly to you about your particular engraving program in the near future.

Respectfully yours,
FINE ARTS ENGRAVING COMPANY

Joseph L. Fontana
President

JLF/dld
3/81

SECTION 3:   COMMERCIAL LOAN LETTERS

1.	Cover Letter for Loan Application	CLIA
2.	Loan Request Letter	LOAN
3.	Asking for Credit Information	CRED
4.	Credit Information	CRIN
5.	Commercial Letter of Credit	CLOC
6.	Advising Letter of Credit Terms	LCRT
7.	Requesting Extension of Loan Commitment	REEX
8.	Agreement to Extend Pay-Off Date of Loan	EXPO
9.	Variation of Insurance Requirement	VARI
10.	Finder's Fee Agreement	FIND
11.	Loan Submission Letter	SUML
12.	Loan Commitment	LCOM
13.	Land Trust Agreement	LTAG
14.	Letter of Direction	LDIR
15.	Letter of Direction—2	LDR2

Whenever you are engaged in a business venture or are involved in the sale or purchase of property, you must protect your interests in every way possible. After the deal is made, it is too late to say that it is not perfectly clear. What you have signed is what you have agreed to do. These letters were prepared to give you a legally sound document to use as a basis whenever you are seeking or supplying a commercial loan.

Points to Remember

- Be aware of all of the pertinent information contained in your letters and documents.
- Do not assume that details are correct. Errors are costly.
- Make a checklist of the points that you wish to cover before you begin to write. Check each one off when your letter is complete.
- When a contract is presented for your signature, reread it before you sign.
- Do not orally agree to anything that differs from the document you sign. The written agreement is enforceable.

COVER LETTER FOR LOAN APPLICATION
CLIA

Dear Mr. Jones:

Thank you for the opportunity to meet with you and Mr. Brown on Thursday to discuss the loan we will need to expand our plant operation. As you instructed, we have prepared all of the documents.

We trust that when you have reviewed the information and projections, you will agree that this is the time for us to enlarge our plant to meet the needs of an expanding market.

Documents enclosed include:

1. Loan application

2. Financial statements for the past three years

3. Income tax returns as requested

4. Earnings projections after expansion

5. Inventory list

6. List of collateral

If you have any questions, please call me.

Cordially,

LOAN REQUEST LETTER
LOAN

Dear Mr. Jacoby:

Pursuant to our recent telephone conversation, I have prepared the documents you requested and I am sending them for your review.

We will need $1,250,000 to carry us through from the time we begin retooling until the first orders are filled and invoices paid.

We are sending you:

- A completed loan application
- Financial statements for the past five years
- Six financial references
- Sales and earnings projections
- Income tax returns of principals
- An inventory list
- A list of real estate, building, and production equipment to be used as collateral valued at $1,750,000.

Thank you very much for the effort you have made on our behalf. If there are any questions, or if you need further information, please contact me.

Very truly yours,

ASKING FOR CREDIT INFORMATION
CRED

Dear Sirs:

Mr. John R. Jones of Acme Manufacturing Company has applied for credit with our firm and has given Greater Savings Bank as reference.

We will be grateful to you for whatever information you furnish regarding Mr. Jones, and you can be sure that we will hold such information in strict confidence. For your convenience in preparing a reply, we are listing below some questions focusing on the answers we need to process this request for extension of credit.

How long has Mr. Jones been a customer of the bank?

Has his account been satisfactory?

What is the general area of the amount on deposit?

Have you extended credit to him? In what amount?

How were the payments handled?

How were the loans secured?

Would you extend credit to Mr. Jones again?

How do you rate the business relationship between Mr. Jones and the bank?

We would like to act on this application and will appreciate a prompt reply.

Sincerely,

CREDIT INFORMATION
CRIN

Dear Sirs:

John Jones has maintained a very satisfactory deposit account with this bank for about twelve years. Recent balances have averaged in five figures in the upper range.

Credit has been extended on numerous occasions with very satisfactory performances. Combined credit reached a high of medium seven figures in three instances. All credit was secured by real estate or supported by secure investment collateral.

Mr. Jones has been a very satisfactory bank customer, reliable in all of the transactions we have experienced with him. We highly value our relationship with him as a bank customer and as a member of this business community.

Sincerely,

COMMERCIAL LETTER OF CREDIT
CLOC

To: Greater Savings
                 100 Main Street
                 Hometown, ID

Beneficiary: John J. Dough
                 456 Cloud Street
                 EasyLife, ID

Date: September 1, 198_

COMMERCIAL LETTER OF CREDIT NUMBER 730

SUM NOT TO EXCEED_____

CREDIT TO EXPIRE_____

We hereby establish our Irrevocable Letter of Credit for John J. Dough. Drafts are not to be presented for collection unless payment is not made within usual terms. Drafts drawn under this credit must be marked with the above number and date and must be endorsed.

This letter of credit is to remain in effect until the unfinished portion of the building is completed, not to go beyond the date entered above.

The Letter of Credit is reducible upon leasing of the area at the rate of $5,000.00 per 500 square feet leased.

This credit shall be subject to the Uniform Customs and Practices for Documentary Credits Commerce Brochure No. 222.

Very truly yours,

ADVISING LETTER OF CREDIT TERMS
LCRT

Re: Cahill/Jones

Dear Ms. Green:

Greater Savings and Loan has informed us that a _____ Letter of Credit will be acceptable. The Letter of Credit is to remain in effect until the existing unfinished square footage has been completed. The Letter of Credit may be reduced in increments of five thousand dollars ($5,000) on the basis of each 500 square feet completed or the rental of the newly constructed area at ten dollars ($10) per square foot. If this is acceptable to your client, please have the documents executed and set up a closing date.

If you have any questions, please do not hesitate to contact the undersigned.

Very truly yours,

REQUESTING EXTENSION OF LOAN COMMITMENT
REEX

Re: James J. Johnson
Mortgage Loan on Property at
100 Main Street, Fairview, ID

Dear Mr. Green:

This morning I talked to attorney William White regarding the above property and he informed me that we would not be able to close on June 1, 198— as scheduled. There are several reasons for the delay, including the fact that the title Commitment Letter and Survey are not completed and the underwriting package is not complete.

We agreed to close on June 10, 198—. This will permit us to get all of the documents needed and will allow Messrs. Johnson and White to reschedule the closing at a mutually convenient time.

Will you please send me a formal letter extending Mr. Johnson's Loan Commitment until June 10, 198— as you agreed to do during our phone conversation?

First Federal holds the existing mortgage on the property and has agreed to the June 10 closing date for payoff.

Thanks very much for your cooperation. If there are any questions, please feel free to call me.

Very truly yours,

AGREEMENT TO EXTEND PAY-OFF DATE OF LOAN
EXPO

Re: James J. Johnson
Mortgage Loan #645804
Property Located at
100 Main Street, Fairview, ID

Dear Mr. Smith:

In reference to the amount required to pay off in full the loan on the above-referenced property, we have agreed to grant your client the extension he needs.

Upon receipt of the $425,000, Greater Savings will issue a release deed of the property. This figure has been extended from June 1, 198— until June 10, 198—, after which this settlement agreement will be null and void.

It is further agreed that this will be the final extension of the payoff of this mortgage.

Funds are to be deposited by wire transfer to —————— Bank for Greater Savings account #8900 and you are to notify Kathryn Brennan, accounting analyst.

Very truly yours,

VARIATION OF INSURANCE REQUIREMENT
VARI

Re: RESTFUL ACRES RESORT

Dear Mr. Wadsworth:

When preparing the documents for closing on the loan for this property, we discussed the amount of insurance called for in the Letter of Commitment. I am aware that it is usual to provide insurance in the amount of the loan, but since the value of this project is in the land, we ask for a variation on this requirement.

The property being developed will have a minimum of permanent buildings that can be destroyed by fire or damaged by campers. Therefore, we believe that a Certificate of Insurance of $500,000.00 and a Certificate of Liability in the amount of $5,000,000.00 should be sufficient security in this instance.

Please consider this variation of the Letter of Commitment terms and conditions and advise me of your decision.

Very truly yours,

Alternate Final Paragraph

If this variation is agreeable to you, please indicate your acceptance of these terms by signing on the line below and returning the original to my attention. The enclosed copy is for your file.

_____   _____
              Signature   Date

FINDER'S FEE AGREEMENT
FIND

Dear Mr. Dough:

This is a confirmation of our previous conversations during which we agreed:

Dough and Associates will compensate Better Financial, Inc., in the amount of 2% of the total loan amount of $1,000,000.00 provided by Greater Savings to Dough and Associates. This is payment for sourcing the capital needed by Dough and Associates and was incorporated into the pricing quote from Greater Savings.

A check for $2,000.00 will be provided by Dough and Associates and will be passed on to Better Financial, Inc., at the time of closing.

_____

George Hunter, President
Better Financial, Inc.

Accepted:

_____

John J. Dough
Dough and Associates

LOAN SUBMISSION LETTER
SUML

    Re: Oak Hills Office/Warehouse
           Oak Hills, OH 00000

Dear Mr. Wadsworth:

In confirmation of our recent conversations, we are sending the enclosed loan submission on the above-referenced building.

Please note that this proposed 35,000 square feet of office/warehouse building will contain 15,000 feet of finished office space. The building will be attractive, aesthetically harmonious with the other buildings in the immediate area, and will be located on the northeast corner of First and Jefferson streets. This is a very desirable location for this type of space.

This $1,750,000 is being offered as a construction loan for 9 months at 2% over the prime rate plus a 1% fee to Greater Savings. The loan will then convert to a permanent loan at 13.5% for 5 years on a 30-year amortization plus a 1½% fee to Greater Savings.

The borrowers, Messrs. Smith, Jones, and Brown, have a combined net worth of $6 million and annual incomes in excess of $400,000.

In summary, we think that this is a very sound loan offering with excellent real estate and a strong base.

Sincerely,

LOAN COMMITMENT
LCOM

    RE: Restful Acres RV Resort and Park

Dear Mr. O'Hale:

It is a pleasure to tell you that the First Mortgage Permanent Loan Application on the property described above has been approved by Greater Savings and Loan Association subject to the following conditions and terms:

Loan Amount:	$2,000,000
Borrower:	Restful Acres, an Illinois Limited Partnership, with Harry Thomas O'Hale and Mary Denise O'Hale as General Partners (80% ownership)

Security:	30.4 acres of real estate property, fully developed as a recreational vehicle resort with 458 R.V. sites plus permanent buildings erected on the property, a boat launching and boat rental business, complete with inventory as listed.
Loan Term:	20 years, 30-year amortization
Interest Rate:	14.5%
Payment Schedule:	Twelve monthly payments of $24,492.00 per month principal and interest. The balloon payment of balance due is the 240th payment.
Escrow:	Borrower will pay monthly payment for tax and insurance to lender as determined on an annual basis.
Loan Service Fee:	Borrower will pay Greater Savings and Loan a $30,000 fee at the time the commitment is accepted.
Interest Rate Adjustment:	On the 5th, 10th, and 15th anniversary dates of the loan, the interest rate for the next 5 years will be determined by adding 200 basis points to the current weekly auction rate for U.S. Treasury Six-Month Bills. If the adjusted rate is not acceptable to the borrower, the loan may be paid off within 60 days with no prepayment penalty.
Prepayment:	The loan may not be prepaid during the first 36 months of the loan term. After the 36th month, the loan may be prepaid subject to a 2% prepayment fee.
Assumption Privilege:	Borrower may sell the mortgaged property at any time during the term of the loan subject to the assumption of the loan. Lender will have the right to approve loan assumption and qualify the new buyer. There will be an assumption fee of 2%.
Due on Sale:	In the event Lender does not grant assumption of this loan to a new purchaser, this loan will be due on sale.

Insurance:	It will be necessary for Borrower to present Lender with copy of insurance agreement showing the amount of coverage and proof of loss payment clause made payable to Lender before the close of loan.
Required Documents:	Borrower will present to Lender's counsel all documents required or requested by Lender's counsel to be executed before the closing date of this loan. Documents will include but not be limited to: Note, Personal Guarantee and Mortgage Assignment of Rents, Assignment of Leases, copies of all leases now in effect, such other documents as Lender's counsel considers necessary.
Appraisal:	This loan commitment is subject to an appraisal establishing real property market of at least $2,400,000. Appraisal must be satisfactory to Lender.
Due and Payable Clause:	This loan will be due and payable immediately if property in whole or in part is transferred without Lender's consent.
Additional Costs:	Borrower will pay for Lender's typical cost in connection with executing this transaction such as title fees, construction loan escrow fees, and recording expenses.

This commitment will be valid until April 1, 198__. After that date, terms will be renegotiated. Lender's fee will be due not later than March 1, 198__.

Very truly yours,

GREATER SAVINGS AND LOAN ASSOCIATION

By:_____

_____, President

Accepted this _____ day of _____ 198__.

By:_____

By:_____

LAND TRUST AGREEMENT
LTAG

TRUST AGREEMENT

DECLARATION OF TRUST

By this Agreement, known as Trust Number _____ and dated this _____ day of _____, 19__, the undersigned certify that the Greater Savings Bank and Trust Company of Metropolis, Illinois, an Illinois Corporation, as trustee, is about to take title to the following described real estate in _____ County, Illinois:

(Insert legal description)

commonly known as (insert street address) . After taking title to the above-described real estate, the trustee will hold it for the uses and purposes set forth below. The following named persons are the beneficiaries of the trust and shall be entitled to the earnings and proceeds of the real estate held in this trust according to their respective interests set forth here:

(Insert names of beneficiaries and percentage
share of the beneficial interest of the property)

RIGHTS AND INTERESTS OF BENEFICIARIES

The parties hereto agree that the interest of the present beneficiaries and any person or persons who may become beneficiaries under this trust shall be limited to a power of direction to deal with the title of the trust property and to manage and control the property as provided herein, and the rights to receive the proceeds from mortgages, sales, rentals or other disposition of the property. The benefits of this property shall be deemed to be personal property and may be assigned and transferred as such. In the event that any beneficiary shall die, his or her interest in this trust shall pass as personal property to his or her personal representative, and not as real estate to his or her heirs at law unless otherwise specifically provided. No beneficiary has, or shall in the future have, any title, interest or right to the real estate as such, either legal or equitable, except those stated herein. The death of any beneficiary shall not terminate this trust or affect the powers of the trustee. No assignment of any interest in this trust shall be binding on the trustee until an executed copy of the assignment is received by the trustee. Any assignment not transmitted to the trustee, fully executed, shall be void as to all subsequent assignee or purchasers without notice.

REIMBURSEMENT OF ADVANCES, DISBURSEMENTS, AND PAYMENTS

The parties further agree that should the trustee make any advances of money or be required to make any payments on account of this trust, whether because of breach of contract, damage to property, injury to person, fines or penalties, the beneficiaries shall jointly or severally pay to the trustee, on demand, all such disbursements or payments, together with expenses and all fees, including reasonable attorneys' fees. Any fees and disbursements remaining unpaid 30 days after demand for payment is made shall bear interest at the rate of ___%. However, nothing contained in this paragraph shall be construed as imposing a duty upon the trustee to make payments or advance money for the benefit of the trust. Nor shall the trustee be required to prosecute or defend any action involving this trust unless it shall first be furnished with sufficient funds in advance.

AGREEMENT NOT TO BE RECORDED

The parties further agree that this trust agreement shall not be placed on record in the Recorder's Office of the county in which the property is located or in any other county, nor shall the recording of this agreement be considered as a notice of the rights of any beneficiary or third party which are in derogation of the title or powers of the trustee.

DUTIES OF TRUSTEE

The parties hereto further agree that the trustee will deal with the real estate held in trust only when authorized to do so in writing by the beneficiaries holding 51% of the beneficial interest in the property or such other persons as shall be designated in writing by beneficiaries holding 51% of the beneficial interest in the property. However, the trustee shall not be required to enter into any dealings whereby it would incur personal liability for damages, costs, expenses, penalties or fines, nor shall the trustee be required to act so long as money is due and owing to the trustee.

RESPONSIBILITY FOR MANAGEMENT OF PROPERTY

The parties further agree that the property shall be managed entirely by the beneficiaries who shall have control of the property. The beneficiaries shall have the power to sell, rent or lease the property and shall collect the rents or other proceeds therefrom. The trustee shall have no duty with respect to the management and control of the property, or the collection of rents or other proceeds nor shall it have responsibility for the payment of taxes, assessments, or other liabilities, unless directed in writing and unless adequate funds are provided in advance.

NOTICE OF RESIGNATION; SUCCESSOR TRUSTEE

The trustee may resign at any time by sending notice by registered mail of its intent to do so to each of the beneficiaries at his last known address. Such resignation shall become effective fourteen days after the date of mailing of the notice. Upon receiving notice of the trustee's intent to resign, the beneficiaries, or those holding 51% of the beneficial interest of the trust shall appoint a successor trustee and the trustee shall then convey the trust property to the successor in trust. Should the beneficiaries fail to name a successor trustee within fourteen days of the mailing of the notice, the trustee may convey the trust property directly to the beneficiaries in accordance with their respective interests in the trust, or seek relief in an appropriate legal forum. The giving of notice of intent to resign shall not affect any right that the trustee shall have to costs, disbursements or fees, including attorneys' fees previously incurred. Successor trustees shall have the same rights, powers, duties, and trusts and obligations of its predecessor.

Greater Savings Bank and Trust Company shall receive for its services in accepting this trust and in taking title hereunder the sum of $_____; also the sum of $_____ per year for holding title after the _____ day of _____ 19__, so long as any property remains in this trust; also its regular schedule fees for executing deeds and other instruments; _____and it shall receive reasonable compensation for any special service which may be rendered by it, or for taking and holding any other property which may hereafter be deeded to it, which fees, charges or other compensation, the beneficiaries jointly and severally agree to pay.

IN TESTIMONY WHEREOF, the GREATER SAVINGS BANK AND TRUST COMPANY has caused this document to be signed by its Trust Officer and attested by its Assistant Trust Officer/Assistant Cashier, and has caused its corporate seal to be attached as and for the act and deed of said Bank, the day and date above written.

ATTEST _____   By_____
     Assistant Trust Office/Assistant Cashier   Trust Officer

And on this day the beneficiaries have signed this Declaration of Trust and Trust Agreement in order to signify their assent to its terms.

_____(SEAL)   Address _____

_____(SEAL)   Address _____

_____(SEAL)   Address _____

_____(SEAL)   Address _____

_____(SEAL)   Address _____

_____(SEAL)   Address _____

Signature of persons having Power of Direction only:

_____(SEAL)   Address _____

_____(SEAL)   Address _____

Shall the name of any beneficiary be disclosed to the public?_____

To whom shall inquiries be sent?_____

May oral inquiries be referred directly?_____ To whom?_____

To whom shall bill be mailed?_____

LETTER OF DIRECTION
LDIR

GREATER SAVINGS BANK & TRUST COMPANY
               Date_____
               Re: Trust No._____

Gentlemen:

We hereby authorize and direct you to execute as Trustee under the above-stated trust number, the following document(s), copies of which are hereto attached.

We certify that the document(s) have been read and approved by the undersigned, and that all statements contained therein are understood by us and are true and correct.

We direct the Trustee to deliver the executed documents to:

Signed _____

_____

_____

_____

_____

State of Illinois)

County of Cook) } SS

If this direction does not contain all beneficiaries, the undersigned, being first duly sworn on oath, depose and say that all of the beneficiaries of this trust are now living.

Subscribed and sworn to before me
this _____ day of _____, 19__.

Signed: _____

_____

_____

Notary Public

LETTER OF DIRECTION—2
LDR2

Re: Trust No. _____

Greater Savings Bank and Trust Company
1 North State Street
Metropolis, Illinois 00000

Gentlemen:

Under the terms of Trust Agreement dated _____
AND KNOWN AS Trust No. _____, you are now authorized and directed to
issue a Trustee's Deed to the grantee listed below:

Grantee: _____

(Please specify if Joint Tenancy)

Address of Grantee: _____
County: _____ State: _____ Consideration to be shown in Deed: _____
Date to appear in Deed: _____

After this deed is executed, will other property remain in this trust? _____
IF NO PROPERTY REMAINS IN THE TRUST AFTER THIS CONVEYANCE, THIS DIRECTION MUST BE ACCOMPANIED BY REMITTANCE FOR ALL FEES INCLUDING FEE FOR THIS DEED.

Is this property in Torrens? _____

Legal description of property:

Also, please issue a letter to Grantee to pay the proceeds of this sale to

Street address of property:

Deliver executed Deed to _____

or hold for pick-up by_____. (Fill in appropriate information)

Actual Consideration $_____   Phone:_____

Date:_____

_____

RECEIVED the above-described

       instrument duly executed _____

_____   _____

If this Direction is not signed by all persons having a beneficial interest in the Trust, the form of Affidavit appearing on the reverse side must be furnished by all persons who have signed this direction.

AFFIDAVIT

Pursuant to Section 9 of the Illinois Inheritance Tax Act

State of _____

County of _____ } SS.

Affiants,_____

Being duly sworn on oath depose and say that all of the persons having a beneficial interest in the trust referred to on the reverse side hereof are living at the date hereof.

_____

_____

_____

_____

Subscribed and sworn to before me this

_____ day of _____, 19__

_____

            Notary Public

SECTION 4: RESIDENTIAL MORTGAGE LOAN LETTERS

1.	Cover Letter with Loan Application	LOAP
2.	Cover Letter with Loan Application—2	ALAP
3.	Residential Mortgage Commitment Letter	RMCL
4.	Residential Mortgage Commitment Letter—2	RMC2
5.	Transmittal Letter	TRAN
6.	Loan Settlement Statement	SETL
7.	Mortgage Collection Letter	MCOL
8.	Mortgage Insurance Change	MINC

These proven letters will serve your clients and save you time. Store them on your word processor and they will be available without delay. They inform, instruct, and confirm.

If you are one of the principals involved in the purchase or sale of property, check each document carefully. In some states—such as Arizona, for example—it is not necessary to have an attorney or to be present at the closing. The closing is executed between the bank issuing the mortgage and the title company. This means that you must be responsible for writing a letter clearly specifying information connected with the sale. Both parties have the obligation to check the details of the sale and agreement carefully.

Points to Remember

- Read all terms and conditions of the sale before you sign any documents.
- Do not assume that promises made will be kept if they are not listed and specified as you want them to read.
- If terms of escrow, occupancy, prepayment, insurance, or any other conditions of sale are not exactly as you expected them to be, take the time to discuss the details and make the corrections. It is faster than having to postpone the closing because of objections to the conditions of sale.

29

COVER LETTER WITH LOAN APPLICATION
LOAP

Dear Mr. & Mrs. Jones:

Re: Unit E10 Lot 277
     6400 Morningside Drive

At the request of Mr. Bob Brown of Castle Builders, we are sending you a Real Estate Loan Application for the proposed purchase of the property referred to above. Please complete this application as fully as possible and return it in the enclosed envelope, which is marked to my attention.

It would be helpful in verifying your savings and checking accounts if you would complete the supplemental information in detail. For verification purposes, also enclose copies of your signed income tax returns for _____ and _____. Please include your check in the amount of _____, which covers the credit search and report and the appraisal fee.

Our mortgage loan rate at this time is _____% and 2 points for <u>owner-occupied property</u>. The commitment on the present rate is for 60 days from date of application. As you are aware, the mortgage market is unstable and subject to fluctuations. If you wish to have the rate quoted in this letter, please complete the application and return it within two weeks from this date.

You may call me if you have any questions or need more information.

Yours very truly,

COVER LETTER WITH LOAN APPLICATION—2
ALAP

Dear Mr. and Mrs. Jacobs:

We are sending you a Real Estate Loan application as requested in your recent letter. Please complete it, so that we can process your application without delay. We will also need to verify your savings and checking accounts. For this information, we are including the supplemental information sheet.

When you return these application papers, please include your check for _____ to cover the appraisal and estimated credit reporting fees.

Our present rate for mortgage loans on <u>owner-occupied property</u> is _____% and _____ points. The commitment on our present rates is 60 days from the date of application. A six-month commitment will be issued for the market rate at the time of completion, not to exceed _____.

Because the mortgage market is expected to change upward in the very near future, it will be necessary for you to complete your application and return it to us within two weeks of today's date.

If you need additional information or have any questions, do not hesitate to call upon me.

Yours very truly,

RESIDENTIAL MORTGAGE COMMITMENT LETTER
RMCL

Dear Mr. and Mrs. Lennan:

We are pleased to inform you that your request for a real estate loan, to be secured by a first deed of trust on the above-captioned property, has been approved. This will serve as our commitment to make a loan under the following terms.

Loan Amount	Term	Service Charge	Interest Rate
$60,000.00	30 years	2%, $1,200.00	Market Rate
			not to exceed 14½%

The principal and interest payment will be $_____. In addition to this amount, your monthly payment will include 1/12th of the annual taxes and hazard insurance premium. Flood insurance and mortgage insurance premiums will be included where required. The terms of this commitment will be in force until _____, 198–. If this loan has not closed by this date, the commitment will expire and the interest rate and service charge must be renegotiated.

This commitment is subject to the following:

1. Greater Savings being insured as first beneficiary by an acceptable title insurance company with all loan proceeds to be disbursed by the title company acting as escrow agent for lender and borrowers per escrow instructions.

2. Insurance coverage in the minimum amount of our loan is required, with Greater Savings being furnished a hazard policy with loss clause favorable to the bank.

3. All requirements referred to in the escrow instructions, purchase contract, preliminary title report, appraisal, and this commitment must be satisfied before funds are disbursed.

If you have any questions regarding this commitment, please do not hesitate to contact us.

Very truly yours,

RESIDENTIAL MORTGAGE COMMITMENT LETTER—2
RMC2

Re: Property Located At
    123 Easy Street

Dear Mr. Dough:

This letter constitutes our commitment to provide a first mortgage loan on the property located at 123 Easy Street, subject to the terms and conditions set forth below.

Amount:	$75,000.00
Repayment Terms:	Graduated Payment Mortgage Rate
	First year 10.25%
	Second year 11.25%
	Third year 12.25%
	Fourth year to thirtieth year 13.25%
Fees:	Loan Origination Fee @ 3% $2,250.00
	Nonrefundable Application Fee 250.00

Evidence of Title to be ordered by Lender as agreed.
Additional Items and Conditions:
. . . Plat of survey acceptable to Lender
. . . Copy of present Evidence of Title showing Legal Description
. . . Flood Insurance required in addition to Home Owner Policy

This commitment is binding until _____, 198 . It can be extended for 30 days @ 1% of the loan request. Maximum extension 60 days after which the commitment is null and void.

Sincerely yours,   Acceptance of terms and conditions
                                    I(We) hereby accept the terms and
                                    Conditions of this Commitment.

                                    _____

                                    _____
                                    Signed   Date

TRANSMITTAL LETTER
TRAN

Re: Loan # _____

Dear Mr. and Mrs. Foster:

The above numbered loan has been paid in full as of May 26, 198_. We appreciate the way you handled your loan and look forward to being of service to you again in the future. The enclosed papers are for your personal records in connection with your paid-off mortgage loan.

_____Promissory Note—Marked Paid in Full

_____Recorded Deed of Trust—Marked Paid in Full

_____Fire Insurance Policy—Policy #_____

_____Flood Insurance Policy—Policy #_____

_____Tax Receipts for the Years:_____

_____Deed of Release and Reconveyance. (PLEASE TAKE THIS DOCUMENT TO THE COUNTY RECORDER'S OFFICE FOR RECORDING.)

_____(other document)

_____(other document)

If you have any questions or if we can be of service, please feel free to call.

Yours truly,

Encl_____

LOAN SETTLEMENT STATEMENT
SETL

Date: Loan Number:
Mortgagor: Property Address:
Mailing Address:
Legal Description
Rate: Term: Mos: Ratio: First Payment Due:
P and I: Impounds   Total Pmt.   By:

Description	Account	Charges	Credits
Amount of Loan			
Interest to			
Escrow			
Taxes: (mos.@)			
Ins. (mos.@)			
PMT (mos.@)			
MIP (mos.@)			
Flood Ins. (mos.@)			
Refinance Old Loan # Date			
Loan Payoff Trans.			
Principal Balance			
Interest to			
Prepayment Fee			
Escrow Balance			
NET PROCEEDS CHECK #			
Loan Settlement Prepayments			
	Totals		

MORTGAGE COLLECTION LETTER
MCOL

Dear Mrs. Green:

Very frequently, we do not realize how important good credit is until we lose it. If you were to need a credit reference at this time, your past-due mortgage account would not permit us to issue a favorable report for you.

This is the present status of your mortgage account:

May Payment Delinquent	$411.00
May Late Charges—5% of $411.00	20.55
June Payment Delinquent	411.00
Total Delinquency on Account	$842.55

Won't you send your check for $842.55 today or come in to make arrangements to bring this account up to date?

Your past payment record has been excellent and we would like to see that rating restored.

Yours very truly,

MORTGAGE INSURANCE CHANGE
MINC

Dear Loan Customer:

Please advise your insurance agent or company that Greater Savings and Loan Association no longer requires customers who pay their own hazard or homeowner's insurance premiums to forward the insurance policy to our office.

You will still be responsible for maintaining at least fire and extended coverage hazard insurance on your property in sufficient amount to pay the sums secured by our mortgage. Such insurance must carry a mortgage clause in favor of:

> Greater Savings & Loan Association
> and/or its assigns,
> Address
> City, State

If you cancel or do not renew your insurance, it will be the duty of the insurer to send us a notice. You will then be required to furnish us evidence of your new insurance and the name of your agent or company. If you do not do so, we will obtain insurance for you, bill you for the premium, and require you to establish an escrow account for payment of all future premiums.

Yours truly,

SECTION 5: HELPING YOU SPEAK "INSURANCE"

1. Informing Building Management of Liability Claim   CLAM
2. Request for Defense in Suit   DEIN
3. Employee Package Revision   EREV
4. Refund Not Issued   NORE
5. Letter Accompanying Home Owner's Policy   AHO2
6. Sales Letter for Insurance Agency   INAG

When we were preparing this section, we were reminded of the friend who reported that his son said to him, "Say something in insurance." Since only those who work in this field can speak the language, we have prepared these letters for the rest of us who must do business with them.

Points to Remember

- When writing to an insurance company, give all of the information you have available. Not doing so will delay your claim until the company gets the needed information.
- Whenever there is an area of coverage that you are not sure of, ask for clarification. After the roof has blown off, it is too late to nail it down.
- Benefit packages for your employees are a large part of your costs. Be sure that your coverage is the best available for your dollar.

INFORMING BUILDING MANAGEMENT OF LIABILITY CLAIM
CLAM

Dear Mr. Cruz:

Mr. John Webster, who is a customer of our firm, tripped and fell when his shoe caught in a ripped seam in the carpet as he exited the elevator on the sixth floor. We know that you were aware of the torn carpet for at least two weeks prior to April 6, 198_, the day on which Mr. Webster was injured. My receptionist, Ann Lind, reported this condition on two separate occasions before this incident.

We have advised Mr. Webster to contact you and have given him assurance that we will verify his statements as to the condition of the carpeting that caused his fall. It is our understanding that you, as the management company of the building, will handle his claim for damages and medical expenses resulting from this occurrence.

We do have liability insurance. However, since Mr. Webster fell in the corridor, not in our suite, our carrier is not liable. Mr. Webster is a valued customer, and we will appreciate your cooperation and prompt handling of this matter.

Very truly yours,

REQUEST FOR DEFENSE IN SUIT
DEIN

RE: Claim Against Policy #85216218

Dear Mr. Kowalski:

In accordance with the terms of the casualty policy that your company has issued for Jackson Heating and Cooling Company, I am requesting that Merchants' Casualty Insurance Company defend my firm and my employee, Keith Jensen, in a lawsuit filed against us by Mr. Joseph Murray.

I am enclosing a copy of the summons and complaint. They were personally served upon me at my office. As you will see by reading the complaint, Mr. Murray, a sales representative for Knollwood Industries, alleges that he was injured on July 24, 198_, when his auto collided with a delivery truck driven by my employee, Mr. Jensen. I personally witnessed the incident which occurred in our dock area, and it is my belief, as well as that of Mr. Jensen, that Mr. Murray was at fault.

Please contact me for any information you may need to pursue this matter.

Yours very truly,

EMPLOYEE PACKAGE REVISION
EREV

Dear Ms. Blaine:

We plan to add a third shift to increase our production. However, our accountants say that we will have to trim back on the cost of our generous health and welfare package in order to do so. We can afford to hire the needed employees if we can keep the cost of insurance to about $140.00 per month for all employees including office personnel.

We want to continue to provide the best coverage we can, but we would like to discourage abuse of benefits by looking carefully at some alternatives. Among the comments and suggestions we have had from employees who have collected medical benefits, we have heard that many would prefer outpatient testing and office procedures instead of hospital requirement to qualify for benefits.

We also have been approached by some employees who want to consider a health maintenance program as an alternative. Please explore this possibility and others that will give us a package that we can present to our management committee. We want to proceed with plans to hire the 30 new employees without delay.

Very truly yours,

REFUND NOT ISSUED
NORE

Dear Mr. Grant:

Is it possible to fire a computer? If not, you had better talk to your employees who are giving your computer a bad image. We have a problem that developed last year when we cancelled our policy with Smith Company and took out a new policy with Jones Fire and Casualty.

According to the terms of our policy with Smith Company, issued through your insurance department, we were entitled to a refund of $200.00 because the policy did not run for the full term.

Despite our repeated letters and calls to your Ms. Ann Brown, we have not been credited with the refund. In addition to this, we have the aggravation of receiving computer notices that we must renew our insurance or our mortgage will become due and payable immediately.

Ms. Brown tells us that the problem is a computer error. Isn't it time someone talked to the computer and told it that it could be replaced by a clerk who keeps accurate records? Better yet, isn't it time someone talked to Ms. Brown?

Sincerely,

LETTER ACCOMPANYING HOME OWNER'S POLICY
AHO2

ATTACHED IS YOUR PROPERTY INSURANCE RENEWAL POLICY
YOUR PREMIUM WILL BE PAID BY YOUR MORTGAGE COMPANY

Dear Mr. Gray:

Is your property underinsured?

An important part of our service to our clients is to inform them of changes taking place that they might not otherwise be aware of. Property in your area has steadily increased in value for the past five years. If you have not increased your insurance coverage to keep pace, your property may be underinsured.

We suggest that you take the time to review your property investment now. Consider the additions and enhancements you have included and the value of your property today. You may find that your present coverage is insufficient. If you need more coverage, call us. We will adjust your insurance to cover your replacement costs.

If you need further information, we can go over your policy with you and evaluate your coverage based on similar construction.

Yours very truly,

SALES LETTER FOR INSURANCE AGENCY
INAG

Dear Mr. and Mrs. Downs:

We enjoy doing business with you!

We sometimes forget to thank you, our clients, for the success we have enjoyed in the past ten years. We like to think that hard work and good service have paid off . . . and they have. However, the third ingredient is you. Your patronage and continued loyalty have made us grow in the community.

Many of our clients are discovering that in addition to homeowners' insurance, we offer highly competitive prices for auto insurance coverage. We may be able to save you money on your auto insurance.

If you will answer the brief questions below, we will give you a quotation.

INFORMATION NEEDED TO GIVE AUTO INSURANCE QUOTATION

Drivers' ages: Mr._____ Mrs._____ Other Drivers_____

DRIVING RECORD PAST 3 YEARS

Citations?_____ Describe_____

Accidents?_____ Describe_____

DESCRIPTION OF AUTOMOBILE(S)

Year_____ Make_____ Model_____

Year_____ Make_____ Model_____

USE OF VEHICLE(S)

Pleasure_____ Drive to and from work?_____No. of miles_____

Business_____ Kind of business_____ Sales?_____

PRESENT COVERAGES

Bodily injury_____ Property damage_____

Medical payments_____ Comprehensive_____

Deductible_____ Collision deductible_____

Towing & labor_____ Uninsured motorist_____

Telephone number_____ Most convenient time_____

We hope to be able to give you a quote that you can't resist. That's how much we enjoy doing business with you.

Cordially,

SECTION 6: GIVING INFORMATION TO BANK CUSTOMERS

1.	Explanation of Escrow Account	ESAC
2.	Notice of Bank Error	BAER
3.	Informing Customer of Change	CSAP
4.	Bank Error—Taxes Paid Twice	TWIC
5.	Explanation of Error	OOPS
6.	Notice of Account Procedure Change	APCH
7.	Letter Accompanying Interest Check	AINT

The relationship between the bank and the customer is one based on trust and communication. Frequently, the customer is in need of information or explanation. These letters are informal, informative, and ready for use. When corresponding with bank customers, take care to use terms that are not intimidating.

Points to Remember

- Create an attitude of cooperation.
- Use language that the public will understand.
- Build the intangible "we" relationship with clients.

EXPLANATION OF ESCROW ACCOUNT
ESAC

Dear Mr. Smith:

We are sorry you misunderstood the reason for the escrow portion of your monthly payment. The FHA requires that the bank collect in advance of the due date sufficient funds to pay for hazard insurance and property tax on your real estate.

The amount of money needed to pay your property tax and the cost of the hazard insurance premiums are added together and the total amount is divided by twelve. This one-twelfth of the total needed to pay these obligations is added to your monthly mortgage payment of principal and interest to arrive at the sum of money you are required to pay each month.

The bank credits your mortgage loan with the principal and interest and places the difference in a non-interest-bearing account to be held in escrow until disbursements for property tax and insurance premiums are due . . . as it is required to do by the Federal Housing Administration.

Because the property tax and the insurance premiums on your real estate are subject to change each year, there is an adjustment of the escrow portion of your monthly payment annually. If you owe a balance, you will be advised to pay it at this time. If there is a refund or a lower sum to be paid, you will be notified.

I hope this explanation will be sufficient, but I will be available to discuss your account at any time that you feel it is necessary.

Yours truly,

NOTICE OF BANK ERROR
BAER

Dear Bank Savings Customer:

The recent Form 1099 you received listing your interest earned from Greater Savings during 198_ is in error. Our computer center just informed us that they mistakenly listed some accounts earning interest in the year 198_ as having earned that interest in 198_.

Please correct Form 1099 by deleting the following:

Account No. 00-000-000   Amount of Interest $2,576.03

This interest, posted in error, and only this item should not be reported on your 198_ income tax return. You will receive a 1099 for the present year that will include this interest-earned amount.

Please attach this letter to Form 1099 so that your records will be complete. I'm sorry for any inconvenience this error caused you.

Sincerely,

INFORMING CUSTOMER OF CHANGE
CSAP

Dear Savings Customer:

For more than thirty-five years, we have provided our customers with the best possible service and the highest possible earnings consistent with sound financial practices. That is why we are making the following adjustments to our regular savings program. Effective January 1, 198—, we will institute the following changes:

- Interest will be credited to your savings account at the end of each month. This will make your interest available to you sooner than the quarterly posting of interest which is our current practice.

- Interest will be paid on your 5¼% savings account as long as the average balance in your account is $100.00 or more for the month. This new policy will affect all savings accounts.

- A minimum deposit of $100.00 will be required to open any new savings account.

- A $2.00 service charge will be charged if at any time during the month your 5¼% savings account balance falls below $100.00.

Please stop in at your nearest office and discuss any questions you may have regarding these account adjustments. Be assured that your satisfaction and service are of utmost importance to everyone on the staff of Greater Savings Bank.

Sincerely,

BANK ERROR—TAXES PAID TWICE
TWIC

Dear Sirs:

The copy of my bank statement enclosed shows my taxes were paid twice. I resent paying property taxes once. Paying twice in the same month is dangerous to my blood pressure! I am sure that this is a computer error. But how could it have happened? Doesn't anyone check the statements? Please correct this mistake without delay and send me a copy of the adjusted balance.

Sincerely,

EXPLANATION OF ERROR
OOPS

Dear Mr. White:

We're sorry! We did make deductions twice from your escrow account during the month of June. The error occurred because our computer was affected by a loss of power during a severe electrical storm. When power was resumed, a few account numbers were inadvertently rerun, causing a duplicate deduction. We thought that we had found and corrected all of the accounts that were involved. As you know, we did not.

Please accept our apologies. We try very hard to give our customers excellent service, but something always happens to keep us humble. Thanks for your understanding.

Sincerely,

NOTICE OF ACCOUNT PROCEDURE CHANGE
APCH

Dear Loan Customer:

We have had to change our accounting procedures in order to align ourselves with the National Secondary Mortgage Market Procedures.

As of January 1, 198—, any prepayments of principal that you have made in the past will be incorporated into your payment schedule. We will no longer be able to consider that money paid is available for use toward future payments.

1. Each and every month a payment is due and payable within the calendar month regardless of amounts previously paid.

2. Beginning January 1, all payments made in excess of your regularly required payment will be held until the last day of the month. On that day, any funds being held will be used to pay the current monthly payment and will advance the payment due date by one month.

3. You can continue to make advance payments on the principal of your mortgage loan to lower the loan balance. However, such prepayments will not release you from the obligation of making a mortgage payment during the next calendar month.

We hope that this change will not inconvenience you. We understand the reason why many of our loan customers desire to prepay loan payments, but we must comply with National Secondary Mortgage Market Regulations. If you need further explanation of how this applies to your specific account, please write to me.

Yours very truly,

LETTER ACCOMPANYING INTEREST CHECK
AINT

Re: Unit 10   Lot 60

Dear Mr. and Mrs. Jacobs:

Enclosed is a check for $66.99. This is interest on your 20% down payment on the above property held by us from time of deposit, February 27, 198—, until March 20, 198—, the date construction was started on your property. This interest represents 1% per month on $9,138.00 for twenty-two days.

Our decision to pay interest was based on the fact that we encountered substantial delay in the start of construction in the area subsequent to our receipt of your down payment. We hope that construction will proceed as scheduled and that you will be enjoying your new home soon.

Very truly yours,

SECTION 7:   BANK PROMOTION LETTERS

1. Bank Promotion Letter   BAPL
2. Bank Promotion Letter—2   BAP2
3. Bank Promotion Letter—3   BAP3

Community awareness and participation are a part of the successful bank. The letters we have prepared for this section will give you examples of how to use information and events to build goodwill and bring more customers into the bank.

Points to Remember

- Encourage new business by showing a human interest.
- Put a good-news letter in every mailbox.
- Let customers know they are not just account numbers but important individuals.

BANK PROMOTION LETTER
BAP1

Dear Mr. Smith:

You will be pleased to know that you have a birthday present waiting for you at Greater Savings. We want to be sure that you, as a member of our community who is approaching the golden years of retirement, are aware of the benefits of our Golden Years Benefit Club.

We have prepared a brochure outlining for you the benefits included in this very special club. All of the benefits and services listed are free to you as long as you maintain a minimum balance of $2,000.00 in Greater Savings. You can help to maintain that balance by signing for direct deposit of your Social Security check when you retire.

Stop in our office at your convenience and ask Tom Green to tell you of the activities enjoyed by the members of our Golden Years Benefit Cub. If you time your visit for the first Thursday of the month, after 12:30 P.M., Tom will introduce you to several of your neighbors who are always in attendance at the popular meetings.

Remind Tom to give you your birthday present at that time also. Tom means well, but we all know that young people are sometimes forgetful.

Cordially,

BANK PROMOTION LETTER—2
BAP2

Dear Ms. Green:

Congratulations on your new business! We are always happy to welcome newcomers to our business community and to show you how we can assist you in many ways to make sure your new venture is a success.

If your business qualifies as a sole proprietorship, you are eligible for an exciting new savings alternative through the use of a checking account. A checking account that pays interest!

Greater Savings will pay you 5% interest on your checking account funds and credit the interest to your account monthly.

- There will be no need to transfer funds from savings to checking account.
- Funds will continue to earn interest until checks clear.
- A call will stop payments lost in transit. A form will be sent immediately for your signature of confirmation.
- Use our night deposit to make deposits after hours or on weekends. Stop carrying cash!
- Automatic cash card service is available at convenient stations.

This sensational new checking account is available to you now. Drop in at your convenience or call me at 000-0000. I look forward to meeting you and welcoming you to Greater Savings.

Sincerely,

BANK PROMOTION LETTER—3
BAP3

Dear Ms. Green:

Thank you for your inquiry about Greater Savings' checking account to be used for your sole proprietorship business. You may not be aware of our Cash Management Account, which I think will be of even more service to you and pay a far higher rate of interest.

With the Cash Management Account, it is necessary for you to maintain a balance of $2,500.00 on deposit, but you will be earning 9% return on your money. In addition to the higher rate of interest, you will have a $5,000.00 Line of Credit established for your use. Your Line of Credit Account will have a separate book of checks issued to you when you open your account. This convenient method of cash management allows you to expand your inventory, pay business expenses, or take advantage of special purchases without delay. There is no charge until the checks are presented for payment. There is an interest rate of 18% charged on the money you use. This is a lower rate than credit-card companies charge for purchases, and you will have the prestige of a personal check when you are paying your suppliers for your selections.

Please feel free to come in or call me to discuss this account or any other of our services at any time.

Sincerely,

SECTION 8: BANK COLLECTION LETTERS

1. Security Pacific National Bank—Collection—1   SPC1
2. Security Pacific National Bank—Collection—2   SPC2
3. Security Pacific National Bank—Collection—3   SPC3

Whenever you are trying to collect money, you are walking a fine line. You want to clear up the delinquency without injuring the dignity of your customer. A successful letter will do both. These proven letters supplied by Security Pacific National Bank are excellent examples of productive collection letters. They ask directly for payment and offer to work out an amicable way to accomplish this.

Points to Remember

- Write a reminder promptly when a bill is past due. It will frequently bring the payment by return mail.
- Consistent action and policy of collection will deter many problem accounts from becoming uncollectible.
- Turn to Sections 37 and 38 for a complete selection of collection letters.

SECURITY PACIFIC NATIONAL BANK—COLLECTION—1
SPC1

SECURITY PACIFIC NATIONAL BANK

HEAD OFFICE, SECURITY PACIFIC PLAZA, 333 SO. HOPE STREET, LOS ANGELES, CALIFORNIA

MAILING ADDRESS: P. O. BOX 2097, TERMINAL ANNEX, LOS ANGELES, CALIFORNIA 90051

July 6, 198—

Jane Doe
49 Lowell
Los Angeles, CA 90071

Re: RRA/MC Account

Dear Jane,

This is to advise you that because of the past due condition of the above-captioned account it has been transferred to the Special Assets Department of this bank for collection and, if necessary, legal action.

Accordingly, we now declare the entire balance, as detailed above, due and payable forthwith.

Any applicable insurance has been cancelled and premium refunds received, if any, have been credited to the balance now due.

The above balance also reflects full credit for the proceeds realized on any assets sold by us or offsets against accounts carried by you in this bank.

It is our sincere desire to bring this account to a close on an amicable and fair basis. We enclose a self-addressed reply envelope for your use. If you find it more convenient, please telephone the undersigned at the number listed below.

Very truly yours,

Mary Jones
(213) 613–0000

MJ/dmj
    wpv
Enclosure

**SECURITY PACIFIC NATIONAL BANK—COLLECTION—2
SPC2**

SECURITY PACIFIC NATIONAL BANK

HEAD OFFICE, SECURITY PACIFIC PLAZA, 333 SO. HOPE STREET, LOS ANGELES, CALIFORNIA

MAILING ADDRESS: P. O. BOX 2097, TERMINAL ANNEX, LOS ANGELES, CALIFORNIA 90051

July 8, 198_

Jane Doe
49 Lowell
Los Angeles, CA 90071

Re: RRA/MC Account

Dear Jane,

Your continued silence indicates to us that you do not have the desire to work this matter out on an amicable basis. Ignoring the debt certainly won't make it go away.

Unless we hear from you immediately to establish a reasonable plan of arrangement, we will be forced to look for recovery under available legal remedies.

We trust that you prefer to handle the matter on an amicable basis, and we ask that you telephone the writer at the number listed below or respond by mail using the enclosed envelope.

Very truly yours,

Mary Jones
(213) 613-0000

MJ/dmk
wpv
Enclosure

**SECURITY PACIFIC NATIONAL BANK—COLLECTION—3
SPC3**

SECURITY PACIFIC NATIONAL BANK

HEAD OFFICE, SECURITY PACIFIC PLAZA, 333 SO. HOPE STREET, LOS ANGELES, CALIFORNIA

MAILING ADDRESS: P. O. BOX 2097, TERMINAL ANNEX, LOS ANGELES, CALIFORNIA 90051

July 14, 198___

Jane Doe
49 Lowell
Los Angeles, CA 90071

Re: RRA/MC Account

Dear Jane,

We are writing in response to your recent letter.

We are willing to accept your proposed plan of arrangement for a period not to exceed six months if supported by the enclosed form and returned immediately. At the expiration of the six months, your ability to increase the payments will be reviewed.

Enclosed is a payment card to assist you in sending your payments.

Very truly yours,

Mary Jones
(213) 613-0000

MJ/dml
   wpv
Enclosure

SECTION 9: REAL ESTATE TRANSACTION LETTERS

The letters in this section represent the variety of side issues encountered in real estate selection and construction. They are not formula letters. Each is presented to illustrate how to handle a specific condition. Use these sample letters as a basis upon which you can develop letters for special situations.

Points to Remember

- Because state laws vary, be sure to check the real estate laws of your community in all transactions.
- Limited partnership letters should be specific in all aspects of investment and benefits to be derived.

RESERVATION OF LOT CHOICE
LOTR

DATE:_____

The CHELSEA GARDENS DEVELOPMENT, a Delaware Corporation, and

_____

agree that CHELSEA GARDENS DEVELOPMENT CO. will reserve a garden apartment condominium in Unit 5 for the prospective purchasers named above.

A deposit of $500.00 is given by the above-named prospective purchasers and accepted by CHELSEA GARDENS DEVELOPMENT CO. However, it is clearly understood that deposit shall be fully refundable at any time prior to the execution of a sales agreement. It is understood by all parties that this is a reservation agreement executed to assure the prospective purchaser(s) a choice of location selection on a first-come, first-served basis prior to construction. It is further understood that a sales agreement will be signed within ten (10) days after notification by CHELSEA GARDENS DEVELOPMENT CO. to the prospective purchasers that said sales agreement is ready for execution.

IN WITNESS THEREOF these parties have signed this reservation agreement on the date written above.

CHELSEA GARDENS DEVELOPMENT CO.
A Delaware Corporation

By:_____

PROSPECTIVE PURCHASER(S)

_____   _____   _____

CONSTRUCTION PROGRESS REPORT
CONR

Reference   Unit:
Bldg:
Job:
Lot:
Seq:

Dear Mr. & Mrs. Smith:

Our work is progressing on schedule here in CHELSEA GARDENS and we are pleased to inform you that we will be starting construction in your area on March 1, 198__. We do not have a definite date for construction of the unit in which your garden apartment condominium is located, but it will be shortly after that date.

Delivery of your new luxury garden apartment condominium will depend on your exact location in the building sequence and as close to your preference date as possible. If you have not yet made application for your mortgage loan and your plans include conventional financing, please do so now. Contact your sales representative if you need assistance or more information.

After construction is under way in your area, we will not be able to make any changes in the standard features or optional choices offered to you. For this reason, it would be advisable for you to review your selections and advise us if you want to make any changes now.

Do not hesitate to contact us if we can be of service.

Very truly yours,

VERIFICATION AND ACKNOWLEDGMENT
VACK

We, the undersigned, hereby affirm and acknowledge that no representation was made to us, nor has our decision to purchase property in the Chelsea Gardens Development been based on any discussion of development of a shopping mall, recreational facilities, or a public park at the intersection of Junction O and County Line Road, Whitewater, OH.

DATED this _____ day of _____, 19____

_____

_____

SUBSCRIBED AND SWORN TO before me this _____

day of _____, 19____

_____

Notary Public

My commission expires:

_____

PROPOSING REAL ESTATE PARTNERSHIP
PREP

Dear Barry:

I enjoyed seeing you at lunch on Wednesday and discussing my plans for the future. This letter is written at your invitation to prepare a solid proposal for a real estate partnership.

As I told you, I am planning to build my own architectural studio with additional office space on the five-acre site that I own at the intersection of Larkin Highway and Route 3. I propose that the building be built and owned by a real estate partnership to be composed of you, myself, and your brother, Jeffrey. Jeffrey would act as the general contractor and would manage the building for the first year. I would contribute my architectural plans as well as the five-acre site. You have indicated your willingness to contribute up to $50,000, but because of your other commitments, you would not have an active role in the building.

Based on fees that I have charged for similar services, I estimate that the value of my services in designing the building would be $35,000. Several real estate agents have looked at the property and have given me estimates of its value averaging $25,000. Thus, my total contribution to the partnership would have a value of approximately $60,000. I will provide you with written documentation to support this statement, if necessary.

I am sending a similar letter to Jeffrey in which I suggest that he document the value of his services. Once we have an idea of Jeffrey's contribution, I will work with him to get some preliminary estimates of the cost of labor and materials for the building and the cost of financing.

It is my intent that once the building is constructed, I would occupy the primary space and would lease it from the partnership at fair market value. The remainder of office space would be leased out to provide additional income to the partnership. My accountant has been suggesting such an arrangement for some time and has convinced me that it would be financially advantageous. I will be happy to arrange a meeting among the four of us so that he can explain the tax advantages to us at the same time.

If you are interested in exploring the possibility of this partnership, please get back to me as soon as possible so that I can begin to make the necessary arrangements.

Sincerely,

_____

Allen

LEASE BACK AGREEMENT
LEAS

Dear Mr. Khrone:

This is to confirm our recent telephone conversation wherein we agreed that following the sale of your building to me on June 25, 198_, I will lease the premises to you at the rate of $23.45 per day for the period of June 26, 198_, to July 27, 198_, at 12:00 noon. You have agreed to tender a check to me totaling $750.40 at the time of closing.

You have further agreed to deposit $500.00 with me at the time of closing to be held until the premises are vacated by you in the condition they were at the time of closing. You have agreed to be responsible for maintaining the premises and permanent fixtures in good condition and to make all repairs for damage that arises during the period of your tenancy.

I have agreed to inspect the premises with you at the time of closing and again at the time you vacate the premises and to return the $500.00 to you within two weeks of the date you move, deducting from it only reasonable expenses incurred by me in making repairs or because of delay in your vacating the building.

If you concur that the above paragraphs accurately reflect our oral agreement, please sign in the space provided. Return the original to me and keep the copy for your files.

Sincerely,

_____

Joseph Marconi

Accepted this_____ day of _____, 198_

_____

Ron Khrone

THANK YOU—REAL ESTATE SALE
RETY

Dear Mr. Jones:

I wish to express my sincere appreciation and that of the management of Anderson Realtors for the privilege of assisting you in the sale of your property in Warrenville, Ohio.

I hope to have the pleasure of assisting you in other real estate transactions in the future. At this time, we have an excellent portfolio of investment and income properties available. I would like to discuss these parcels with you now while the market is so favorable for buyers. Please feel free to call on me without any obligation.

Sincerely,

PERMISSION TO SELL PROPERTY
PERM

Dear Mrs. Jacobs:

We are sending the signed contract giving you authorization to sell our property located as 1234 Echo Lane, Hometown, Indiana.

You will note that we have attached a rider that excludes us from paying the broker's fee of 7% in the event the house is purchased by Mr. Gregory Anderson. The reason for this exclusion is that Mr. Gregory Anderson and his wife, Margaret, looked at the house in response to an ad I placed in the <u>News</u> before listing the property with Century 21.

Mr. Anderson is being transferred to the area and said he was interested in buying the house. However, I was not able to get him at the telephone number that he gave me. He may be somewhere enroute.

I discussed this exclusion with your agent, Mary Grzyb. She instructed me to ask for the variation of the contract in writing.

Thank you for your efforts and cooperation. I wish you every success in selling our property.

Cordially,

SECTION 10: SHAREHOLDER'S LETTER AND INVESTMENT INFORMATION

1.	Dividend Report Problem	DIVR
2.	Shareholder's Check Returned	SCRE
3.	Reply to Shareholder Complaint	SHAP
4.	Shareholder Inquiry—IRA	SIRA
5.	Reply to Inquiry	RIRA
6.	Shareholder Inquiry IRA—2	SIR2
7.	Reply to Inquiry—2	RIR2
8.	Follow-Up Letter to IRA Inquiry	FIRA
9.	Shareholder Tax Information	STAX
10.	Reply to Investment Questions	RINQ

The letters in this section were supplied to us by the management of T. Rowe Price Funds. They were included to give you examples of the kinds of letters clients write and tactful and informative ways to answer them. The questions raised are valid, and the response to each is straightforward. It is important to give accurate information in all matters pertaining to financial investment.

Points to Remember

- Be sure the answers you give in your responses are specific to the needs of the writers.
- Use the opportunity to correspond, to increase goodwill and to reassure your shareholders of your concern for their investments.
- Do not be evasive. The hard truth is the best answer.

DIVIDEND REPORT PROBLEM
DIVR

Dear Sirs:

I have a problem with the way in which you handle your report of distribution of dividends to shareholders. Please enlighten me.

Form 1099 includes distribution paid to holders of record on December 31. However, the checks mailed to shareholders do not reach the shareholders until some time in January. This causes a problem for those who report on a cash basis. Form 1099 shows earnings in 198__, but we do not get the earnings until 198__.

You could get around this problem in more than one way. You could change your reporting procedures or you could send the check out a few days before the end of the year by changing the record date. You could also send the checks after December 31 and report accordingly.

Please let me know if you intend to consider the need for a change in the way that you handle the end-of-the-year distribution and report.

In any case, if I have trouble with the IRS, I will be sticking pins in a doll representing your fund.

Very truly yours,

SHAREHOLDER'S CHECK RETURNED
SCRE

Gentlemen:

Please find enclosed a check in the amount of $2,000.00. This is a contribution to my Prime Reserve Fund IRA Account.

I also wish to complain about the service from your transfer agent. On December 30, 1981, I mailed the enclosed check and remittance coupon to the transfer agent. On January 2, 1982, I received the enclosed mailgram (dated December 31, 1981), which informed me that my check was to be returned to me. On the 4th (Monday), I tried three times to reach your transfer agent via the telephone number in the mailgram, but the line was always busy. Several days later, I received the returned check and coupon.

Your transfer agent is a clear example of the mindless, faceless, computer-run bureaucracy that is increasingly dominating our society. My check is dated January 1, 1982, the coupon is clearly marked 1982, yet your "representatives" could not hold them from December 31, 1981, until the first business day of 1982!

Please reprimand your transfer agent. Instruct them to change their ways before they lose many customers, including me.

Sincerely yours,

REPLY TO SHAREHOLDER'S COMPLAINT
SHAP

Dear Sir:

Thank you for writing.

I regret the inconvenience you experienced last month when trying to invest your 198__ IRA contribution. However, my investigation of the issues detailed in your letter supports our transfer agent's position in returning your check.

Internal Revenue Service's regulations require that IRA contributions be made "at any time during the tax year." The last day to make a contribution is the due date for filing the tax return for that year—April 15 or later for extensions. However, an investment cannot be made prior to the tax year of the contribution.

Additionally, the increased contribution deduction allowance of $2,000 permitted by the Economic Tax Recovery Act of 1981 was effective for tax years beginning after December 31, 1981.

I have enclosed a copy of the transfer agent's time-stamped internal routing slip which confirms receipt of your check at 9:20 A.M. on December 30, 1981.

Securities and Exchange Commission regulations prohibit the Fund from holding checks for investment and page ten (10) of the prospectus states that "orders will become effective when an investor's . . . check is converted into federal funds." This conversion is generally 24 hours following receipt of the check. Since your check was received on the 30th, the investment would have become effective on the 31st.

Since State Street Bank was unable to invest the $2,000 prior to January 4, 1982 and also was prohibited from holding the check, there was no alternative but to return the check.

Please accept my apology for the frustration you experienced in trying to reach the transfer agent on January 4. Telephone delays are more likely to occur on Mondays, which usually are our busiest phone days. If you experience such delays in the future, please feel free to contact the Shareholder Services Office in Baltimore.

I have welcomed this opportunity to investigate this matter for you and trust that I have reassured you of the proper handling of your investment.

Sincerely,

Enclosure

SHAREHOLDER INQUIRY—IRA
SIRA

Dear Sirs:

I am a client of T. Rowe Price Associates, Inc., and of T. Rowe Price Prime Reserve Fund, Inc.

The attached article entitled "An Oversight Overseas?" in the February 17, 198—, Wall Street Journal has been brought to my attention. It discusses how many Americans abroad can't invest in IRAs.

I am currently an American working overseas. At the same time, I have already made a 198— participant contribution to my IRA account with T. Rowe Price Prime Reserve Fund, Inc.

I would appreciate your reading the attached article. Kindly advise me of my options. As I will not obtain any beneficial tax deductions for making an IRA contribution in 198—, am I able to withdraw the principal amount, plus interest that I have mistakenly contributed for 198— without penalty? If so, whom do I contact at T. Rowe Price and how do I go about it? What is your opinion and recommendation vis-à-vis my current predicament?

I look forward to hearing from you.

Sincerely,

REPLY TO INQUIRY
RIRA

Re: T. Rowe Price Prime Reserve Fund, Inc.
 IRA Qualifications for Overseas Citizens

Dear Mr. Blank:

Thank you for writing. Your letter to Mr. ———— has been referred to me for response.

As ———— confirmed in his letter of March 12, and in accordance with the International Operations Division of the Internal Revenue Service, one can qualify for both the IRA deduction in 198— and the new Foreign Tax Exclusion of $75,000. Your IRA deduction would be based on earned income in excess of $75,000—that is, the amount of taxable income that is not eligible for the Foreign Tax Exclusion. For further clarification on the Foreign Tax Exclusion and IRA Eligibility/Deduction, I suggest that you contact the IRS International Operation Division in Washington at 202-566-5941.

Should you decide to redeem the shares purchased as your 198— contribution, please send a letter to our transfer agent, State Street Bank and Trust Company, Post Office Box 2357, Boston, MA 02107, instructing them to redeem the shares plus any related earnings. Since the contribution was for tax year 198—, there would be no tax liability.

I hope the above information is helpful.

Sincerely,

SHAREHOLDER INQUIRY IRA—2
SIR2

Dear Sir:

I would like to take this opportunity to thank you for your letter of March 11, 198__. I highly appreciate your attentiveness and research on this matter.

I am a client of T. Rowe Price Associates, Inc., and of T. Rowe Price Prime Reserve Fund, Inc.

The attached article entitled "An Overseas Oversight?" in the Feburary 17, 198_ Wall Street Journal has been brought to my attention. It discusses how most Americans abroad can't invest in IRAs.

I am currently an American working overseas. Furthermore, I do qualify for Subtitle B—Income Earned Abroad of the Economic Recovery Tax Act of 1981. This entitles me to a Foreign Tax Exclusion of $75,000. I will not surpass this amount in 198__.

At the same time, I understand that all contributions (principal plus interest and/or capital gains) to an IRA are subject to income tax upon withdrawal. Is this correct?

I have already made a 198_ Participant Contribution to my IRA account with the T. Rowe Price Prime Reserve Fund, Inc.

I would appreciate your reading the attached article. Kindly advise me of my options. As I will not obtain any beneficial tax deductions for making an IRA contribution in 198_, am I able to withdraw the principal amount plus interest of the amount that I contributed thus far for 198_ without penalty. If so, who do I contact at T. Rowe Price and how do I go about it? What is your opinion and recommendation vis-à-vis my current predicament?

I look forward to hearing from you.

Sincerely,

REPLY TO INQUIRY—2
RIR2

Re: Individual Retirement Account Foreign Investment

Dear Mr. Blank:

Thank you for writing again. I believe that Mrs. _____'s letter of March 23, which I trust you have received, answers most of the items in your most recent letter. However, I am glad to reclarify them for you.

The Wall Street Journal article you included agrees with the information the Fund has obtained from the International Operations Division of the Internal Revenue Service. Although one can be eligible for both the Foreign Tax Exclusion and the liberalized IRA deductions enacted by the Economic Recovery Tax Act of 198_, the IRA deduction is based on earned income over $75,000. Since you state that your 198_ earned income will not surpass this figure, you do not qualify for the deduction.

You may have your 198_ contribution plus any earnings refunded to you by writing to the State Street Bank and Trust Company. I have enclosed a self-addressed envelope for your convenience. Please advise State Street Bank that you were not eligible for the deduction. There will be no premature distribution tax penalty.

I hope the above information has sufficiently resolved this matter. However, if you desire more detailed information you might want to contact the IRS International Operations Division at 202-566-5941.

Sincerely,

FOLLOW-UP LETTER TO IRA INQUIRY
FIRA

Re: Individual Retirement Account Foreign Investment

Dear Mr. Blank:

The following information follows up our discussion of February 26. Please accept my apology for the delay in responding, but the matter required more research than I had anticipated.

I have confirmed with the International Operations Division of the Internal Revenue Service in Washington that one can quality for both the $2,000 IRA deduction in 198_ and the new Foreign Tax Exclusion of $75,000. Of course, I cannot advise you whether you are eligible to exclude your foreign income under the new rates, but your eligibility to qualify for the Foreign Tax Exclusion does not preclude you from making the IRA contribution.

I have, therefore, included our IRA kit for your consideration.

If I can be of any additional service, please call me collect at 000-000-000.

Sincerely,

SHAREHOLDER TAX INFORMATION
STAX

Dear Sir:

Thank you for your letter of February 15, 198_, concerning 198_ income dividends and dividends qualifying for exclusion.

I have enclosed the 198_ tax letter on the Prime Reserve Fund. Your income dividends of $467.49 should be reported on line 8-B of your federal income tax form 1040. The dividends qualifying for exclusion should be placed on Line 8-d of the 1040 form. (NOTE: This amount should not exceed $100.00 if you are filing individually or $200 if you are filing a joint return.)

The difference between the total dividends received and the dividends qualifying for exclusion is taxed as ordinary income.

The $313.22 (dividends qualifying for exclusion) is 67% of your total dividends of $467.49, because only 67% of the Fund's 198— dividend income qualified for the exclusion. Interest earned by the Fund from foreign securities did not qualify.

I hope that the above information has been helpful. Please write or call me collect in Maryland at 000-000-000 should you have any further questions.

Sincerely,

Enclosure

REPLY TO INVESTMENT QUESTIONS
RINQ

Dear Mr. Blank:

It was nice hearing from you again. I welcome this opportunity to answer your follow-up questions to my last letter.

You stated that you are not sure of what questions to ask of our investment advisors. The following are some considerations to keep in mind.

- Is my investment objective still long-term capital appreciation?
- Would I prefer stability of principal?
- Am I likely to retire soon and, therefore, need income?
- How soon will I need the money?

The information that you are requesting on when or if to switch your money really depends on your present financial situation and your investment objectives. Our investment advisors would be more than happy to go over these objectives with you and help you decide which T. Rowe Price Fund would best meet your needs.

If you are not presently concerned with income and desire capital appreciation it would be advisable to invest in one of our four other common stock Funds that seek to achieve long-term capital appreciation with little or no emphasis on current income. You should be aware, however, that along with these Funds' potential for strong capital appreciation there is an inherently greater risk to principal. The Price Organization also sponsors income-oriented funds that are designed for the investor who has a need for a higher current rate of return, and desires stability of principal. I am enclosing a T. Rowe Price Family of Funds brochure that explains in more detail our various Funds.

In regard to your questions concerning any brokers or agents in the United Kingdom, I am afraid I will have to reiterate the information in my previous letter. Because we are a No-Load Mutual Fund regulated by the Securities and Exchange Commission, we cannot recommend any outside brokers or advisors.

I wish I could be of more help to you, but we are limited in the advice that we can offer. I trust, however, that the above considerations will be of some help to you in reaching your investment decisions.

Sincerely,

Enclosure

SECTION 11: STOCKHOLDER AND PROXY LETTERS

1.	Response to Stockholder's Letter	RNSH
2.	Response to Stockholder's Letter—2	RNS2
3.	Letter to Stockholders	TOST
4.	Reply to Stockholder's Letter	RSTL
5.	Reply to Stockholder's Letter—2	RST2
6.	Reply to Stockholder's Letter—3	RST3
7.	Reply to Stockholder's Letter—4	RST4
8.	Proxy Letter and Explanation of Issue	PROX
9.	Proxy Letter and Explanation of Issue—2	PROX2
10.	Proxy Reminder	PREM

Communication with stockholders and explanation of issues that are of vital concern to them are necessary and, at the same time, enlightening. A small matter can disenchant a lot of people and it is through correspondence that these matters of unrest are settled.

Points to Remember

- Use every opportunity to enlighten stockholders regarding issues on which you need support.
- Send a message of cooperation and concern.

RESPONSE TO STOCKHOLDER'S LETTER
RNSH

Dear Mrs. Burns:

We are happy to know that you plan to attend our stockholders' meeting again to vote your shares personally. It will be held, as usual, in our corporate offices on Thursday, October 28, 198—. You will receive your announcement of the meeting together with the Stockholders' Report and other pertinent information within a week or ten days. Your name has not been omitted from the mailing list as you feared. However, I will personally ensure that you receive this information, and I invite you to contact me if it fails to arrive in the mail as scheduled.

Our meetings and open discussion of company policy and goals are intended to keep all shareholders apprised of our development, and we welcome your participation. It is the right and privilege of all stockholders to ask questions during the meeting. During these sessions, valuable information is exchanged. This leads to better understanding on both sides of the corporate aisle.

Thank you for your interest. If I can be of assistance to you, please do not hesitate to write again.

Sincerely,

RESPONSE TO STOCKHOLDER'S LETTER—2
RNS2

Dear Mr. Sayburn:

It is always a pleasure to receive letters from interested stockholders, and we welcome your suggestions and comments. We understand your frustrations at company earnings for the past year, but the general economy has improved and our sales are reflecting a pattern of growth. These signs bring a sigh of relief.

We are pleased to be able to show our shareholders that prudent management and conservative policies have resulted in an excellent financial position and a very optimistic projection for the coming fiscal period.

With regard to your comment that we should increase earnings for stockholders and cut salaries of officers of the company who ride around in limousines . . . I can only say that the limousine that was parked in our lot during our last meeting was hired to transport members of the Board of Directors to the airport. Since two of the members had flown in from Houston for the meeting and our company treasurer was leaving to attend a meeting in New York at about the same time they were departing, this was the most practical method of transportation.

If I can be of service to you or if you have any other questions regarding company policies or practices, do not hesitate to write.

Yours very truly,

LETTER TO STOCKHOLDERS
TOST

To Holders of Our Common Stock Purchase Warrants:

This is to remind you that the option to purchase shares of common stock on the basis of one warrant plus $30 for one share of common stock expired on April 30, 198—. Thereafter, your unexercised warrants continue to be convertible into shares of common stock at a conversation rate of three warrants for one share of common stock. Cash dividends on common stock are being paid at a current annual rate of $2.60 per share.

If you wish to convert your unexercised warrants into common stock, the procedure for doing so is described on the reverse side of this letter.

Sincerely,

REPLY TO STOCKHOLDER'S LETTER
RSTL

Dear Mr. Blank:

This is in reply to your letter telling me of the assistance you received from our Stockholder Records Department in obtaining Mrs. —————'s errant dividend check.

That employee who assisted you was Miss ————, and I shall see that she is commended for the courteous and efficient manner in which she did so.

It was good of you to bring this matter to my attention.

Sincerely,

REPLY TO STOCKHOLDER'S LETTER—2
RST2

Dear Mr. Blank:

This is in reply to your August 3 memorandum suggesting the inclusion of certain information in (company name) future annual reports to stockholders.

Over the years, we have received many suggestions from stockholders on information they would like to see included in our reports. While we carefully consider such requests, we must also consider the usefulness and importance of such information to all stockholders as a group. In addition, we must consider the increased costs associated with providing additional information to our stockholders.

We appreciate receiving your memorandum and will consider your suggestion in planning for our 198— annual report.

Sincerely,

REPLY TO STOCKHOLDER'S LETTER—3
RST3

Dear Mr. Blank:

Thank you for your recent letter and suggestion to reduce costs by encouraging customers to read their own meters. In Mr. _____'s absence, your letter has been referred to me.

We are always seeking ways to reduce costs and can appreciate your concern as a stockholder in these days of inflationary prices.

Historically, we have provided meter-reading cards to those customers who chose to read their own meters, but it has been our experience that customers do not always adhere to the timely requirements of our meter-reading schedule. It is essential to our billing procedure that we follow a timely meter-reading schedule in order to maximize cash flow.

In some cases, customers are unfamiliar with an electric meter and may read it incorrectly or even prefer not to read the meter at all. These situations cause bill adjustments and/or delayed bills with attendant increased operating costs.

I have asked Mr. _____, Coordinator of System Meter Reading, to contact you to discuss these issues in detail.

We thank you for your suggestion and for expressing your concern.

Sincerely,

REPLY TO STOCKHOLDER'S LETTER—4
RST4

Dear Mr. Blank:

This is in reply to your August 1 note to Mr. _____ regarding the multiple copies you received of his July 29 letter.

The letters were machine-inserted. Occasionally, a malfunction will occur, causing more than one letter to be inserted into an envelope, as happened in your case. We have operators watching for such malfunctions, but they are not always able to correct the problem in time to prevent some improperly inserted letters from being mailed.

We appreciate your bringing this matter to our attention as it affords us the opportunity to review our operations.

Sincerely,

PROXY LETTER AND EXPLANATION OF ISSUE
PROX

Re: T. Rowe Price New Era Fund, Inc., Acct.
    Registered:

Thank you for returning your proxy card. Your comments have not gone unnoticed, and we are pleased to have this opportunity to respond to your concerns.

In determining the Fund's management fees, we examine the total assets, objectives, portfolio, and operating costs of the Fund. The history of the Fund and stability of the net asset value per share are also considered.

Because the management expenses are calculated as a percentage of assets, the fees are performance-related. When the Fund's assets rise, the advisory fees increase, and when assets decrease, the fee paid to the adviser is less. For example, in 1980 when the Fund's total assets were $577,799,196, the advisory fee was $2,188,755; but in 1978, the Fund's assets were $190,486,412 and the advisory fee was only $961,406.

I believe the reasonableness of the advisory fee is evident when viewed from the perspective of the Fund's expense ratio. This figure is an expression of the Fund's total operations expenses related to the average net assets and is regarded as the most accurate barometer of the Fund's expense liability. The ratio of operating expenses to average net assets has changed little over the last several years and tends to be low in comparison to other mutual funds of comparable size with similar investment objectives.

Sincerely,

PROXY LETTER AND EXPLANATION OF ISSUE—2
PROX2

Dear Shareholders:

Thank you for returning your signed proxy card for the T. Rowe Price Prime Reserve Fund, Inc. I trust the following comments will further clarify our reasons for seeking to lift the restriction on nonvoting securities.

Certain investment restrictions are imposed upon the Fund to insure compliance with State security regulations. One restriction limited the Fund's purchase of outstanding securities to <u>any</u> class of <u>any</u> issuer to 10 percent, except that of the United States Government. To insure that their regulations comply with the provisions of the Investment Company Act of 1940, the states have amended these regulations to provide for the 10 percent restriction on the <u>voting securities</u>. The Fund seeks to amend its investment restrictions, therefore, to allow investment in more than 10 percent of the <u>nonvoting</u> securities of any issuer. The Fund views this proposal as important since it permits greater flexibility in managing the portfolio and offers the potential for higher return. By lifting the restriction, the portfolio would not be limited to the purchase of only 10 percent of high yielding, nonvoting securities. Most of the securities in our Fixed Income Fund's portfolio are nonvoting securities.

I appreciate this opportunity to discuss the Fund with you. Please feel free to contact us at any time we can be of assistance to you.

Sincerely,

PROXY REMINDER
PREM

Dear Stockholder:

IMPORTANT—PROXY REMINDER

We would appreciate receiving your signed proxy for our annual meeting of stockholders to be held April 21, 198_. However, as yet we have not received the proxy mailed to you in March or it was returned without your signature.

Accordingly, for your convenience, we have enclosed a *second* proxy and a return envelope which requires no postage. Even if you have already mailed the original proxy, we ask you to send in this one also, because the original may have been lost or returned unsigned.

Please sign and return this proxy as soon as possible. The meeting is only about two weeks away, and it is important that we have your vote.

Sincerely,

B O O K 2

**PERSONNEL LETTERS GUARANTEED
TO MAKE YOUR JOB EASIER**

SECTION 12:   HIRING PROCEDURES

A job offer and acceptance is sometimes like a marriage proposal—you are so anxious to get one that you do not look closely at what you are getting. A good working relationship starts with mutual respect and cooperation. The job offer and acceptance procedures should result in a basic understanding of what is being offered and what is expected in return. For example, don't forget to mention duties that the employee is expected to perform, compensation, and probation period or salary review.

Your company policy or philosophy is basically what you expect and what you will or will not tolerate. It does not have to be long or involved, but it should be clearly written.

Points to Remember

- Attendance and tardiness.
- Performance of duties.
- Grounds for immediate dismissal.
- Grounds for dismissal if continued after warnings.
- Miscellaneous statements that pertain to your company and its philosophy.

JOB OFFER
JOCL

Dear Mr. Clifford:

This letter will confirm our telephone conversation of this morning. We are happy to be able to offer you a position as a member of the office staff at the G&H Carpet Warehouse. As we discussed in your interview, your duties will be varied, but we feel you are the man who can handle the job. I have attached a job description that was prepared by the Office Manager, Bill Sprecht. If you accept this offer, we will assume that you are agreeing to perform the duties assigned to you by the Office Manager from time to time.

Your starting salary will be $240.00 per week for 40 hours. You will be a probationary employee for ninety days, after which your work will be reviewed and I will decide whether to make you a permanent employee.

You will be entitled to all the employee benefits offered to our employees, as outlined in the attached Statement of Benefits.

Please let me know by Friday, June ——, 19——, whether you wish to accept this offer.

Yours very truly,

George Hilbert, President

JOB DESCRIPTION
JODS

Job Description for Office Help G&H Carpet Warehouse

Hours: 8:30 A.M. to 5:00 P.M.

Lunch: 1/2 hour

Breaks: Two 10-minute breaks, one between 10:00 A.M. and 11:00 A.M. and one between 2:00 P.M. and 3:00 P.M..

Duties: Answer the Phones: Includes taking orders from dealers; sending out information requested; providing assistance necessary to help dealer make correct purchase.

Transmit Orders: Includes entry of order information into computer; check on credit history to make sure dealer is up to date on payments, etc.

Two week follow-up: Includes checking order two weeks after it is placed to make sure goods were shipped or to find out why goods were not shipped. Order taker must write follow-up letter to dealer to confirm order shipped or to state reason for delay. Order taker must continue to follow up on delayed orders on a weekly basis until filled.

Miscellaneous: Includes filling in at switchboard or reception desk; taking care of supply cabinet; keeping sample books in order; keeping showroom area neat and orderly.

Service Walk-Ins: Includes greeting dealers who may come into showroom; solving problems; taking orders and processing same as telephone orders.

COMMENT: This letter is a job offer and also an offer of an employment contract for ninety days. Notice that the employer can decide not to hire the employee permanently if he or she so chooses. The employee, in accepting the offer, agrees to the terms of employment, including the performance of all tasks that are a part of the Job Description.

The Job Description is short and to the point. It informs the employee what is expected of him or her so that there is no confusion later on.

CONFIRMING ACCEPTANCE OF JOB OFFER
CAJO

Dear Mr. Clifford:

I was happy to receive your phone call this morning accepting the job I offered you on May __, 198_. Welcome to our staff.

Please report to our supervisor, Bill Sprecht, on Monday, June __, 198_, at 8:30 A.M.. He will begin training you on that date.

For your information, I am attaching the G&H Performance Policy. It is our way of monitoring and training our employees to make sure that G&H customers always get the best service possible. Bill Sprecht will be discussing this information with you as he trains you. He will be happy to answer any questions you may have.

Congratulations again.

Yours very truly,

George Hilbert, President

STATEMENT OF PERFORMANCE POLICY
SPER

G&H CARPET WAREHOUSE PERFORMANCE POLICY

In order to ensure that both employees and management are treated fairly, G&H Carpet Warehouse has set up the following policy regarding performance of job duties and discipline for failure to perform.

Probationary Employees
Probationary employees may be dismissed at any time during the 90-day probationary period.

Permanent Employees
Permanent employees are a valuable asset to G&H Carpet Warehouse and will not be dismissed except for a justifiable reason.

Grounds for Immediate Dismissal

The following acts of serious misconduct are grounds for immediate dismissal.

1. Acts that reflect badly upon G&H Carpet Warehouse or are detrimental to our relationship with our customers

2. Stealing

3. Dishonesty in dealings with customers or with the management

4. Falsification of employment records

5. Falsification of financial records

6. Refusal to perform duties as outlined in Job Description or as fairly assigned by supervisor.

Employees who commit such acts will forfeit all benefits, will be terminated immediately, and will receive one week's severance pay.

Grounds for Dismissal If Acts Are Repeated

The following acts of misconduct will lead to dismissal if not corrected:
1. Excessive tardiness

2. Excessive absences where the employee fails to produce a doctor's letter to verify illness

3. Drinking or use of drugs on the job

4. Poor performance of assigned work duties

5. Carelessness on the job that endangers the safety of any employee

An employee who commits one of the above acts shall be given an opportunity to improve his behavior at the discretion of his or her supervisor.

SECTION 13:   EQUAL OPPORTUNITY POLICIES

1. Answer to Charge of Discrimination   ADIS
2. Answer to Charge of Discrimination Follow-Up   ADS2
3. EEOC Charges of Sex Discrimination   ESDE
4. Answer to EEOC Charges of Sex Discrimination   RSD2
5. Answer to Sex Discrimination Charge   RSDC
6. Equal Employment Opportunity Letter   EESH
7. Reply to Equal Employment Opportunity Commission   EERH
8. Response to EEOC Request for Information   REGA

The letters in this section are legally sound examples of how to respond to charges of noncompliance by an agency of the federal government. They are strong letters. They show you how specific you have to be in response to unfair charges of discrimination. There is no way to insure that you will not be cited for noncompliance by a disgruntled employee but you can protect your company from further action of this kind by keeping accurate records.

These letters, which were taken from actual cases, will give you an outline to follow if you are called upon to defend your actions in response to a former employee's charges. You will notice that you have to have facts and dates to substantiate your statements. These facts and dates are too important to trust to anyone's memory. It is better to build your employee file carefully and not need it than to need it and not have it.

Points to Remember

- Treat employees fairly. It is in your best interest.
- Do not depend upon hearsay.
- Document your reasons for dismissal carefully.

ANSWER TO CHARGE OF DISCRIMINATION
ADIS

Mr. William Redford
Investigator
Department of Human Rights

Re: Complaint of Andrew Conklin

Dear Mr. Redford:

This letter will confirm the telephone conversation we had this morning. You called to inquire whether the complaint of Andrew Conklin, our employee, can be settled amicably.

As you know, Mr. Conklin, who is black, has alleged that he was suspended for five days because of absenteeism, while white employees were not suspended for similar conduct. He also claimed that his immediate supervisor makes racially derogatory remarks to him.

I told you in our telephone conversation that Mr. Conklin's accusation comes as a complete shock to me as I have always emphasized the need for fair and impartial treatment of all employees by management, as well as the need for strict discipline. For this reason, before discussing the possibility of settlement, I would like to investigate Mr. Conklin's allegations from within and discuss the matter with my attorney.

I will contact you within two weeks to let you know whether I think Mr. Conklin's claim can be settled amicably.

Yours very truly,

ANSWER TO CHARGE OF DISCRIMINATION FOLLOW-UP
ADS2

Mr. William Redford
Investigator
Department of Human Rights

Re: Complaint of Andrew Conklin

Dear Mr. Redford:

In response to your request of two weeks ago that I consider settling the claim of discrimination lodged by Andrew Conklin against our company, I am at this time informing you that I will not settle the claim.

Mr. Conklin alleged that he was improperly suspended for absenteeism while white co-workers were not suspended. Upon investigation, I determined that Mr. Conklin was suspended for 5 days when he missed his tenth day of work since the beginning of the fiscal year on July 1. Further, Mr. Conklin failed to call in to report that he was sick and failed to produce a doctor's note indicating treatment for illness, both of which are required by the employment policy of the company. Mr. Conklin has a long history of such behavior.

By contrast, the white employee who was not disciplined, who had been cited by Mr. Conklin, had been absent only twice since the beginning of the fiscal year. He was able to document that the reason he failed to call in on the day in question was because his telephone had been disconnected. His illness was verified by a note from his doctor.

As for the allegation that Mr. Conklin's supervisor makes racial derogatory remarks to him, the supervisor vigorously denied he did so. This fact was substantiated by other blacks in the same department who have had no such experience.

However, based on the possibility that some supervisor may at any time be guilty of such behavior, I have issued a memorandum warning against such conduct and asking that any such incident immediately be reported directly to me.

Based on his previous record and this investigation, I can only wonder why Mr. Conklin's supervisor has not asked to have him terminated rather than suspended. I cannot agree that he was discriminated against based on his race, and I cannot offer to settle this matter amicably.

Very truly yours,

EEOC CHARGES OF SEX DISCRIMINATION
ESDE

Edited Sample of Form

In response refer to:
Gwendolyn Banks v.
Thomas Electrical Co.
Charge No. 00000000

Mr. Thomas B. Burns
Personnel Director
THOMAS ELECTRIC COMPANY
211 Industrial Drive
Commercial Park, PA

QUESTIONNAIRE REGARDING CHARGE NUMBER 00000000

The information described and requested by this questionnaire is necessary to the United States Equal Employment Opportunity Commission's investigation of charge number 00000000. Please supply the information specified to the Commercial Park District Office on or before July 9, 198—. If there are any questions, if any discussion is needed, or if, for some substantial reason, an extension of time is required to the time specified for response, please contact Mr. Clark Jones at 000-000-0000.

If alternative documents are available that will satisfy the purpose of some item requested and can be supplied with greater convenience or less expense, please supply them as alternatives; if there is doubt as to the appropriateness of a possible substitution, discuss the matter with the person identified above.

We appreciate your cooperation in supplying the following:

1. Supply a copy of the most recently filed EEO-4 for the organizational unit or facility or unit named in the charge. If your organization (or this unit or facility) is not subject to filing requirements, explain.

2. Are applications given to all persons who attempt to apply for the position of Packer I or II? If not, indicate by whom (identifying job title, name and sex for each person) the determination is made as to which applicants are given applications and which are not. Specify what factors are considered in making such determination.

3. Describe all attempts, if any, to seek out female employees.

4. Are the duties, responsibilities, effort, and skill requirements of the Packer I substantially the same as those of Packer II? If not, explain the difference in detail and submit copies of formal job descriptions, if any, during the period from 1980 to the present.

5. Submit the personnel files of every Packer I and Packer II employed by the organizational unit or facility since 1980.

6. In addition to any of the information requested herein, submit a written response to each of the allegations of the charges, accompanied by documentary evidence, affidavits, and other written statements, where appropriate, including any additional information and explanation you deem relevant to the charge.

ANSWER TO EEOC CHARGES OF SEX DISCRIMINATION
RSD2

Mr. Clark Jones
EQUAL EMPLOYMENT OPPORTUNITY COMMISSION

> Re: Gwendolyn Banks v.
> Thomas Electrical Co.
> Charge No. 00000000

On behalf of the respondent, Thomas Electrical Company, I am making the following response to the questions submitted in your questionnaire dated June 18, 198—.

1. See our most recent EEO-4 form attached as Exhibit A.

2. No, not all applicants are given application forms. Either Joan Walters, female, Assistant Director of Personnel, or myself, Thomas Burns, male, Personnel Director, screens all applicants who come in to apply for any job. We consider the following factors in determining to whom an application is given for any job:

appearance, attitude, behavior, apparent suitability for the job sought, and availability of the job sought. Because Packer I and Packer II positions are the final chance for inspecting and rejecting defective merchandise, applicants must have the aptitude necessary for training as inspectors.

3. Our firm does not seek out employees for any type of job, with the exception of a very few highly technical, specialized jobs. We have many, many applicants, both male and female for every type of job.

4. No, the duties and responsibilities, effort and skill requirements of Packer I and Packer II are not substantially the same. As you will see by the job descriptions for each job, attached as Exhibits B and C, they are quite different. Packer I is a heavy lifting job. Persons empoyed as Packer I must stand at the end of a conveyor belt and off-load heavy products and large electrical components manufactured by our company. After removing each item from the conveyor belt, the packer places it in a shipping carton labelled to correspond to the item. We consider any item that weighs more than 50 pounds to be a heavy item, and only Packer I employees are assigned to lift and pack those items. Packer I employees are also assigned to work the night shift because most of the heavy items that we manufacture are produced on all three shifts.
    Packer II is a light, no-lifting job. Packer II employees are assigned to work at long tables. They are seated while they inspect wall outlet components, light switches, and other small electrical items. The parts are dumped on tables in lots of several gross at a time. Defective parts are rejected and carried away on slow-moving conveyor belts. Approved items are packed into boxes which are also carried to shipping department by slow moving conveyor belts. Also, Packer II employees are not required to work the night shift. Whenever any light items are produced on the second or third shift, they are held until the following workday for packing. Packer II employees do no lifting. Packer I employees remove any light items from conveyor belts to sorting and packing tables and do whatever other lifting is necessary. Other than that, the jobs do not overlap in any way.

5. I object to this request. This action would place an extreme financial burden upon our company to photocopy the personnel records of every Packer I and Packer II we have employed since 1980. Our orders determine the number of our employees, and since the number of orders fluctuates there is a relatively high turnover rate. This means that we would have to copy hundreds of files to respond to a complaint that I believe is completely without merit.

6. The response of the Thomas Electrical Company to each of Ms. Banks charges is as follows:

    a. Ms. Banks has not been employed as a packer by our company since 1978, as she claims. She was hired in January 1978 and quit on September 15, 1978. At that time, she told Joan Walters that she was going to Las Vegas to work as a cocktail waitress. She returned to the area and reapplied for the position of Packer II on May 18, 1979. She was rehired. In July 1981, she took a leave of absence for six months for personal reasons. She returned in January 1982, and since that date has taken 175 sick days, vacation days, and personal leave days. This information is all documented in her employment attendance record and personnel file, which is attached as Exhibit D.

b. Ms. Banks was not denied a promotion to Packer I. We do not consider the job of Packer I to be a line promotion, above Packer II. The two jobs are distinct. The ability to perform as a Packer II employee is not a qualification for a job as Packer I. In May, 1979, when Ms. Banks applied for the position of Packer II for the second time, she was informed by Joan Walters that there was an opening for a Packer I on the night shift and was offered that job. Ms. Banks refused the job, even on a trial basis, and waited approximately three weeks until there was an opening for Packer II. At the time that she refused the Packer I job, Ms. Banks told Joan Walters that she liked to have her evenings free. Ms. Walters distinctly remembers this conversation with Ms. Banks because the two women attended high school together and Ms. Walters has known Ms. Banks personally for many years.

c. Ms. Banks is not paid less than men for performing a job of equal skill, effort, and responsibility. As pointed out in our response to question #4, the two jobs are distinct, and the Packer I employee does more strenuous work and heavy lifting. It is also more difficult to box the heavier items.

I sincerely hope that you will find the foregoing responses and attached Exhibits helpful in determining that Ms. Banks has no claim against Thomas Electrical Company for a violation of the Equal Pay Act or for any other type of discrimination.

Yours very truly,

ANSWER TO SEX DISCRIMINATION CHARGE
RSDC

Mr. Robert L. Baker
Commission Representative
Equal Employment Opportunity Commission
Denver District Office

> Ref: Charge No. 0132400T
> Charging Party: Ms. Linda T. Brown

Dear Mr. Baker:

Following is Western Energy Company's response to your questions regarding the sex discrimination charge of Ms. Linda T. Brown:

<u>Western Energy Company Position Statement</u>

1. On April 29, 198_, Ms. Brown's employment was terminated because of company-wide reduction in force.

a. Ms. Brown's date of hire was May 1, 197_.

b. Western Energy Company had 647 employees as of September 1, 198_.

c. At the time of the reduction in force, sixteen persons were employed in the Land Department. Of the sixteen persons employed, one was the department manager, three were supervisors, six were professionals, and six were office and clerical employees.

2. On April 26, 198—, Mr. Robert L. Johnson, Manager of the Land Department, telephoned Ms. Brown at the Houston office and informed her that she was going to be terminated effective April 29, 198—. She was told that she would receive severance pay, vacation pay, and that her medical benefits would be continued for an additional 30 days after termination.

Mr. Lawrence Fey, Vice President of Human Resources, sent a letter to each affected employee confirming the termination and outlining the pay and benefits to be received. This letter was mailed on April 26, 198—.

Ms. Brown was not terminated because of her sex. She was terminated because her level of performance was unsatisfactory, which was in accordance with the criteria established for the reduction in force. The criteria for termination are listed below in order of priority.

> Employees in jobs identified as nonessential
> Employee's individual job performance
> Less senior employees

Ms. Brown was not offered reassignment because her level of performance was not up to the required standard as evidenced by her past performance appraisals. There were no open positions in her job classification in any of our other offices.

4. On May 10, 198—, Ms. Brown was given the opportunity to appeal her dismissal in accordance with company personnel policy No. E–7. Ms. Brown did discuss her termination with Mr. Kenneth R. Green, Vice President of the Law Department, who is Mr. Johnson's immediate supervisor. Mr. Green suggested that he, Mr. Johnson, and Ms. Brown meet to discuss the termination. Ms. Brown declined saying that she would call later to set a time for a meeting. Ms. Brown did not call again for a meeting.

Western Energy Company feels that there is no basis for Ms. Brown's charge of sex discrimination. Her termination was justified and was in accordance with the reduction in force criteria that the company established.

If you have further questions, please give me a call.

Sincerely,

Mary F. Cook
Director Human Resources
WESTERN ENERGY COMPANY

EQUAL EMPLOYMENT OPPORTUNITY LETTER
EESH

Notice: This case is simulated for your sample letters and is <u>not</u> an actual case.

Dear Ms.

QUESTIONNAIRE REGARDING CHARGE NO. 00000000

The information described and requested by this questionnaire is necessary to the United States Equal Employment Opportunity Commission's investigation of charge number 00000000. Please supply the information specified to the Chicago District on or before July 00, 0000. If there are any questions, if any discussion is needed, or if for some substantial reason an extension is required to the time specified for response, please contact Joan Doe at 000-0000.

If alternate documents are available that will satisfy the purpose of some item requested and can be supplied with greater convenience or less expense, please supply them as an alternative; if there is doubt as to the appropriateness of a possible solution, discuss the matter with the person identified above.

We appreciate your cooperation in supplying the following:

1. Has Charging Party ever alleged to an official, orally or in writing, that your organization engaged in unlawful employment discrimination against her in the form of sexual harassment? If so, explain the nature of the allegations, their dates, the names and titles of the persons to whom the allegations were made, and what action, if any, was taken with respect to the allegations.

2. Who measured Charging Party's performance during the period of her employment with your firm. Identify that person by sex.

3. Submit respondent's written policy regarding sexual harassment.

4. Submit the personnel file of the Charging Party.

5. In addition to any of the information requested herein, submit a written position statement on each of the allegations of the charges, accompanied by documentary evidence, affidavits and other written statements, where appropriate, including any additional information and explanation that you deem relevant to the charge(s).

(Editor's Note: The edited and shortened questionnaire above is the kind an employer would receive after a female employee filed a complaint with the EEOC alleging sexual harassment by her immediate supervisor. This complaint supposedly alleges that many of her job responsibilities were taken away and that she was given menial tasks and snubbed by her boss after she had refused his sexual advances. Sample answers to the questionnaire are set out for you in the document that follows.)

REPLY TO EQUAL EMPLOYMENT OPPORTUNITY COMMISSION
EERH

Re: Nancy Cartwright v.
Elite Feet Shoe Store
Charge No. 00000000

Ms. Joan Doe
Investigator
EQUAL EMPLOYMENT OPPORTUNITY COMMISSION

Dear Ms. Doe:

The following responses are filed on behalf of the respondent, Elite Feet Shoe Store, to the questionnaire submitted by you in the above charge. If you need any further explanation regarding the information contained in this reply, please call me a 000-000-0000.

1. Yes, Ms. Cartwright came to me in December 1982 and complained that her immediate supervisor, Joseph Blount, manager of the Big Foot branch store was harassing her because she had not responded to his sexual overtures. That was the one and only time that she complained to me about harassment. I offered her a transfer to another store, located in a nearby town, but she stated that she did not like the idea of driving any distance to and from work. I further stated that if she decided to stay there would be no further harassment. I told her that I would immediately call Mr. Blount into my office and tell him that I would not condone this type of behavior.

    I did call Mr. Blount into my office and told him that in no respect would I tolerate his harassment of Ms. Cartwright or any other female employee. I told him that I did not approve of such goings on and that if he wished to get ahead with Elite Feet Shoe Stores he had better change his ways. He promised to keep his personal life out of the business. I was shocked to hear that this matter had continued for almost a year after my speaking to Mr. Blount.

2. Ms. Cartwright's performance during the period of her employment with the Elite Feet Shoe Company was measured by Mr. Blount her immediate supervisor, a male. Mr. Powers, a male, our vice-president in charge of retail stores, also measured Ms. Cartwright's performance to some extent, but he did not see her on a daily basis.

3. The Elite Feet Shoe Stores do not have a written policy regarding sexual harassment.

4. I am sending you Ms. Cartwright's personnel file along with this letter. It consists of 6 pages of documents.

5. The following is the position statement of the Elite Feet Shoe Stores responding to each allegation of Ms. Cartwright:

    a. Ms. Cartwright has been employed by Elite Feet Shoe Stores since 1978 as a stock clerk, then salesperson and finally assistant manager of our Big Foot store, as she states. She did not make repeated complaints about harassment by Mr. Blount. As previously stated, she only lodged one complaint with me in December 1983 that she was being punished by Mr. Blount because she had refused his sexual advances. Mr. Blount, when questioned by me, denied that he retaliated further against Ms. Cartwright after I called him in and lectured him on his behavior. Ms. Cartwright never complained to me that Mr. Blount was retaliating against her for making her first complaint, even though I had told her to let me know if the problem continued.

b. I deny that Ms. Cartwright is presently being sexually harrassed by Mr. Blount or any other employee of the Elite Feet Shoe Stores. It is my suspicion that these two employees were once very close personally and that they had a falling out. I personally responded promptly to Ms. Cartwright's complaint the one and only time that she complained. Further, I am on record as being opposed not only to sexual harassment, but also to fraternization between sexes at the workplace. However, I cannot control people's personal and private lives.

In conclusion, I would like to offer my services to cooperate in arranging a mutually agreeable resolution to this matter. It is my opinion that one of these employees should be transferred so that they will be apart, but I do not wish to punish one person when both are at fault. Please telephone me at your earliest convenience to discuss the role that I, as an employer, can play in resolving this matter.

Yours truly,

RESPONSE TO EEOC REQUEST FOR INFORMATION
REGA

Mr. Halcolm Holliman
Acting Denver Area Director
U. S. Department of Labor
Employment Standards Administration
Office of Federal Contract Compliance Programs

Dear Mr. Holliman:

In compliance with our equal employment opportunity obligations under Executive Order 11246, as amended, under Section 503 of the Rehabilitation Act of 1973, as amended, and under Section 402 of the Vietnam Era Veterans Readjustment Assistance Act of 1974, we are submitting the following information and exhibits in response to your request dated August 16, 198_:

Exhibit A   EEO-1 forms for the years 1976, 1977, and 1978.

Exhibit B   Work force analysis for January 1, 198_.

Exhibit C   Progression line charts as of January 1, 198_.

Exhibit D   198_ job group and availability analysis.

Exhibit E   Goals and timetable charts for 198_ and 198_.

Exhibit F   Analysis of our selection process.

Exhibit G   Analysis of promotions for 198_ and 198_.

Exhibit H   Analysis of terminations for 198_ and 198_

Exhibit I   Affirmative Action Plan for Handicapped and Veterans.

These exhibits should provide you with all the information you seek; however, if we can furnish further information and answer questions that come up in your review please give us a call.

Sincerely,

Mary F. Cook
Director Human Resources
WESTERN ENERGY COMPANY

SECTION 14: PERSONNEL: FOLLOW-UP LETTERS AFTER INTERVIEW OR APPLICATION

1.	Welcome to New Employee	WNEM
2.	Secondary Interview	SEIN
3.	Not Selected for Interview	NOIN
4.	No Position Available	NOPO
5.	No Position Available—2	NOP2
6.	Promotion	PROM

There are very few people who cannot recall the agony of waiting to hear the results after applying for a position.

For all of those who have waited for the mail, we are giving you these friendly positive letters.

Points to Remember

- Send negative letters promptly. The applicant will not be building up hope.
- If you have doubt . . . check it out.
- Hire or promote the best-qualified person.

WELCOME TO NEW EMPLOYEE
WNEM

SECURITY PACIFIC NATIONAL BANK

HEAD OFFICE, SECURITY PACIFIC PLAZA, 333 SO. HOPE STREET, LOS ANGELES, CALIFORNIA

MAILING ADDRESS: P. O. BOX 2097, TERMINAL ANNEX, LOS ANGELES, CALIFORNIA 90051

July 6, 198_

Dear Jane,

Congratulations! We are very pleased that you have accepted our offer of employment as a Management Associate in our Banking Office System for the Southern Division. Your beginning salary will be $1,000 monthly.

The starting date will be August 1, 198_. On that day, please report to 333 South Hope Street for Orientation at 8:30 A.M. in Training Room C on the 19th floor. If you wish to take advantage of the early-bird parking rate, be sure to park on level H and have the attendant by the elevator stamp your ticket.

We look forward to your joining the bank and wish you great success. If you have any questions, please feel free to contact me at (213) 613-5555.

Sincerely,

John Smith
Personnel Relations Officer
Personnel Department

JS:dmi
    wpv

SECONDARY INTERVIEW
SEIN

Dear Jane:

We enjoyed the recent opportunity of talking with you and of reviewing your background with respect to our employment opportunities at Security Pacific National Bank.

As a result of our interview with you on campus, we are interested in considering you for our Management Associate Program, which begins in September 198__.

We will be contacting you in two weeks to coordinate a secondary interview.

Please do not hesitate to contact me if you should have any questions regarding your interview. I can be reached at (213) 613-5555.

Sincerely,

John Smith
Personnel Relations Officer
Personnel Department

JS/dmf
   wpv

NOT SELECTED FOR INTERVIEW
NOIN

Dear Jane,

Thank you for your interest in career opportunities at Security Pacific National Bank.

We have completed our evaluation of your qualifications as outlined in your resume. After carefully reviewing all the responses to our campus interviews, your resume was not one of those selected for further consideration.

Again, we appreciate your interest in Security Pacific Bank, and wish you well in your future career search.

Sincerely,

John Smith
Personnel Relations Officer
Personnel Department

JS/dme
   wpv

NO POSITION AVAILABLE
NOPO

Dear Jane,

Thank you for your interest in employment opportunities with us at Security Pacific National Bank.

Your qualifications have been given careful consideration by this department and presented to the various operating divisions to which your background and experience might be applicable. At this time, it has been determined that we are unable to locate a position suitable to your interests. We are retaining your application in our files should a position commensurate with your qualifications become available.

We appreciate your interest and the opportunity to review your background. We wish you well in your future career search.

Cordially,

John Smith
Personnel Relations Officer
Personnel Department

JS/dmg
   wpv

NO POSITION AVAILABLE—2
NOP2

Dear Jane,

Thank you for your interest in employment opportunities with us at Security Pacific National Bank.

We have completed our evaluation of your qualifications and have taken into consideration the importance of a position that would be of mutual benefit. At the present time, we do not have a position that would meet this objective.

We appreciate your interest and the opportunity to review your background. We wish you well in your future career search.

Cordially,

John Smith
Personnel Relations Officer
Personnel Department

JS/dmh
   wpv

PROMOTION
PROM

Dear Jane,

It is my pleasure to advise you that the Chief Executive Officer has appointed you Vice President, in lieu of your present title, Assistant Vice President, and approved an increase in your salary rate to $30,000 a year, effective from the 1st of August, 198__.

Congratulations upon this recognition and, in appreciation of your efforts, we extend best wishes for your continued success and happiness.

Sincerely,

JS/dmd
    wpv

SECTION 15:   MORE . . . PERSONNEL LETTERS

1. Offering Enrollment in Training Program   OETP
2. Recruitment   RCLR
3. Welcome to New Employee   WNE2
4. Offer of Interview   OFIN
5. No Offer   NOFF
6. Position Filled   IAPF

It is not difficult to write a letter offering an applicant a job or an opportunity to join a training program. The most difficult letter is the one that contains no offer but is positive and encouraging.

Points to Remember

- State the reason for the decision as courteously as possible.
- If you plan to keep the application or resume on file, say so.
- Wish the candidate success in the employment search.

OFFERING ENROLLMENT IN TRAINING PROGRAM
OETP

Dear Jane:

You have been recommended by your store manager to be considered for enrollment in our Retail Manager Associate Training Program. This program is a part of our effort to provide capable, ambitious employees with the opportunity to train for advancement.

We are particularly interested in your college courses in Marketing and Sales. Combined with your work experience and attendance record, they indicate that you will be a qualified candidate for assignment when you graduate.

Because of your work and class schedule, we will try to give you an interview at a time convenient to you. Please call Ms. Smith on extension 3456. She will arrange the interview and answer any questions you may have about the program.

My very best wishes to you for your future success.

Sincerely,

RECRUITMENT
RCLR

Dear Jane:

We are sorry that you were not contacted for an interview when our recruiters visited your campus recently. There were so many student applicants that your name was inadvertently left off the list.

We have completed our evaluation of the resume and application that you mailed to our personnel office. You are invited to come to our offices for an interview on Monday, May 26, at 9 o'clock. At that time, we will give you complete information about the Retail Manager Training Program, which will begin on June 15.

If there is any reason that you cannot keep this appointment, or if you have any questions, please call Ms. Paula Conroy at 345-6789.

Sincerely,

WELCOME TO NEW EMPLOYEE
WNE2

Dear Lynn:

You will be pleased to know that you have been selected to fill the position of Technical Writer. Anne Breen, who will be your supervisor, was very impressed with the writing samples you submitted. She will train you in the specific style of writing required in the position.

Your starting salary for the first ninety days of employment will be at the rate of $15,000.00 per year, as agreed. After that probationary period, your salary will be reviewed.

Please report to the personnel office on September 1, 198_, at 9:00 A.M. for orientation. Your working hours will be from 8:30 A.M. to 4:30 P.M. Monday through Friday.

Welcome to Acme. We wish you every success in your new job.

Sincerely,

OFFER OF INTERVIEW
OFIN

Dear Mrs. O'Hara:

Thank you for your interest in Acme Metalcasting. We are interviewing for a position as assistant to our Vice President in Charge of Marketing and Sales. This is a dynamic new position on a fast-paced team. Since you indicated that you are looking for a job that is a challenge and has potential, we are sure that you will be well suited for this opening.

We are an Equal Opportunity Employer and have already interviewed other candidates for this position. We assure you that we will make an impartial decision based on the qualifications of the applicants. Please call me at 000-0000 to arrange an interview without delay.

If I can be of further assistance to you in preparing for this interview, do not hesitate to contact me.

Sincerely,

Bernard Anderson
Personnel Manager

NO OFFER
NOFF

Dear Ms. Callahan:

Thank you for sending your resume to us for consideration. We do not have any openings at this time. Due to a cutback of government funding for our research and development programs, there is a temporary freeze on hiring.

Your information will be kept on file in our personnel office, and you are encouraged to update it periodically. We are sorry that we cannot be more encouraging to you and we wish you success in your search for employment.

Sincerely,

POSITION FILLED
IAPF

Dear Mrs. Petry:

I am sorry to have to tell you that the position as Nuclear Medicine Technician has been filled. After we placed the ad, but before the paper was printed, a former employee returned. She had previously worked in this position and was well-qualified. She started to work immediately.

In the same mail that brought your request for an interview, we received a glowing letter of your qualifications, written by Dr. Robert Jacobs. Please come in to see me as soon as you are settled in Houston. With your skills and experience, we should be able to place you. If we do not have an opening at that time, we can refer you to our colleagues in the area.

The best of luck to you and your husband in your move to Texas. It will be the start of an exciting new way of life.

Cordially,

SECTION 16: DISCIPLINARY ACTIONS

There is always the risk that an employee will not be satisfactory. Because labor laws are designed to protect the interest of the employee, it is necessary to defend your actions if you ever have occasion to reprimand, suspend, or terminate anyone.

The letters in this section are samples of what should be kept in an employee file.

- Date of the infraction of company policy
- Nature of the infraction
- Counseling of employee
- Warning of pending action
- Simulated case history of unsatisfactory employee
- Suspension

There is no formula for this type of correspondence, because there is no formula for human reaction to circumstances. Some personalities and behavior are stimulating in sales and disruptive in production departments. These letters will give you examples of how to deal with problem situations and protect yourself from unfair charges.

Points to Remember

- Establish a clear company policy for hiring and follow it fairly.
- It is better to be short an employee than to be saddled with one who is not performing satisfactorily.
- An unsatisfactory employee is a disruptive force in the company.

CONFIRMING END OF PROBATION PERIOD
CEPP

Dear Bob:

As I indicated at our meeting yesterday, I am pleased with your work. Your supervisor, Bill Sprecht, has given you good ratings. I am, therefore, making you a permanent employee at the salary of $_____ per 40-hour week. You are to continue to work under Bill with the same job duties. Your work will continue to be supervised in accordance with our Performance Policy.

Keep up the good work, Bob.

Sincerely,

George Hilbert, President

WARNING LETTER TO EMPLOYEE—1
WLE1

Dear Bob:

This letter will confirm that you received a verbal warning from me today for the poor manner in which you cleaned up the showroom Monday evening. Failure to perform your assigned tasks properly can be grounds for termination if not remedied. Please take my warning to heart.

Sincerely,

Bill Sprecht

cc. Employee file

WARNING LETTER TO EMPLOYEE—2
WLE2

This letter will confirm that you received a verbal warning from me today when you returned from lunch with the smell of alcohol on your breath and slurred speech. You were drinking at lunch and your work suffered this afternoon. Drinking on the job can be a cause for termination if not corrected. Please don't let it happen again or I will be forced to suspend you.

Sincerely,

Bill Sprecht

cc. Employee file

INFORMING COMPANY PRESIDENT OF WARNING LETTER TO EMPLOYEE—3
WLE3

Date_____

To: George Hilbert, President
From: Bill Sprecht
Re: Bob Clifford

I had to give Bob Clifford a verbal warning today for excessive absences. When he called in sick for the fifth Monday in the last twelve weeks, I told him to bring me a letter from his doctor when he returned to work. He did not do so. He said he will try not to miss any more days until the end of the year.

cc. Bob Clifford

    Employee File

SUSPENSION LETTER TO EMPLOYEE—1
SLE1

Certified Mail—Return Receipt Requested

April_____

Mr. Bob Clifford:

On _____, you were issued a verbal warning by me because of your failure to clean up the showroom area properly before 5:00 the day before. Yesterday, you again left early and allowed the showroom to remain disorganized. You are only asked to be responsible for cleaning up the showroom and putting the samples back one day out of ten, and you can trade days with the other employees if you have a conflict. There is no reason for you to shirk this important part of your job. Frankly, I think you believe that this is "woman's work" and that you should not have to do it. That is an attitude that creates bad feelings in the office and that must be corrected.

Because this is the second time in twelve months that you have failed to perform your work duties properly, I must suspend you for one day, April __, without pay. Please return to work on April __, and try to improve your attitude regarding your work. Your job depends on it.

Alternative Conclusion:

You are a valuable employee. Do not let this type of thinking impede your progress with the company.

Very truly yours,

REPRIMAND TO EMPLOYEE
RERM

Dear Mr. Clifford:

This written letter of reprimand is being sent to you because of your performance below acceptable standards.

On the morning of _____, Mr. Hanover and Mr. Bergman found you in the Cluster I conference room with others, and an inspection of your assigned work area indicated that an acceptable amount of work had not been done.

Your abusive language toward Mr. Hanover has also been noted. A recurrence of either of the above will result in further disciplinary action—namely, a one-day suspension, three-day suspension, and finally a recommendation for termination.

Very truly yours,

John Smith
Personnel Manager

cc. L. Hanover
    T. Bergman
    Employee File

SUSPENSION LETTER TO EMPLOYEE 2
SLE2

Dear Bob:

On _____, you received a verbal warning and on _____ you were sent a letter suspending you for one day for failure to clean up the showroom on your assigned day. Again yesterday you failed to put the showroom in order on your assigned day. I have no choice but to suspend you without pay for three days for this failure to perform your work duties properly. Your suspension is for August _____, _____, and _____, 19__.

Bob, I know from your conversations with me that you feel you are a better order taker than some of the others and that you think straightening out the samples and arranging the chairs in the showroom cuts down on your ability to do the rest of your job effectively. However, it is just as important to the image of the company that the showroom be neat as that orders be serviced.

You are a good employee in almost all respects, but so are the others. It is not fair to the other members of the office staff that you do not pitch in and clean up the showroom on your assigned day.

If you do not change your attitude regarding this area of your job, I will have no choice but to terminate your employment.

Yours very truly,

Bill Sprecht

SECTION 17:   TERMINATION LETTERS

1.	Failure to Perform Assigned Tasks	TER1
2.	Alcohol on Job	TER2
3.	Stealing	TER3
4.	Unexcused Absence	TER4
5.	Reduction of Staff	TER5
6.	Missed Deadlines	TER6
7.	Nonproductive Salesperson	TER7

Termination of an employee is never a pleasant task, but when it becomes necessary, these letters will show you how to get the job done. It is important that the employee know why this action is being taken.

Points to Remember

- Is this action consistent with your company policy?
- Have you read the employee file and determined that he or she has been given due process?
- Have you discussed the action with your superior or a fellow manager?
- Are you in compliance with governmental regulations regarding racial, sex, or age discrimination?

FAILURE TO PERFORM ASSIGNED TASKS
TER1

Dear Bob:

Effective November ___, 198__, your employment with G&H Carpet Warehouse is terminated. For the fourth time in twelve months, you failed to clean up the showroom properly, which is one of your assigned tasks. As is the policy of the company, all employee benefits are hereby forfeited. Enclosed with this letter is one week's severance pay.

Yours very truly,

Bill Sprecht

ALCOHOL ON JOB
TER2

CERTIFIED LETTER RETURN RECEIPT REQUESTED

Dear Mr. Blough:

Yesterday, one of our customers called to report seeing your delivery truck parked in George Washington Park at 2:00 o'clock in the afternoon. Your supervisor drove to the park and found you inebriated and sleeping amid the rolls of carpeting in the back of the truck.

This conduct is an act that reflects badly upon G&H Carpet Warehouse and cannot be tolerated. Therefore, your employment is terminated immediately. All employee benefits are withdrawn. You will find one week's severance pay enclosed with this letter.

Yours very truly,

George Hilbert, President

STEALING
TER3

Dear Miss Johnson:

This letter will confirm that your employment is terminated upon receipt of this letter. You were found removing an adding machine from the office at 6:30 P.M.. Stealing will not be tolerated at G&H Carpet Warehouse.

Your employee benefits are terminated and you will receive one week's severance pay as soon as the payroll department can draft a check.

Yours very truly,

Bill Sprecht

UNEXCUSED ABSENCE
TER4

Dear Jason:

Your failure to return from own-time vacation to work on August 24, 198—, as agreed upon previously and your failure to contact me with a reasonable explanation of your action has forced me to discharge you from Ellandee's employment. You have been warned on previous occasions that the next time you were not back at work after an own-time vacation, you would be terminated.

Your last paid day was August 13, 198—. Your last two paychecks, covering July 16 through August 15, are being held pending return of Ellandee's materials and your identification badge. Please contact the personnel office to finalize your departure from the company.

Yours very truly,

REDUCTION OF STAFF
TER5

Dear Fred:

Because of current economic conditions and our inability to finalize several of our current projects on a timely basis, we have found it necessary to have a reduction in force. Therefore, we are terminating your employment effective October 8, 198—. The company agrees to pay you, however, for an additional 30 days through November 7, 198—; all unused 198— vacation and accrued 198— vacation; plus severance pay at the rate of two weeks for each year of service up to a maximum of 26 weeks.

You understand and agree that this severance payment is in lieu of all other payments and benefits due to you as a result of your employment at Western Energy Company and its affiliate companies except those payments and benefits specifically identified in this letter.

In addition to termination pay, severance pay, and vacation pay, the company will pay your medical insurance coverage through December 198—. All other benefits cease October 8, 198—.

The company is also prepared to provide job search counseling and resume assistance to those employees who request it. Please notify us that you wish to receive these services no later than October 15, 198—.

A letter reviewing specific details of your particular benefits and severance pay will be mailed to your home on October 10, 198—.

Sincerely,

Mary F. Cook
Director Human Resources
WESTERN ENERGY COMPANY

MISSED DEADLINES
TER6

Dear Rowland:

You may remember that when we hired you last December, there was a clear need for an individual in the firm who could work closely with our outplacement clients. Although you have been extremely sensitive toward and flexible to their needs, you have experienced difficulty in responding to the urgency of their situation. In fact, on August 2, 198_, a manufacturing client; on September 16, 198_, a financial institution client; and on November 22, a military client came to me to discuss the fact that you had failed to complete the resume on the day on which it was promised.

I spoke with you about the missed deadline after the first two infractions, and you will remember that I gave you a written warning of termination on September 17 if the same situation should arise another time. In addition, I referred to the first infraction on the performance evaluation that we discussed on August 16 and you signed the evaluation to indicate that you understood the recommendations and warning inherent in it.

You are asked to complete the projects that you have begun. On December 1, we will then begin your own outplacement process. Due to your otherwise good service to the company, we will assist you in your search by providing outplacement services through April 1, 198_. As part of your severance package, we will continue to provide your health and insurance coverage until June 1, 198_.

My understanding of your management style is that you belong in a more fluid, less time-oriented work environment. Your interpersonal skills suggest to me that you are a natural in a position in which you will be developing others over an extended period of time. I would be happy to communicate this to a future employer.

We appreciate the service that you have given to Executive Resumes.

Always the best,

Mildred Louise Culp, Ph.D.
Director

km

NONPRODUCTIVE SALESPERSON
TER7

Dear C. J. Johnson:

The Monday mail has been received and your weekly sales report is not in it . . . again.

I have no choice but to terminate you and send someone into that area to service our customers. I have repeatedly told you that the company cannot operate without orders. You evidently do not consider customer orders important. We do. We have to!

Jack Sendar will meet with you at your home to pick up your samples and other company materials. Your account will be credited and a settlement check will be mailed to you as soon as an audit of your account is completed.

Yours truly,

SECTION 18: RECOMMENDATIONS THAT REFLECT WELL ON YOU AND YOUR EMPLOYEES

1.	Former Employee	RECO
2.	Assistant—1	REA1
3.	Assistant—2	REA2
4.	Consultant	RECC
5.	Programmer	REPR
6.	Secretary	RESE
7.	Former Employee	REFE

Personal recommendations were never more important than they are today. Since many firms are reluctant to give more than the dates of employment and workers are more mobile, prospective employers must rely on recommendations to assess the capabilities of applicants.

Points to Remember

- Write an honest evaluation of the applicant's ability.
- Include character traits that are favorable.
- If applicant interacts well with other employees, mention this ability.

FORMER EMPLOYEE
RECO

Dear Mr. White:

Thank you for giving me the opportunity to recommend Mr. John Anderson for employment as plant superintendent with your company. He is capable, dependable, and very personable.

He has risen through the ranks at Newport Van, Inc., and in each position he has done an outstanding job. His ability to work with and relate to plant employees is a unique talent that you will not find in many men.

In response to your asking whether or not I would hire him again, I can honestly answer an enthusiastic "yes." However, I think he is capable of success and growth that we can no longer offer him.

He leaves our employ with an excellent record and our personal best wishes.

Sincerely,

ASSISTANT—1
REA1

Dear Mr. Findley:

Your letter asking for recommendation of Coleen Carroll was on my desk when I returned from a three-week vacation. I hope that the delay in answering the request does not jeopardize Ms. Carroll's consideration for the position of research technician.

She is very capable and works hard. It was with reluctance that I suggested that she look for a company in which she would have more room to develop her skills. She has patience, diligence, and basic honesty in her approach to solving any lab problem. Her work always exceeds my expectations, and other technicians praise her thoroughness when working with her.

You will never regret having her on your staff. She is destined for success in her field.

Sincerely,

ASSISTANT—2
REA2

Dear Mr. Moore:

Lisa Petry has told me that she is answering an ad for a position as a Nuclear Medicine Technician with your hospital.

Do not pass up the opportunity to hire this capable young woman. She will be a valuable worker on your team. She is bright, energetic, and very dependable. What is more, her personality has a remarkably calming effect on patients who are being tested. They immediately feel her warmth and caring spirit and are comforted.

I will hate to lose her. I understand that she is moving because her husband has been transferred to that area. We will be able to get another technician; but there are very few like Lisa Petry.

My professional assessment is that she is extremely qualified. My personal recommendation to you is to look no further.

Cordially,

CONSULTANT
RECC

Dear Mr. Jacobs:

We welcome the opportunity to recommend Dianne C. Morr as an editor and corporate writer. She has worked for us on several projects in the past five years.

Dianne has never disappointed us. Her work is excellent. Each assignment was carefully planned, thoroughly researched, and completed on schedule.

She has tactfully interviewed employees on sensitive issues, respected the confidence of the people she worked with, and presented intelligent analysis of the material she was given.

You will be thoroughly satisfied with any project she does for you.

Sincerely yours,

PROGRAMMER
REPR

Dear Mr. Swanson:

Your request for information about the employment of Joanne White has been referred to me by Mr. Blazer. I am happy to recommend Joanne who worked as a programmer under my supervision for three years.

She is well qualified for a position in research and development. This is her strength. She works very well alone and is always goal-oriented. She needs almost no supervision because she is industrious and uses her time very well.

She has the personality and methodical attention to detail that signify a good programmer. She tests and retests as she develops her programs. As a result, there are a minimum of problems to be "debugged."

I highly recommend her.

Sincerely,

SECRETARY
RESE

Dear Sirs:

Ms. Linda Richardson was my secretary for three years. During that time, she attended Northwestern University and earned her MBA. She was one of the most efficient and intelligent secretaries I have ever had.

She will be excellent in any capacity in personnel management. Her background experience as a secretary will be an asset in understanding the problems of office management. She is a rare blend of outgoing friendliness and dignity. I recommend her highly.

Sincerely,

FORMER EMPLOYEE
REFE

Dear Sirs:

 Your letter asking for personal recommendation of Mr. Richard Jackson arrived in the morning mail. I want to answer immediately so you will not delay in your decision to hire this worthy applicant.

He is efficient, trustworthy, and cooperative. While he was in our employ, I had several opportunities to observe him with other employees and I was impressed with his ability to get the best effort from each one.

He has a likable personality and can relate to people on all levels. He is an excellent candidate for the position of Branch Manager. He has unlimited potential, and I am happy to see him seeking a new challenge.

Cordially,

SECTION 19:   EMPLOYMENT VERIFICATION

1. Employment Verification—Unenthusiastic Response   EVUR
2. Employment Verification—Suggests Problem Record   EVPR
3. Employment Verification Request Form   EFEV

It is the ethical responsibility of a member of the business community not to attempt to mislead a prospective employer who inquires about the work record of an applicant for a job.

If an employee has been unsatisfactory or has been encouraged to leave your employ, your best course of action is to verify the dates of employment. This does not indicate an endorsement of his or her qualifications.

Points to Remember

- Consult your labor attorney if there is cause to believe that your former employee may initiate action for information that you may disclose.
- In some instances, the best response is no response at all.
- If you receive a noncommittal response to a request for employment verification, delay hiring procedures until you check further.

EMPLOYMENT VERIFICATION—UNENTHUSIASTIC RESPONSE
EVUR

Dear Sir:

Mr. Raymond Smith was employed with Smith Van, Inc., at the same time I was employed in their offices in Toledo, Ohio.

During the twelve years that I know him to have been in the employ of Smith Van, I cannot recall any incident that would cause me to discourage you from hiring him.

Sincerely,

EMPLOYMENT VERIFICATION—SUGGESTS PROBLEM RECORD
EVPR

Dear Sir:

When I was employed in the offices of Smith Van, Inc., Mr. Raymond Smith was plant manager. My association with him was limited and I can only verify that I know he was an employee.

I'm sorry I cannot be of more assistance to you, but I can only refer you to the personnel office of Smith Van, Inc., for specific details of his employment record.

Sincerely,

EMPLOYMENT VERIFICATION REQUEST FORM
EFEV

To Whom It May Concern:

We are considering the application of _____ for employment as _____.

We will appreciate any information you have that will verify his/her employment record. He/She has signed the release form below and given us permission to seek this information.

Thank you very much for your cooperation.

Carla Cooper,
Personnel Manager

This is my permission for you to release any and all pertinent information regarding my employment with your firm for the purpose of verifying my previous employment record.

Signed _____ Date _____

Dates of Employment: From _____   To _____

Job title _____

Duties _____

Performance _____

Attendance _____

Reason for leaving _____

Comments _____

_____

_____

Signed by: _____   Date _____

Name of company _____

Position held _____

SECTION 20:   MANAGEMENT MEMOS FOR A UNIFIED COMPANY SPIRIT

1.	Teamwork	TEWK
2.	Performance Appraisal Seminar	PERS
3.	Equal Employment Opportunity and Affirmative Action Statement	MMAA
4.	Identification of Disabled Veterans and Veterans of the Vietnam Era	MMVV
5.	Communication	TALK
6.	Attendance Policy	TEND
7.	Absenteeism	ABSE
8.	Alcoholism	ALCO
9.	Dress Code	DRES
10.	Schedule for Docking Tardy Employees	DOCK
11.	Cleanliness Is Next to Godliness	NEAT

Open lines of communication are the lifelines of a company. These management memos will help you start the information flowing from the corporate office to the employees and back again.

Points to Remember

- They point out sound business management principles to use.
- The language is easy to read and understand for all levels of employees.
- They can be used as presented or as a basis for discussion.

TEAMWORK
TEWK

To: All Supervisors
From:
Re: <u>Teamwork</u>

We have read a great deal recently about the superiority of the Japanese worker over the American worker. This is thought to be why the Japanese economy is outperforming the American economy and why they have an edge on their competition. I do not agree with this thinking. I think that the American worker is, and always will be, the epitome of an ideal worker in a free society, and if he has a goal he will exceed it every time. I also think that the American worker is as good as we demand him to be and we have not been providing the challenge necessary for an all-out performance in the past few years.

The Japanese peace-time industrial structure was strengthened by General Douglas MacArthur during the occupation of Japan after World War II. He used the good old Yankee teamwork as his basis. Maybe it's time we tried it again ourselves.

We are going to have a meeting of supervisors in four weeks. From now until then, you will have time to evaluate the workers in your department. Consider each and every one from the standpoint of his good points and how he relates to the other workers. You will find leaders. I hope you will also find followers. We will need them for your team. At the meeting, you will be asked to give us the results of your observations and to make suggestions for improving production in your department.

If each one brings something to contribute to the meeting, we will all go away with a lot of valuable information that we can use to save time, cut costs, and improve production. This is one time that you can be sure management will be listening to what you have to say.

Let's get rid of the stagnation. Let's start the challenge of achievement and appreciation circulating through our shops. It will be interesting to know what you discover about your department as a team. It will be rewarding to learn what you discover about yourself as a supervisor.

PERFORMANCE APPRAISAL SEMINAR
PERS

To: Section Supervisors—Departments 101, 102, 105
From:
Re: Performance Appraisal Seminar

You have been selected to attend the Performance Appraisal Seminar to be conducted by the Employee Relations Department. The seminar consists of two sessions which will be held in the personnel meeting room on March 5 and 8 from 1:00 P.M. until 3:00 P.M..

To assist you to gain the greatest benefit from this seminar, please observe and fill out an appraisal form for your two least cooperative employees. Use fictitious names in all references to these individuals, and use no identifying information on the form.

The purpose of the seminar is to raise the performance level of all employees through education and self-image. The information provided on the appraisal forms will be used to build case stories for the meetings.

If you have any questions or are unable to attend, please come into the personnel office without delay.

EQUAL EMPLOYMENT OPPORTUNITY AND AFFIRMATIVE ACTION STATEMENT
MMAA

MEMORANDUM TO: All employees of
                              WESTERN ENERGY COMPANY

SUBJECT: Equal Employment Opportunity and
                 Affirmative Action Statement

Western Energy Company subscribes to the concept of equal employment opportunity and affirmative action. We judge individuals on job-related factors, without regard to race, color, religion, sex, age, or national origin. We believe this is the most positive way to attract and retain good employees. Fulfilling this belief in nondiscrimination is a real and vital part of everyone's job; a commitment shared by all of us at Western Energy Company.

Since the company's inception, we have subscribed to the letter and the spirit of equal employment opportunity and affirmative action. It's more than just a matter of legal compliance—it's our philosophy.

It's also our objective to make sure that all employees have an equal opportunity to progress within the company. Our Affirmative Action Programs are an important tool in meeting this objective. As part of our continuing efforts to upgrade our employment practices for minorities, women, handicapped, and veterans, we monitor their utilization within the company and periodically reaffirm our commitment to Affirmative Action and Equal Employment Opportunity.

After reviewing the progress we made in our Affirmative Action Programs last year, I'm please to report that our efforts have had a positive effect. We still have more to accomplish, however. We will strengthen our efforts to increase our representation of women and minorities at professional and managerial levels.

WESTERN ENERGY COMPANY
Wilson F. Jones
President

IDENTIFICATION OF DISABLED VETERANS AND VETERANS OF THE VIETNAM ERA
MMVV

MEMORANDUM TO: All Employees

SUBJECT: Identification of Disabled Veterans and Veterans of the Vietnam Era

The Joynson Computer Company has an Affirmative Action Program designed to employ and advance in employment qualified disabled veterans and veterans of the Vietnam era.

If you are a disabled veteran or a veteran of the Vietnam era, please tell us. Submission of this information is voluntary, and refusal to provide it will not subject you to discharge or disciplinary treatment.

A disabled veteran is defined as a person who:

. . . is entitled to disability compensation under laws administered by the Veterans' Administration for disability rated at 30% or more, or a person whose discharge or release from active duty was for a disability incurred or aggravated in the line of duty.

. . . a person capable of performing a particular job with reasonable accommodation to the disability.

A veteran of the Vietnam Era is defined as a person who:

. . . served on active duty for a period of more than 180 days, any part of which occurred between August 5, 1964, and May 7, 1975, and was discharged or released therefrom with other than a dishonorable discharge, or

. . . was discharged or released from active duty for a service-connected disability if any part of such active duty was performed between August 5, 1964, and May 7, 1975, and who was so discharged or released within 48 months preceding the alleged violation of the Act, the affirmative action clause, and/or the regulations issued pursuant to the Act.

> Mary F. Cook
> Director Human Resources
> Affirmative Action Officer
> WESTERN ENERGY COMPANY

COMMUNICATION
TALK

To: All Department Supervisors
From:
Re: Communication

Communication is not complete until you receive a response.

Often managers and supervisors think they are communicating when they issue orders or edicts. These same managers may then wonder why they get no cooperation or why the morale is so low in their departments. This silent communication of the dissatisfaction of the people that they supervise is the only way the workers have to "interchange thoughts." They are sending a message even though no one is listening.

Be sure that you are open to the people in your department. You are their link with management, and it is important to keep the channels of information flowing freely in order to have satisfied workers with high productivity.

This does not mean that you are to spend all of your time mollycoddling whiners. But do try to recognize legitimate requests for improvement of conditions. Also, encourage suggestions among people who work with the systems. They are usually time-saving, cost-saving methods that increase productivity and work satisfaction. In the final analysis, isn't that what good management is all about?

ATTENDANCE POLICY
TEND

To: All Employees
From:
Re: Employee Attendance

Twice during the past six months, I informed all Section Supervisors of the management's dissatisfaction with some employees' attitudes. They are not getting to work on time; not starting to work promptly; leaving the building for excessive periods of time when they are expected to be working.

To ensure that all employees understand exactly what is expected of them each day, the rules for attendance are repeated in this bulletin. Please read them carefully. If you feel that you cannot abide by them, please come into my office at your earliest convenience.

1. Office hours are from 8:00 A.M. to 5:00 P.M. Lunch time is one hour. That hour is from 11:45 A.M. to 12:45 P.M.. You are expected to be at your desk and to begin working at 8:00 A.M. and 12:45 P.M..

2. There are two 20-minute coffee breaks scheduled into each day: one in the morning and one in the afternoon. You are not permitted to leave the building during your coffee break.

3. You are expected to be in your office during working hours. If it is necessary to leave your office to go to another department or part of the building, you are expected to inform the office secretary, department supervisor, or assistant supervisor. It is often impossible to track down employees if something comes up when they are not at their desks.

4. Any employee who is absent for the day will telephone the department supervisor between 8:00 A.M. and 8:30 A.M. If the line is busy or no one answers, wait a few minutes and try to call again. If after two attempts you still cannot get the line, call me.

This attendance policy is reasonable and is not a hardship for most of our employees. If that is a hardship on you, I will discuss your compliance with you.

ABSENTEEISM
ABSE

From: All Employees
From:
Re: Absenteeism

It is time to restate our attitude toward excessive absenteeism and to discuss it frankly with the few employees who are making it a problem. Being too tolerant of those who abuse the privileges of fair employment is increasing the burden of those who take up the slack when someone does not report for work.

Our figures indicate that 10% of our employees are responsible for more than 50% of the absences. This means that we have a responsibility to the 90% of our employees who recognize their obligations and report to work on time, every day.

To fulfill this responsibility, we are asking each supervisor to observe the absentees in his/her department. If there is a pattern of absence or tardiness, the supervisor will speak to the employee about it and send a report of the problem, action, and response to the personnel office.

ALCOHOLISM
ALCO

To: All Department Supervisors
From:
Re: Alcoholism

If one of the employees in your department showed up for work on crutches, you would immediately recognize that he or she needed particular consideration to avoid being a hazard or causing an accident in the plant. However, how many times have employees reported for work on the mental crutch of alcohol and you turned away from having to recognize the danger?

There are many men and women in our company, and the number seems to be growing, who are being treated for various illnesses but who are not being treated for the cause . . . excessive drinking. Alcoholism and its effects drain off 75% of the accident and illness benefits paid to workers during a calendar year. Recent figures indicate that problems related to drinking cost industry as much as $60 billion a year.

We can now offer help to those who have drinking problems. If you observe anyone, and I do mean anyone, under your supervision whose work habits, absenteeism, appearance or production errors indicate alcoholism; please help us help him/her. Pass the name on in confidence to Larry Cantwell in Personnel. He is qualified to deal competently with this problem and will offer professional counseling and support services.

We would all rather cover up for our friends. We all know that alcoholism frequently affects very sensitive and compassionate people. However, we should make an effort to restore our employees to full productive lives and not make work harder for the employees who work with such individuals. For this reason, I hope you will give those who need rehabilitation services an opportunity to be included in our program.

Incidentally, if there is a work-related accident or illness traced to alcohol in your department, you may be asked to explain why you had chosen not to enroll this employee in the program.

DRESS CODE
DRES

To: All Employees
From:
Re: Dress Code

Our clients judge our firm by its employees as well as by its services. That is one of the reasons why an employee's personal appearance is so important. We are in a very competitive market. If a client forms a negative impression of our employees, it can seriously effect our success.

If we fail, our employees will not have jobs! That is why we established the dress code as stated in the employee handbook. It is based on common sense and moderation. It requires that employees wear clothes that are appropriate for a professional office and not draw undue attention to the individual.

We ask that you observe this dress code. It will give you acceptance in the offices of our clients. This is good for you and good for the company. If you have any questions as to what is considered inappropriate, please discuss it with your supervisor.

SCHEDULE FOR DOCKING TARDY EMPLOYEES
DOCK

TO ALL EMPLOYEES

THE FOLLOWING SCHEDULE IS TO BE USED FOR DOCKING EMPLOYEES FOR BEING TARDY. IT IS TO BE USED WITHOUT EXCEPTION TO ENSURE FAIRNESS TO ALL PERSONNEL. EVERYONE IS EXPECTED TO BEGIN WORKING AT STARTING TIME.

Starting Time	Arrival Time	Time Docked
8:00 A.M.	8:16 A.M. to 8:45 A.M.	½ hour
	8:46 A.M. to 9:15 A.M.	1 hour

DEPARTMENT SUPERVISORS ARE ADVISED TO SEND ANY EMPLOYEE WHO QUESTIONS THIS PAYROLL DOCKING SCHEDULE TO PERSONNEL WHERE THE STARTING TIME AND PROCEDURE WILL BE EXPLAINED.

CLEANLINESS IS NEXT TO GODLINESS
NEAT
MCI TELECOMMUNICATIONS CORPORATION

DATE: July 8, 198_

FOR: Sales/CSC
FROM: Larry Kampwirth
SUBJECT: "Cleanliness Is Next to Godliness"

I don't know if that really is true. The nuns taught us to believe that in grade school.

However, in touring the office last night, I was amazed at what some of the work areas looked like.

In anticipation of the new modular desk arrangements that will be arriving in about six weeks, let's get into some good habits now.

Do me a favor; clean up your area each night before you leave.

Remember, the nuns taught Tom Wynne the same lesson in grade school. Look at his office sometime.

cc: Tom Wynne
    The Cleaning Lady

SECTION 21:   EMPLOYEE INTERACTION MEMOS

1. Absence and Tardiness   ABTA
2. Lack of Cooperation   LACO
3. Use of Telephone   PTEL
4. Leave of Absence   LEVA

Most of the time, problems can be solved before suspension or other drastic action is necessary. A letter, memo, or word to the wise will alert the employee whose behavior is not satisfactory that a change is expected.

Act quickly. If the action is repeated until it becomes a habit, it is much harder to remedy. Make a record of the date and the problem and what interaction takes place whenever it is necessary to call an employee on the carpet.

Points to Remember

- State the problem clearly.
- Explain how it affects fellow employees.
- State what change you expect or whatever message you want to deliver.

ABSENCE AND TARDINESS
ABTA

Dear Leslie:

In many ways, fellow employees are similar to a family. They are interdependent and frequently called upon to "take up the slack" for each other. They are also apt to respond with "It's not fair" if one gets more consideration than the rest.

That is what is happening in your department. The employees who are asked to do your work when you are absent and those who notice that you often come in late are getting resentful. They are complaining.

Frankly, I can't blame them; but I do not want this attitude to continue or to spread. I suggest that you come into my office Wednesday morning before 9:00 o'clock. You and I can talk this out. Maybe there is some way we can resolve the problem.

C. Jacobs

LACK OF COOPERATION
LACO

Dear Cindy:

The antagonism and lack of cooperation between you and Ruth has had a depressing effect on the rest of the people who must work with you. When Laura retired, I thought that we made it clear which duties each of you was to assume from the position that was eliminated.

Several staff members have come to me recently with the complaint that they are having trouble trying to get either of you to do the simplest tasks. The indignation created by this behavior is radiating to other departments.

This condition cannot be ignored. On Friday morning, we will have a staff meeting in my office. Ruth, you, and I will go over the distribution of duties. The object of the meeting will be the fair distribution of work. However, we will also discuss the alternatives open to me. The harmony and goodwill of the employees are of paramount importance to everyone.

Between now and Friday, will you please make a list of the duties performed by you each day and the person who gives you the work? This will assist me in evaluating the distribution of the assignments fairly.

Yours truly,

USE OF TELEPHONE
PTEL

Dear Alice:

It has been brought to my attention by some of the sales representatives that they cannot get my telephone line to check prices during the day.

This is of utmost importance to them because being able to quote an accurate figure to a prospective customer affects their ability to sell our services.

There are two incoming lines for their exclusive use. If anyone else uses these lines, I want to be informed of the practice. There are to be no exceptions. We have made it clear on more than one occasion that these two incoming phone lines are not to be used for outgoing calls. Also, at no time are they to be used for incoming personal calls.

Copies of this memo are being sent to all section supervisors. They will know that you have my permission to refuse to connect calls to anyone who uses these price-quote lines for any other purpose.

Thank you for your cooperation.

Mary Brennan

LEAVE OF ABSENCE
LEVA

Dear Joel:

The personality clashes between you and Burt are beginning to take their toll on the people working with you. I am sure they are taking their toll on you also. After the meeting we had on Friday, I agonized over the best way to resolve this problem.

It was a mistake to try to combine your responsibilities when the companies merged. A better solution should have been worked out at that time. In fairness to both of you, we tried to share responsibilities and combine the positions. Unfortunately, the personalities did not mesh.

Although you have both tried very conscientiously to make the best of it, the stress is dividing employees into two camps.

You are overqualified for the position you are in, and we cannot create a spot for you at this time. For this reason, I suggest that you take a ninety-day leave of absence starting on the first of the month. The personnel office will work out the details of your vacation time, insurance, and so on.

During that time, you would be relieved of the stress and could use the time to begin exploring the job market outside the company. Meanwhile, I will have time to review other areas of the firm in which attrition may be creating a job you could fill.

You have said that your job has no future. It is the individual who has the future. I'm sure you have the ability to see beyond this impasse to make a better future for yourself.

Good luck! I envy you the challenge.

Sincerely,

SECTION 22:   COMMENDATION

1. Restraint under Pressure   CRES
2. Cooperation during Emergency   CCOP
3. For Winning Award   FWIN
4. For Assisting Fellow Employee   CAEM

An individual adjusts to the dynamics of team effort and responds to the encouragement of a pat on the back. It works on the football field, in an orchestra pit, and it will work in your business. Letters of commendation should be a regular part of your in-house communication.

Points to Remember

- These letters should be personal and specific.
- They pay big dividends in loyalty and dedication.
- Write to individual employees for outstanding effort and keep a copy in the personnel file for reference.

RESTRAINT UNDER PRESSURE
CRES

To: All Employees

Congratulations! The restraint you demonstrated last week when we had outsiders harassing employees in the parking lot was commendable.

The management team is meeting with environmentalists to clear up the misinformation and untruths that brought about this demonstration. We know that we are doing nothing to harm the environment or pollute it in any way. Our problem is that we must convince the public of this fact. It will not be easy to do after the unfortunate publicity we received.

We think that the demonstrations are over, but we cannot be certain. We are working with the leaders of the group and will keep you informed.

Meanwhile, thank you for not "losing your cool." It was provoking, but you responded magnificently. Please continue to do nothing to complicate the problem if pickets return.

Thanks for your cooperation.

- - - - -

Alternate sentences for second paragraph.

A.   The management is trying to find out who the vandals were who splashed paint on the building and cars in the lot.

B.   The management is trying to work with the police to have the rowdies apprehended.

COOPERATION DURING EMERGENCY
CCOP

To: All Employees

Take a bow! Hear my applause!

You will all agree that Monday was the most wretched day we have ever experienced. I hope we never go through another one like it.

The continued cold weather has been enough to cope with these last few weeks. The failure of the heating plant and the bursting pipes were enough to send anyone over the edge.

Thanks to all of you, we made it. Now that we are all back in our own offices, warm and comfortable, I can't believe that we all endured it so well. My appreciation to those who so graciously shared office space with others. A very special thanks to those of you who pitched in to carry typewriters and equipment out of the frosty area. You made it possible to conduct business, in a fashion, in the annex.

It is teamwork and cooperation that have always made Gray Engineering a great place to work. Once again, you have come through and made everyone in management proud to be associated with you. The comradeship and cooperation were remarkable.

Now, could we settle back and enjoy a little monotony?

Roy Gray

FOR WINNING AWARD
FWIN

To: Jim Randolph

Once again, your department has the best safety record in the plant. You and the men and women you supervise are to be congratulated. Not only are you consistently ahead of other departments in the areas of safety and production, but you set standards that improve the overall performance of other departments.

Notice of the award has been posted on the bulletin board. I would like to extend my appreciation to you personally. I know the effort and vigilance that went into this fine record.

Thank you and all the employees of your department.

The following letter is more explicit than you would ordinarily write to thank an employee for an act of heroism. However, if you do not include all of the details and record it in the employee file, it will be forgotten when the employee asks for a letter of recommendation. Write the information in the form of a letter and put a copy in the record. It will be available after people in the personnel department have forgotten the incident.

FOR ASSISTING FELLOW EMPLOYEE
CAEM

To: Tom Ryan

There was no emergency yesterday when the fire alarm went off as a result of a malfunction. But you did not know this and you acted heroically. You took the time to escort Lana Brown, who is handicapped, out of the building. I hope that everyone noticed, as I did, that you took the time to help someone you thought might be in danger. I was touched when I saw you coming slowly but resolutely through the door with Lana holding on to your arm, and I was proud of you.

If young people continue to act so admirably, older people may be forced to concede that the world will not go straight to hell when you take over.

SECTION 23: CONGRATULATIONS

Letters of congratulations are easy to write. They convey your best wishes. One of the most important elements of the letter should be sincerity.

Points to Remember

- How well do you know the recipient? If he or she is a close friend, show your enthusiasm and joy for this recognition or success.
- Send the letter while your feelings are fresh and genuine.
- The length is not important. Dash off a sentence or two if you are pressed for time. It is much better than sending a long letter after the enthusiasm is gone.

TO CEO
CCEO

Dear Chris:

I have just heard that you have been chosen to serve as CEO. Please accept my warmest congratulations upon recognition of the skill and leadership you have always demonstrated to your colleagues.

You have the dedication and the zeal to serve in an excellent manner. It is my fervent hope that you enjoy complete success in this new responsibility.

Cordially,

UPON JOINING NEW FIRM
CONF

Dear Tom:

Congratulations on being asked to join the firm of Smith and Jones. I hope that it is the beginning of a long and satisfying association.

I hope that your fulfillment is even greater than your expectations.

Sincerely,

PROMOTION
CPRO

Dear Pat:

I read of your promotion in the trade papers yesterday and was elated. You have the tenacity to succeed and the grace to wear it well.

Go get 'em!

PROMOTION—2
CPR2

Dear Matt:

You got the promotion!

We heard the news in this office with unabashed joy. We know that you are the best man for the job and that you will work well with management. We feel that we have a friend in court.

We all hope that this is only the first of many moves upward.

Congratulations!

"The Girls in the Back Room"

B O O K 3

LETTERS TO HELP IN THE CARE
AND FEEDING OF YOUR SALES FORCE

SECTION 24: SALES REP LETTERS GUARANTEED TO OPEN DOORS

Sales are the manna that feeds your firm. Without sales and service, there would be no need for your company to operate. That is why we have devoted several sections to the care and feeding of your sales representatives.

Points to Remember

- Whenever possible, transfer inside salespeople to outside sales. They know the line and the customers and do not lose time getting acquainted.

- Prepare your accounts for a new representative. It makes them "a part of the family," prepares them for the new rep, and keeps contact until the new rep gets to them.

HIRING INFORMATION FOR SALES REP
HISR

Dear Jim:

This letter confirms the discussion we had in my office this morning regarding your assignment as sales representative in the Middle States Area.

1. You will continue your present position as Customer Service Rep until June 30, 198__. As of July 1, 198__, you will be picked up on the Direct Sales Payroll and will report to Jack Day, Regional Sales Manager, in Aurora, Illinois.

2. Because of your previous training and experience as Customer Representative, you will start getting commissions as of July 1, instead of waiting 30 days— which is the usual training period for new salespersons.

3. You will be scheduled for a performance and salary review after 90 days in your new assignment.

4. You will be assigned a company car by Jack Day when you meet with him. He will also furnish you with a telephone-answering device. This can be installed in your home to record all incoming calls when you are out in your territory.

5. The company will pay for a business telephone to be installed in your home, separate from your family phone.

6. The company will also pay for two file cabinets, each two drawers deep, and a wood top to cover them to create a desk-type work area.

We are very pleased to offer you this opportunity for promotion, Jim, and we want you to succeed. You are the first in-house service representative to be promoted to outside sales through our new policy of employee preference to fill available openings. As I told you earlier, if you make it, there will be new upward mobility offered to other entry-level employees.

Go get 'em.

Steve Jefferson
General Sales Manager

INTRODUCTION OF NEW REP
NEWR

Dear Mr. Gray:

Doug Brown will be your new Acme representative and will be calling on you within the next two weeks. We are very happy to make this announcement because we thought we were never going to find a representative who could fill Jim Bowen's shoes.

As you know, Jim has retired after 22 years with Acme. He had built a great relationship with our customers, and we wanted to continue that tradition. Doug Brown can do it . . . for us and for you.

We know that he will give you excellent service. We will continue to give you prompt delivery and low, low prices. Won't you welcome Doug Brown with a smile and a handshake when he calls on you? He can help you build your sales volume in the Acme tradition.

Sincerely,

NOTICE TO EMPLOYEES OF NEW ASSIGNMENT FOR REP
NUSS

To: All Employees
From: Sales Manager
Re: New Employees

Jeanne Smith is joining the Sales Department of our company on September 1, 198—

Jeanne has been a Customer Representative for four years. She knows the line and the competitors' lines thoroughly and completely. And, as those who have enjoyed the telephone contact with her know, she can get things done. She was a consistent winner in the Customer Representative Awards Program. Her inside sales were frequently in the top five in total volume. We have a folder of customer letters of commendation and praise for her efforts.

Welcome, Jeanne. We wish you every success.

PERSONAL INTRODUCTION—NEW REP
INNU

Dear Bob:

I'm sorry that I will not be calling on you after the first of the month. I have had my leash shortened by the doctor. Instead of going all the way to Maple Grove, I will be staying closer to Madison.

Mike Martin will take over your part of my territory. Believe me, Bob, if I had hand-picked my replacement, I would have chosen Mike. He is pleasant, personable, and works hard to give good service. He is eager to succeed; this reminds me of the enthusiasm I had when I started with Lathrup. He will do a good job for you, and I am sure you will welcome him as you did me when I came to you.

Think about it for a while; you'll have a new audience for your stories. He laughs at every story I tell him. And you know what corn I peddle. But watch it on the golf course. He plays well and he counts accurately; two deadly sins.

I know that Mike will serve you well. I wish I could accompany him and introduce him to you, but the doctor has not released me to return to work yet. In case you need me, I will be happy to help in any way I can. I will be Mike's crew chief and I will keep an eye on my old customers.

Take care.

Bud Terrell

SECTION 25: CARE AND FEEDING OF SALES REPS

1. Rep Bonus Plan   RBON
2. Advice on Cutting Fees for Service   SACF
3. Advice on Written Contract   SAWC
4. Notice of Inventory Closeout   INCO
5. Complaints and Adjustments   COAD
6. Sales Advice—Prep and Discount   SPRE
7. Expense Account Itemizing Memo   EXIM

Frequent calls cost money. Save time and money by letting your sales reps know what procedures you want them to follow, how to react to sharpies, and how to handle complaints and dissatisfied customers.

Points to Remember

- A well-informed rep with the authority to act saves time and money for you.

- A rep who knows the line and the limits makes fewer mistakes.

REP BONUS PLAN
RBON

TO ALL CUSTOMER SERVICE PERSONNEL

Our customers frequently tell us that our customer service representatives are the best in the business . . . and we agree that they are.

We have thought for some time of a way we could stimulate more small repeat orders. We feel that we now have devised a way to do this and to give our service reps a little recognition and bonus at the same time.

Starting March 1, 19___, each of the five customer service reps will be teamed with the three salespersons whose territories they service. They will receive one award point for each dollar of repeat telephone sales generated from their conversations with established customers. This will not be taken from the commission of the salesperson whose customer places the order. It will be a separate accounting procedure.

To stimulate telephone sales, we will have a special promotion regularly. These promotions will be designed to encourage small repeat orders, over and above the regular orders written by the salesperson calling on the distributor.

Customer service reps will receive one dollar for each ten award points. With three territories to work with, this will be a substantial monthly bonus. You have earned this opportunity. Let's see you double your income.

Steve

ADVICE ON CUTTING FEES FOR SERVICE
SACF

Dear Mitch:

It was good to read your report and know that the percentage of sales resulting from personal calls has increased. In these economic times, it is hard to get anyone to spend money. So, I know you are exerting a great deal of effort to show an increase. Keep up the good work. The more calls you make, the more sales you make. That is the basic truth in salesmanship.

In answer to your question of shaving our fee for services, I strongly advise against it. We set the fees fairly after the estimates of time and materials are calculated for each job. If there is a difference, it will be shown on the final statement. No one will be overcharged and costs will be substantiated by figures kept accurately.

When a client asks for a cut and you agree, you are giving the impression that the fee was inflated or the services are not worth what we are asking. This is a bad image to project and seriously undercuts the client's respect for you and for your company.

Set the fees after you have figured the project, and write up the contract before you return to the client's office. If the client begins to haggle, leave the contract with him and tell him that you understand his need to consider the project and that you will return to pick up the contract on the next day. If you remain and haggle, you will lose credibility.

See you in Dallas!

Roger

ADVICE ON WRITTEN CONTRACT
SAWC

Dear Mitch:

You are really running into every artful dodger in the state. The prospect who asks you to service the account but who will not sign a contract is a good one to avoid.

We are a professional company and we work professionally. We take our clients seriously and perform services exactly as outlined for the fees quoted. The contract is a legal protection for you and for the people you do business with. When you are dealing with a client who suggests that you work without a contract, take that as a warning. Make the contract very specific and be sure you can deliver what you promise. Also, be sure to spell out the client's obligations very clearly. You are protecting yourself from a sharpie. A good client wants a firm contract. It protects both ways.

My advice is to be cautious. Good luck.

NOTICE OF INVENTORY CLOSEOUT
INCO

To: All Sales Personnel
From: Sales Manager
Re: Sale of Inventory of Discontinued Products

In answer to the many requests you have been getting for this announcement, you may now contact your key accounts and tell them that the clearance is going to begin on Monday.

The enclosed inventory sheet, price quotation, and other pertinent information are to help you dispose of this inventory.

We will honor requests for color, size, or model (as each case may be) as long as we can do so. Since there are limitations, however, we cannot guarantee that all requests will be filled.

If you have any questions, call Jay Smith at the Lexington Warehouse, 000-000-0000.

Thanks. Your help in disposing of this merchandise is greatly appreciated.

J. Clark.
Encl.

COMPLAINTS AND ADJUSTMENTS
CCAD

To: All Sales Personnel
From:
Re: Customer Relations, Complaints and Adjustments

You have to take complaints seriously. The distributors take them <u>very</u> seriously. They frequently change suppliers because of a grievance.

We spend a lot of time and effort in building customer relations. This is useless if we do not deliver the goods and service as we promise. It is your responsibility to investigate all complaints and claims for adjustment. Find out what the problem is, what it will take to solve it, and see that it is done, promptly.

Satisfied customers are repeat customers. They are the base on which you can build your commissions. Keep that in mind when a customer has a complaint. As soon as a distributor starts to tell you of unsatisfactory products or service, get your Complaint Report pad out and be ready to write. Turn in the report and, if necessary, follow it up.

Many times, the responsibility is with the manufacturer. We have the job of collecting the sample and the facts. We can then charge the costs of replacement to the plant that shipped the goods. Without this information, we take the loss. Sometimes, the shipper is at fault. In these cases, we can file claims for reimbursements. If we do not get the information, we eat another loss. If the consumer is not satisfied, we lose the account.

This brings me back to the beginning of this letter. <u>You</u> have to take complaints seriously.

J. Clark

SALES ADVICE—PREP AND DISCOUNT
SPRE

To: All Sales Reps

This year, we have to make extra efforts to close each and every sale. Competition is tough. Sales are tough. Times are tough.

We have a few suggestions that we have gleaned from studying the orders and reorders that have been coming in.

First, know your competition. Study their lines and their prices and beat their prices if you can! I know this sounds elementary, but sometimes we forget that they are out there working hard too. So, if you have a hot-shot working your territory and breathing down your back, consider this. Are you giving your distributor the best price and the best discount you can to beat out the sale?

Next, know your costs like the back of your hand. If you know them, you can sometimes shave the set-up or preparation charges on large quantities, and bring in a better price quote. The days of writing up the order are long gone. You have to sell each distributor each time you call.

If you run into a situation that needs special handling, take the time to call the home office and get special consideration. We want to help you land every sale.

Keep plugging!

EXPENSE ACCOUNT ITEMIZING MEMO
EXIM

To: Regional Sales Managers
From:
Re: Expense Account Itemizing

<u>All</u> employees are to use the Expense Report forms whenever they request reimbursement or report travel expenses and other expenses incurred while attending company conferences and trade conventions.

Employees who do not travel regularly should submit a request for reimbursement immediately upon return from the trip. Send the report to the Accounting Department and be sure to fill out the form and document all expenses properly. Receipts for all expenses must accompany the completed form and only those expenses that are documented or have receipts will be considered for reimbursement or payment.

Sales personnel who travel regularly should submit a weekly report, mailed to arrive by Monday morning in the Accounting Department. Please file a report every week, even if no expenses were incurred. If employee is on vacation, on sick leave, or not working for any other reason, file a report and indicate this fact. This will avoid confusion and looking for reports that were not mailed.

Business-personal trip combinations are contrary to company policy and must not be planned without prior knowledge and approval by proper company executive. There are absolutely no exceptions to this point. Please avoid disappointment by getting clearance before the trip is planned.

SECTION 26: ASSIGNMENTS: THEY GO WITH THE TERRITORY

1.	Territory Reassignment	TERE
2.	Plans to Reorganize Sales Force	SFRO
3.	Territory Division	TERN
4.	Explaining Division of Territory	EXDT
5.	Follow-Up to Salesman after Territory Division	SATD
6.	To Sales Rep Who Is Not Producing	SNPR

When you say "It goes with the territory," you are not using a cliché. You are stating a fact. Some territories are better than others, just as some sales reps are better than others, and bringing them into balance and developing each to the highest potential is the dream of every sales manager.

Points to Remember

- Review your territory assignments on a regular basis.
- Some reps enjoy the challenge of new ground. Others produce better in familiar territories. Know your employees and reward them for their efforts.
- Weed out dead wood to give your customers good service.
- Good service—more sales—better profits.

TERRITORY REASSIGNMENT
TERE

To: All Regional Sales Managers
From:
Re: Territory Reassignment by Zip Code

Attached is a revised listing of territory assignments by Zip Code that will be in effect on June 1, 198__. It reflects the rapid increase in the number of our distributors in the past fiscal year. It was designed to bring the volume of sales in each territory into closer balance for most of the areas.

We are very happy that there have been expansions in most of our regions, and these assignments make room for additional sales staff. There are also several accounts that have been designated as National Accounts. In fairness, these accounts have been assigned to the salesperson who originated the account even if that corporate address is no longer in the Zip Code assignment of that salesperson.

We have numbered National Accounts as #50. Please be sure that all National Accounts are set up with this number designation to avoid any conflict in the future.

PLANS TO REORGANIZE SALES FORCE
SFRO

Dear Jim:

We have told you many times that we are dissatisfied with the performance of your sales staff. Sales totals in your area are down sharply. This contrasts with the figures of other sales teams for the same period. We added incentives to stimulate sales, but nothing helps.

I'm sorry, but we cannot continue to carry this nonproductive team any longer. We are sending Cy Jensen and Robb Hertig to St. Louis on Thursday to reorganize the sales force for that territory.

Please advise your staff that instead of mailing their weekly reports, they are to bring them to a meeting at the Holiday Inn on Friday morning at 8 o'clock. After a brief meeting explaining the losses, each person will be interviewed and evaluated on the basis of past sales performance. Each one will then be advised of employment status. We have to turn this area around without delay.

In view of your past sales record, we are offering you a sales territory in Milwaukee, Wisconsin, that is productive and can be built up. You will not be a manager, but you will be doing what you do best—selling.

I'm sorry that this venture did not work out. You are a good salesman, but you have a problem motivating others. If you decide to take the Milwaukee offer, please let me know. Ray Wierzen is the manager of that office and I think you will do well with him.

Sincerely,

TERRITORY DIVISION
TERN

Dear Garrett:

When you and Bob were in my office last month, I thought I was clear enough in my instructions to both of you about the division of the territory in Oklahoma. Evidently I was not, because he has questions and so do you.

The enclosed map should solve the problem. The lines are drawn and marked very clearly. We have had three copies made. One is being sent to each of you and the third is being filed in the office for future reference.

The area is new to both of you and you will have to build it up. I tried to divide the territory to give some of the good customers and some of the dead wood to each of you.

The sales rep who had this area was let go. He did not make the effort needed to overcome the competition. The competition is doing very well here and there should be enough sales for both.

I wish we had several more eager, productive salespeople like you in the field. You have done a tremendous job in your territory, and this additional area is a chance to increase your income substantially.

Sincerely,

EXPLAINING DIVISION OF TERRITORY
EXDT

To: Regional Sales Staff
From: Sales Manager
Re: Territory Realignment

Many of you are concerned because we have had to realign our territories. This action does not indicate that we are planning a major change in staff. It is the result of vacancies occurring through attrition. Two members of our staff have retired after long careers with the company; one has been promoted to management; and one has been terminated.

Because of current economic conditions, we have chosen to give our sales staff the chance to keep up their sales and commissions by not refilling these positions immediately. They will be filled as trainees are ready to take them over.

As you all well know, the trainees for sales positions are selected from our staff of Customer Service personnel. These are the inside sales and service positions that most of you had when you started with the company.

We have several qualified people who are ready to go out into the field as sales trainees. We are waiting to give them assignments until the financial climate improves. This will ensure them of success with a good territory. Now there is too great a potential for lean months and discouragement.

I hope this puts the rumors of lay-offs to rest. The new territories will be a temporary assignment until growth demands another change. We hope that will be soon.

Best regards,

FOLLOW-UP TO SALESMAN AFTER TERRITORY DIVISION
SATD

Dear Garret:

You are doing a great job! We are pleased to see the increase in the new area. We knew that the sales were there. You are the person we needed to reap them. The weekly sales charts should be pleasing you. You have moved up into the top five sales reps.

We are sending fact sheets on our new telemarketing service. Please distribute them to all of the people you call on. It will enable you to concentrate on getting new customers while your repeat orders are handled for you.

Some accounts are too small for you to spend time calling on. They can now place orders directly. Our in-house sales staff will handle any returns, credits, or pickups. They will give complete service to these users; the commission is yours.

As you make your rounds, pick up names and addresses of potential users of our telemarketing service. That will generate additional sales for you.

TO SALES REP WHO IS NOT PRODUCING
SNPR

Dear Mike:

We are sending the printouts of your latest sales figures. I'm sure that you are as disappointed as I am to see the steady decline in the totals.

You will recall that when you were given your present territory, the gross sales were in excess of $50,000.00. It was this base that made it possible to give you the generous guarantee of $500.00 per week. Sales have not reached $50,000.00 since you have been working that territory.

It is natural to assume that there would be some adjustment to a new salesman by some of the customers. With the firm base on which you had to build, it is reasonable to expect that by this time you would have recovered the momentum and gained enough new business to exceed previous totals. Our marketing analysis indicates that the potential is there. Our spies tell us that your competition is beating us out in handy fashion. Shouldn't you be trying harder?

Because of the cost factors involved, we must insist that each salesperson generate enough sales in the territory to justify the compensation. Otherwise, we would not be fair to the men and woman who are building the sales base. For this reason, starting on October 1, we will have to renew your contract on a straight commission basis.

We are confident that this change will give you the incentive to develop your talents into a top sales rep and generate more income for yourself. You have excellent potential there. Don't let competitors keep you from going over the top. You have my best wishes for your success.

Sincerely,

SECTION 27:   SALES REP NOTES

1. Offer to Help Fellow Salesperson   HEFS
2. To Customer—Thanks for Patronage   TYPA
3. To Customer—Thanks for Contract   TYDC
4. Invitation to Customer   INRE
5. Invitation to Newcomer   IGLF
6. Thanks to Crew   TYWC
7. Thank You for Order   TYFO

The letters in this section are miscellaneous letters that some people will not write because they do not do any more than they have to. You will write them because you know that they will promote goodwill, create a friendly atmosphere for you to work in, and increase your sales.

Points to Remember

- Every letter you write is a sales letter.
- It is a personal contact when you do not have the time to visit a client.

OFFER TO HELP FELLOW SALESPERSON
HEFS

Dear Larry:

Can I help? I heard that you will be out of commission (in more ways than one) for the next few weeks. I have my accounts pretty well under control and will be able to call on some of your more important accounts for you.

If you will get an itinerary ready and any other information that you want to have given to your customers, I will be by on Saturday morning to pick it up. That will save me from trying to plan a route in an area that I do not know.

Try to set it up so that I will be able to leave on Monday morning and cover the territory by Thursday afternoon. I have to be back on Friday morning for an important meeting.

It would help a great deal if you could call your customers and tell them that I will be in and when to expect me. In that way, I will not have to spend time telling each one that you have a broken ankle . . . and that you have not fled to Bali with a beautiful exotic dancer.

Good luck and take care.

Jack

TO CUSTOMER—THANKS FOR PATRONAGE
TYPA

Dear Mrs. Hafner:

Of all of the letters that I have written since starting in business many years ago, none has given me more satisfaction than this letter of thanks.

You have been an excellent customer, and our business is a success because of customers like you. Without such dependable repeat business, we would not have grown and prospered in the community.

We are in a program of expansion. We hope to be able to open our new enlarged facilities next month. We are enclosing cards to admit you to our Pre-Opening Sale. It is scheduled for September 15 and 16. It is our way of showing you how much we appreciate your faithful support.

Sincerely yours,

TO CUSTOMER—THANKS FOR CONTRACT
TYDC

Dear Mr. Jones:

I wish to express my sincere appreciation and that of the management of Byrne's Decorating Studio for the privilege of decorating and furnishing your executive offices and reception area.

We hope that you are as pleased with the finished rooms as we are. From concept to completion, we have enjoyed working with your staff. We are particularly grateful to you for your cooperation, time, and effort.

I would be very happy to have the pleasure of assisting you on some future occasion and hope that you will feel free to call upon me whenever I can be of service.

Sincerely,

INVITATION TO CUSTOMER
INRE

Dear Phil:

The Thank God I'm a Buckeye Club is having a party on February 18 at the Old Barn, and you are invited.

Every year about this time, a group of Buckeyes who are living in exile here in Arizona get together. I'd like very much for your wife and you to be our guests. Dianne and I are having a cocktail party before the main event. Plan to be at our house about 6:30 P.M. That should give us enough time to have a drink and a little conversation as you meet our friends Bob and Jean White, who are also attending.

Start tonight to practice your "Remember Whens." See you on the 18th.

Regards,

INVITATION TO NEWCOMER
IGLF

Dear Leo:

George Butler, who was my roommate at Purdue, has written to tell me that you and your family have recently moved to Springfield. Welcome to the Ozarks. I hope you will enjoy your new home.

George has told me you play golf and might be interested in joining a club. I would like you to join me for a game Saturday morning at Cress Creek. We tee off at about 8 o'clock. One of the members of our foursome is on a business trip, and we would be delighted to have you fill in.

Besides enjoying the fresh air and the exercise together, we will get a chance to exchange a few "George" stories. He is a great guy and I miss him.

Cordially,

THANKS TO CREW
TYWC

Dear "Gang":

The first object my eyes focused on as I was coming out of the anesthesia was this lush greenery. Naturally, I thought I was in the Garden of Eden. Having lived a good life, I felt like that is where I would end up.

Later, I realized that I was in my hospital bed and that you had sent me a beautiful planter. It was just what I needed. You will have to take my word for it that I was almost moved to tears.

Take a bow! You are truly a wonderful (though motley) crew.

And I love ya.

Ben

THANK YOU FOR ORDER
TYFO

Dear Mr. White:

Thank you for your order. It will be shipped without delay.

We also want to welcome you as a customer and tell you that we hope our business relationship will be long and satisfying to you and to Master Sales.

Our reputation has been built order upon order as a result of our high standards of quality and service. We are available to you around the clock through our automatic order and service phone. Do not hesitate to call us toll-free whenever we can be of assistance.

Sincerely,

SECTION 28:   SALES APPOINTMENT LETTERS

1. Sales Introduction—Prior to Appointment Call   SAIN
2. Asking for Appointment   ADEM
3. Thanks for Appointment   TYAT
4. Setting Appointment   ASHO

Getting to talk to the customer when he or she is receptive is half the battle. Don't drive for several hours and arrive to find the buyer gone for the day! Set appointments. Confirm appointments. Follow up appointments. Keep your product and your company visible by writing on letterhead. In that way, the customer is not trying to remember the name of the product when placing an order.

Points to Remember

- You will get more appointments if you offer to solve a problem than if you ask for a sale.
- Do not just sell a product. Tell your prospect how to use it.
- A "Thank You" is never thrown in the basket before it is read. It sits on the desk working for you longer than most letters.

148

SALES INTRODUCTION—PRIOR TO APPOINTMENT CALL
SAIN

 **ROYAL BUSINESS MACHINES, INC.**
Word Processing

October 29, 198—

Dear Ms. Blank:

Many hotel owners and managers are concerned not only with getting a regular return from their present customers but more importantly with securing new business.

The key to developing new business is to reach personally as many potential customers as possible. To be successful, this can be done with a minimum amount of investment and effort.

We have developed a lost-cost system that will be operated by hotel employees that can enhance the image of your hotel and also provide you with a means of attracting additional customers.

This newly designed system has tremendous potential and certainly warrants your consideration. I will call you to set an appointment at a mutually convenient time.

Royally,

Neal Schawel
Account Representative

ASKING FOR APPOINTMENT
ADEM

Dear Mr. Whiteside:

Have you ever thought about all of the things you have to do and concluded that an octopus would be short-handed in your job?

We would like you to meet our octopus. More accurately, we have a mechanical substitute for the many hands needed to make your business a smooth-running operation.

Our representative, Pamela McMahon, is ready to give you a demonstration of how many ways a computer can work for you. THERE IS NO OBLIGATION!

We would like to show you what everyone else is talking about . . . word processing, inventory control, automatic order taking, accounts receivable management. Pamela will explain how a computer can help you in a very short time. After all, she knows how busy you are.

Sincerely,

THANKS FOR APPOINTMENT
TYAT

Dear Mr. White:

Thank you for the courteous way you received me when I visited your company last week. I think you know that a sales representative frequently faces hostility and rejection. It is a heartfelt pleasure to be greeted warmly and treated with genuine interest.

I have discussed your needs for a solvent with our chemist, and he is sending you several samples to determine which formula best suits your problem. He is confident that two or more of them are capable of dissolving the residue left from the undercoating. This method of testing will save you time and money rather than having you order without knowing for certain that the product will do the job.

I will be in touch with you after you have had time to test the products. Meanwhile, if you have any questions or if I can help in any way, please call me. We are here to serve you.

Cordially,

SETTING APPOINTMENT
ASHO

Dear Mr. Greenfield:

I am sorry I was not in when you called my office today. But, I was elated to hear that you did call to invite me to show our line of athletic equipment to your staff members.

I will be in your school on Monday, March 16, at 7:45 A.M. This will give me time to set up the display of athletic equipment before classes start. I will stay through lunch periods to give all teachers and coaches a chance to inspect the equipment. If there is any reason why March 16 will not be convenient for you, please call my office and give my secretary an alternate date.

You and your staff will be impressed with the improvements that we have made this year. Each article has been designed to give maximum service with emphasis on safety, comfort, and durability.

Thank you for giving me this opportunity. I can assure you of excellent price consideration and service.

Sincerely,

SECTION 29:   SALES INCENTIVES

1. MCI Sales Incentive Letter   SELL
2. MCI Sales Report Update   DATE
3. Sales Quota Report   SSQT

Each sales rep usually works alone. Write notes frequently to let each one know that he/she belongs to a team and is appreciated.

Points to Remember

- If you want to be a winner, you must try harder . . . and then try harder.
- A sales rep is usually a competitive person. Be sure to give your sales rep regular incentives.
- Even an old dog likes a pat on the head. Let your team know when they have done a good job.

MCI SALES INCENTIVE LETTER
SELL

MCI

875 N. Michigan Ave., Chicago, IL 60611 (312)751-0400

DATE: July 20, 198_

FOR: All Commercial Reps - Central Region
FROM: Larry Kampwirth
SUBJECT: "Summer Spectacular"

Here it is!! The long-awaited and much talked about Summer Sales Contest.

This warm weather wallabaloosa will determine once and for all who the Number One (!!) Star is on the Central Region All-Stars.

The winner will be entitled to a night out on the town (dinner, drinks, entertainment) with his or her guest, compliments of MCI.

In addition, that rep's name will be engraved on a plaque which will hang in the lobby of our regional office for everyone to see.

Of course, he or she will already have a leg up on qualifying for the Number One Club, which will be a trip to Florida next April, a plaque, and all of the recognition that goes along with membership in this special group.

The contest runs from July 1st through August 31st. The winner will be that person with the most gross Commercial Execunet installations over ninety (90).

Success to all of you!!

LK/ck

cc: Tom Wynne

Distribution: S. King
                C. Languirand
                L. Weintraub
                J. Obermayer
                S. Shiner
                F. McGuire
                D. Waltman
                T. Raczynski

**MCI SALES REPORT UPDATE
DATE**

MCI

8/5 N. Michigan Ave., Chicago, IL 60611 (312)751-0400

DATE: July 23, 198_

FOR: All Commercial Execunet Reps
            Central Region
FROM: Larry Kampwirth
SUBJECT: Month-to-Date Sales

Through July 22, this is how each of you is going in gross orders:

Snell King	19
Cary Languirand	32
Francine McGuire	34
Jessica Obermayer	14
Tom Raczynski	26
Shelley Shiner	36
Lori Weintraub	41
Dave Waltman	30
	232

Based on 15 working days, this activity amounts to 15.46 sales per day, and 340 projected sales for July (based upon 22 working days).

Divided by 8 reps, this is 42.5 sales each. As you can see, this number is below the targeted quota and needs to be improved. You should plan to sell about three accounts per day over the last seven working days for our region to meet quota.

Let's all raise the intensity these last few days and exceed our goals for July.

Good selling!!

LK/ch

cc: Tom Mullaney
     Tom Wynne

Distribution: S. King
               C. Lanquirand
               F. McGuire
               J. Obermayer
               T. Raczynski
               S. Shiner
               L. Weintraub
               D. Waltman

**SALES QUOTA REPORT
SSQT**

To: Sales Manager
From:
Re: First Quarter Sales

We have six salespeople who are ahead of their sales figures for the same period last year. Our thanks to them for this accomplishment.

Roy Gray	1.28%
Jack Anders	1.25%
Greg Green	1.22%
Lois Randell	1.17%
Bernie White	1.10%
Ann Ryan	1.04%

These figures prove that hard work, perseverance, and more hard work can get the job done.

We have had a tough time, but we proved our mettle. We want to thank all of you. We need every order. The pressure is on each one of us. We have to keep the plant open and keep our work force working. We are trying not to lay off anyone. It is not easy; success never is. But with all of you making such a valiant effort, we will succeed.

Best regards,

SECTION 30:   BUSINESS AND COMMERCIAL TRAVEL

Business and commercial travel is a very desirable part of hotel and motel occupancy. It is not limited to special events or vacation time. Neither is it to be taken for granted. Of course, the number of rooms occupied by business or corporate guests depends on the location, but in those areas that are convenient to large cities, airports, and expressways, the weary traveler is wooed.

Sales offices aggressively seek this share of the market, and the letters in this section show you the services and considerations that are emphasized in an effort to invite the business traveler. The aura of comfort and luxury of each hotel or motel, the service, the ambiance—these are the areas you should emphasize in your letters.

INQUIRY LETTER
INLE

Dear Sirs:

Our firm has decided to establish a program to accommodate our management executives and corporate guests who travel to and through Chicago frequently. Because of our expanding foreign market, we have found that Chicago has become the hub of our corporate travel. We would like to arrange meetings and appointments to be held there.

Please have a member of your sales department contact us and give us the information that we will need to decide what type of program will best serve our needs.

Sincerely,

RESPONSE
ESP1

Dear Beth:

It was such a pleasure sharing lunch with you last Friday. I'm glad we had the opportunity to discuss personally your Chicago hotel requirements.

Beth, I know that making your out-of-town guests feel welcome and comfortable is one of your top priorities. I do hope that your brief visit to the Ambassador East was long enough to assure you that your guests will receive the finest in hotel accommodations and service.

We at the Ambassador East appreciate Planmetrics' patronage and look forward to welcoming many more of your guests.

Warm regards,

Elizabeth A. Callahan
Account Executive
EXECUTIVE SERVICE PLAN

EAC:pk

EXECUTIVE SERVICE PLAN RESPONSE—2
ESP2

Dear Ms. Quaka:

It is a pleasure to learn of your interest in the Ambassador East Hotel, and I am delighted to introduce myself to you as your contact for group reservations.

As you discussed with Ann Hessert, the Executive Service Plan is our corporate program, which is designed with the individual traveler's needs in mind. This plan offers Pilot Corporation of America the corporate rate and many other personalized services.

Because of several factors involved in negotiating group rates, it is necessary for us to review the specific requirements. After I have had the opportunity to discuss this information with you, I will then be able to offer your company the best possible group rates.

Ms. Quaka, we genuinely value your business and look forward to establishing a long-term relationship with Pilot Corporation of America. Early next week, I will be in touch with you to follow up on your group needs. In the meantime, please give me a call if you have any questions.

Sincerely,

Cathy Sorenson
Senior Account Executive

CS:pk
Enclosure

bcc: Ann Hessert

EXECUTIVE SERVICE PLAN RESPONSE—3
ESP3

Dear Ms. Hammergren:

Let me take this opportunity to tell you how much I enjoyed speaking with you and discussing Budget Rent-A-Car's hotel needs over breakfast. It was nice of you to take the time from your busy schedule, and I hope you feel your time was well spent.

Lillian, I know it's important to you that all of your guests feel welcome and comfortable while in Chicago. I'm hopeful that our brief tour reassured you of the Ambassador East's ability to fulfill your expectations.

We would truly appreciate and value Budget Rent-A-Car's patronage and hope to have the opportunity to accommodate your Chicago guests. I'm looking forward to speaking with you soon to set up a luncheon date at your convenience. In the meantime, if I may be of further service to you in any way, please feel free to give me a call.

Warm regards,

Timothy B. Juliusson
Account Executive
EXECUTIVE SERVICE PLAN

TBJ:pk

AMBASSADOR EAST RESPONSE—4
AER4

Dear Ms. Masters:

We are interested in participating in your future tour group and F.I.T. programs.

Our recent multimillion-dollar restoration has recaptured a bygone era for one of Chicago's most elegant landmarks. We have restored everything from our stunning lobby to our lovely suites with gleaming marble bathrooms, crystal chandeliers, antiques, AM/FM radios, color televisions, plush towels, and countless other touches. Our sleeping rooms are tastefully refurbished in a restful contemporary fashion. The famous Pump Room restaurant is still attracting celebrities and serving excellent cuisine. Our multilingual concierge helps guests with many facets of their stay.

The Ambassador East is just a short walk from Lincoln Park, Lake Michigan, and lively Rush Street. The surrounding neighborhood, known as the "Gold Coast," is perhaps the city's most prestigious area. Best of all, our guests appreciate the safety of this area.

Net rates through 198_ are:

Group		F.I.T.
Single	$____	$____
Double, Twin	$____	$____
Triple	$____	$____
Tax	____	

Baggage handling at $.75 per bag each way
Complimentary room ratio is 1 per 25

You are most welcome to be our guest for a site inspection of the Ambassador East.

We hope to accommodate your clients who desire a first-class property. Please let me know how I may be of assistance.

Sincerely,

Janet Hunter
Sales Manager

JCH:pk

EXECUTIVE SERVICE PLAN RESPONSE—5
ESP5

Dear Ms. Silva:

Thank you for taking the time to speak with me recently regarding our corporate program, the Executive Service Plan.

I'm sure you're familiar with the often difficult and time consuming task of securing hotel accommodations. With our Executive Service Plan, we can minimize your efforts by offering you a private unpublished reservation line: (312) 000-0000. This line automatically identifies you as a member of our corporate program.

We know that making your out-of-town guests feel welcome and comfortable in Chicago is one of your top priorities. Our Executive Service Plan offers the special amenities that can do just that! Your travelers will be pampered in the classic European tradition, with Courvoisier at bedside, turn-down service with Godiva mints, and the Wall Street Journal at their door each morning. Our concierge can provide the distinctive touches that even the most discerning guest might require!

We wish to extend the special corporate rate of $____ single and $____ double occupancy to all travelers of Control Data.

We look forward to welcoming each one of your guests to the Ambassador East Hotel, as it affords us the opportunity to demonstrate that our staff and service are the finest in Chicago!

Kind regards,

Elizabeth A. Callahan
Account Executive
EXECUTIVE SERVICE PLAN

EAC:pk
Enclosure

AMBASSADOR EAST RESPONSE—6
AER6

Dear Molly:

I was pleased to speak to you today regarding your annual meeting. Thank you for the extensive information.

We are very interested in participating in next year's array of hotels providing sleeping rooms. Our attractive Gold Coast location is the first stop in from the airport on the Continental bus and is close to your normal shuttle-bus route. We will gladly extend reasonable room rates in "double digits" per our discussion.

I will contact you in January in order to put forth our bid for the 198_ meeting. In the meantime, I hope to make your acquaintance. You are most welcome to drop by for a hotel tour at your earliest convenience.

Cordially,

Janet C. Hunter
Senior Account Executive

JCH:pk

PALMER HOUSE RESPONSE—7
PHR7

Mr. Hagen Dettmer
INTERCERAM
Verlag Schmid Gmbh.
Hartkirchweg 24
Postfact 1722
D–7800 Freiburg (Breisgau)
WEST GERMANY

Dear Mr. Dettmer:

We have been informed by the Chicago Convention and Tourism Bureau of your interest in bringing a group to Chicago in 198__. This group is to consist of managers and engineers in the ceramic industry.

The Palmer House would welcome the opportunity to accommodate this group, and if you can furnish us with the exact dates and whether or not the group will be attending a Congress or is strictly on a pleasure tour, we will confirm availability and rate.

The Palmer House is located in the heart of downtown Chicago, on the all-new State Street Mall. We are convenient to the theatre and financial districts, large department stores, Michigan Avenue and the Magnificent Mile, and public transportation to most major sightseeing attractions. We are in the midst of a $35 million renovation program to maintain the hotel as one of the finest in the world.

We look forward to hearing from you, and please do not hesitate to contact us if we can be of any further assistance.

Yours truly,

Fred Schmitz, Director
Agency and Tour Sales

cc - Mr. Paul Sturms, Director of Sales
    Corporate Accounts-Central/Southern Europe
    Hilton Hotels Corporation - Frankfurt

B	O	O	K		4

PURCHASING LETTERS
DESIGNED TO HELP YOU DELIVER

SECTION 31:   PURCHASING POLICY

1. Statement of Purchasing Policy   STPP
2. New Blanket Order Issued   BLAN
3. Offer to Sell on Cash Basis   SCSH
4. Offer to Ship C.O.D.   OCOD

Are you reasonably sure that your employees are not stealing merchandise or ideas and plans? Well, just to be certain, establish a purchasing policy. This will ensure that employees are not tempted to make purchases that are not authorized by the company. When it is necessary to use blanket purchase orders, set limits and let the suppliers know exactly who is authorized to use them and for what purpose.

Points to Remember

- Designate purchasing agents who are accountable.
- Inform suppliers of your policy and that there are to be no exceptions.
- Control access to purchase orders and keep a record of the numbers issued.

STATEMENT OF PURCHASING POLICY
STPP

Gentlemen:

With reference to the recent incident in which there was a discrepancy between our records of purchases and your billing, please note and follow our purchasing policy.

1. In all dealings between CCA and R & R Supply Company, authority to purchase supplies and obligate CCA has been delegated to Purchasing Department personnel only. There are to be no exceptions to this rule.

2. The normal procedure for routine procurement will remain the same. A buyer will phone your sales department or your automated telephone order number. When placing the order, our buyer will give our P.O. number and all other forwarding and billing information. The buyer will also give his or her name and phone number.

3. When parts or supplies are needed immediately, an employee will be sent to pick up the order. The employee making the pick-up will have a valid Purchase Order, signed by the buyer who placed the order. The pick-up will be confined to items listed on the P.O. These items will have to be ordered by phone by the buyer before the employee is sent.

4. All CCA employees carry identification badges complete with name and photograph. Please be sure that this identification is presented every time a pick-up is made. If there is any reason to doubt the authenticity of the individual, call the buyer and verify the transaction before giving out the material.

5. Merchandise should not be given to any employee who cannot furnish you with a valid Purchase Order specifying the material and the quantity being purchased and signed by a buyer who has personally placed the order.

Thanks for your cooperation in this procedure. We are all a little sadder and wiser than we were before the billing problems beset us. Fortunately, our education was not too costly.

Sincerely,

NEW BLANKET ORDER ISSUED
BLAN

Dear Ms. Leahy:

Thank you for bringing to our attention the fact that our blanket purchase order #S39077 will expire on August 31. We are issuing a new blanket purchase order #S64145 to be used starting September 1, 198__. This new blanket purchase order will be good for parts and service for one year as the previous ones have been.

The Purchase Order lists the projects, by number, that are to be serviced by this order. Any other project or equipment that is serviced needs a separate purchase order. This is necessary in order to charge the work to the proper account.

Please tell your service clerks and technicians to make no exceptions to this use of purchase orders. The auditors are very careful to check that we are not using funds improperly. Some of the projects we work on are government funded. Therefore, we must ask your cooperation in avoiding improper posting of charges.

Sincerely,

OFFER TO SELL ON CASH BASIS
SCSH

Dear Mr. Neff:

Thank you for the order. We like nothing better than to receive orders from new customers. The only exception to this is that we enjoy repeat orders even more and will try very hard to earn your repeat order.

Right now, we have a problem. We checked the references you supplied us and are sorry that the replies indicate you are overextended at this time.

I suggest that we ship you half of your order now, on a cash basis. This will give you the merchandise you need for the sale you have scheduled. We will fill the second half of the order as soon as you indicate the need for items to replace your stock.

In this way, you can sell what you have on hand, pay for the delivery, and have a better cash position. It will be cost-effective for you, because there will be no finance charges involved. In fact, you will have a savings of 3% cash discount. On this order of approximately $5,000, it will amount to about $150.00.

Please let us know of your decision. We will ship immediately.

Sincerely,

OFFERING TO SHIP C.O.D.
OCOD

Dear Mr. Green:

We have your order ready for shipment, but we cannot release it because our credit manager has not received your financial statement. Until we receive permission from him to ship the merchandise, it is here in our warehouse instead of in your stockroom.

If there will be a further delay in the processing of your credit application, we will ship this order C.O.D. in order for you to have it in time for your sale.

Please let us know how you want to handle this initial order. We value you as a new customer and know that you will be pleased with your merchandise and its price.

Yours truly,

SECTION 32: COMPLAINTS AND RESPONSES TO COMPLAINTS

1.	Unsatisfactory Serviceman	UNSE
2.	Asking for Review of Charges	RECH
3.	Challenging Charges	CHCH
4.	Wrong Material	WRMT
5.	Cards Not Received on Time	PRCD
6.	Response to Complaint	RECP
7.	Explaining Cost Difference	DIFF
8.	Incomplete—Improperly Done Work	INIM
9.	Defective Workmanship	DEWK
10.	Wrong Material—2	WRFE
11.	Wrong Part Shipped	WRPS
12.	Careless Delivery	CADR
13.	Response to Claim for Stolen Merchandise	RECO
14.	Response to Complaint—2	REC2
15.	Response to Complaint—3	REC3
16.	Response to Complaint—4	REC4
17.	Wrong Shipment	WRSH
18.	Apology and Adjustment	APAD
19.	Follow-up Letter of Thanks	FOLL

The time will never come when everyone is perfect and your business day runs smoothly and without frustration. That is why you will probably use these letters of complaint and responses to complaints frequently.

A letter is a part of the file records if you have to take legal action to claim insurance settlement. A letter addressed to an officer of the company will reach the person for whom it is intended and will remain on the desk demanding action.

When your letter is a response to a complaint, it establishes that you take complaints seriously. It outlines what steps you are taking to remedy the problem. It offers a reasonable explanation of the error. Most of all, it keeps your customer.

Points to Remember

- Take all complaints seriously and investigate the problem
- "I am sorry" costs little to say. Not saying it may cost you a valuable account.
- When you are making a complaint, be specific.
- Give all of the details that will affect a prompt resolution.

UNSATISFACTORY SERVICEMAN
UNSE

Dear Mr. Newsom:

When we decided to put our payroll on a computer, we asked for proposals from several companies. Your firm did not bid the lowest price, but you were given the contract for program design and maintenance. The deciding factor was your assurance that you would supply dependable service and support. You claimed that the prime reason for the expansion of your firm was the excellent service rendered to your clients.

I regret to say that we have not had this service from your representative, Jack Caulfield. The computer has been down several times in the past two weeks, and we have lost time and money because Mr. Caulfield is not available when we call. Not only is he unavailable when we call, he delegates the return calls to an employee who is not familiar with the system and who cannot give us any help.

I suggest that you have a meeting with Mr. Caulfield and read the contract to him . . . line by line, if necessary. If you have another representative who would be more responsive to our request for service, please reassign our account. The present lack of cooperation is not an acceptable performance of your contract.

Sincerely,

ASKING FOR REVIEW OF CHARGES
RECH

Dear Sirs:

Will you be kind enough to review your Invoice #56430 for service charges to our San Francisco Data Center?

There is a difference in your engineer's time record and our shop foreman's log. For your convenience, we are sending you copies of our shop log for the days in question.

You will notice that in the travel time for your serviceman, we have estimated the time to get to the airport, flight time, car rental time, and drive to the data center to be 9 to 10 hours. This estimate was based on two previous billings. On both trips, the travel time was 9 hours. This time, the serviceman billed 4 additional hours spent searching for his luggage. We do not think this charge can be justified at time-and-a-half.

4 hours at $75.00 per hour $300.00

The balance of the time difference is shown on the log for July 17, 18, and 20. Our shop records shows that the equipment serviced was under warranty. Some of the time billed for service was for correcting design and functional errors. The warranty time and service time are shown separately on our log entries.

According to our records, there is a difference of:

8 hours at $50.00 per hour	$400.00
6 hours at $75.00 per hour	$450.00
	$1,150.00

Please compare these entries for service warranty time and travel time, and send us an invoice reflecting the new total.

Sincerely,

CHALLENGING CHARGES
CHCH

The next letter challenges cancellation charges of a manufacturer. The letter was written by an interior decorator who accompanied the buyer to the display room. It is a good example of an explanation of why a charge is not in the best interest of the manufacturer at this time.

Re: Your Invoice #13650
    Amount $45.00

Dear Jason:

Sorry, but we feel that this charge is unjustified. We are also confident that you will cancel it when you review the circumstances.

Our customer, John Grant, ordered a sofa but cancelled the order before selecting fabric. It could not have been in production and should not be subject to cancellation charge.

Mr. Grant has many major items to purchase and is considering several from your collection. On Tuesday, we will be in the Merchandise Mart and plan to visit your showroom. At that time, he intends to make final selections. I am confident that he will place a large order. Whether or not that order is with your firm will undoubtedly be influenced by this controversial charge.

We have emphasized when bringing customers to your display rooms that your staff is courteous and your business ethics superior. We make it a point to bring clients to see your collection as one of the first stops in the Mart. It will sometimes happen, as it did in this case, that a client will change his mind or will want to take more time.

We are sure that you will cancel this charge because no fabric was cut or labor expended on this sofa. Mr. Grant will probably order this sofa. This time, however, he will be certain.

Sincerely,

WRONG MATERIAL
WRMT

Dear Les:

When I arrived at work today, I was in a good mood and I am sure that it would have been a good day. However, the first call I received was a complaint, so I think my euphoria has ended. Your company shipped the wrong merchandise to one of our clients, and this error was really a beaut.

Our client, Callahan Funeral Directors, ordered several pieces of furniture from your display in the Merchandise Mart. You will recall that you accompanied us on our tour of the display rooms and wrote the order. You particularly recommended the pair of blue matelasse love seats for the front of the fireplace in the foyer.

The furniture arrived late yesterday afternoon, Les. The blue matelasse love seats were replaced by a pair that were covered in RED SATIN.

Fortunately, Callahan has a sense of humor. He wants to have the love seats replaced immediately. He says that if he ever changes his establishment to a house of happiness, he will be sure to reorder the red satin love seats.

Now that you have had your laugh for the day, please take care of the pick-up and replacement without delay. All of the information is on the original order, a copy of which is enclosed.

Cordially,

CARDS NOT RECEIVED ON TIME
PRCD

Dear Sirs:

On October 23, we issued our Purchase Order #L–46053 to you for a quantity of 2,000 Holiday Greeting cards to be imprinted with our company name and logo.

When we did not receive an order confirmation or shipping date, we called your office on November 8. The customer-service employee who spoke with us acknowledged that the mail order had been received and was in the process of being filled. She estimated that the order would be shipped within one week.

On November 17, we called and spoke to Mr. Yates. He said that the order could not be found and that there would be no further production of the card that we had selected. He also said that there was a strong possibility that the order had been filled and shipped. He promised to trace the order and call us when he had information. He did not call back.

Through November and early December, we called a total of four times in an attempt to get the information regarding the shipment of this order. Finally, on December 5, we issued a written cancellation. We had verbally cancelled during a telephone conversation with Mr. Yates.

On December 21, the cards arrived with our firm name misspelled and no address imprinted on the envelope. Your invoice, which accompanied the order, had the name of the firm spelled correctly.

Because the order had been cancelled, we have no intention of paying the charges. We request that you cancel the invoice.

Sincerely yours,

Phillip Moore

RESPONSE TO COMPLAINT
RECP

The reply that Mr. Moore received is printed below. It is a gesture of apology and goodwill. If I received a letter and gift like this from a supplier, I would be tempted to keep my account open and continue to do business with him. I think you will agree. The silent cancellation of the charges would guarantee that the printer would never get a nickel's worth of business from Mr. Moore.

Dear Mr. Moore:

I apologize sincerely for the aggravation and disappointment your company endured. I hope you were able to get cards locally and that they were ready in time for mailing.

Your experiences with our company reads like a classic chronicle of a patient individual who is rewarded with abuse.

You will have no problems with your cards next holiday season. Today, I supervised the shipment of 2,000 cards. They should arrive in a few days via Courier Express. I am sure you will be satisfied with the selection. They are our number 3289. This card is an updated version of the card you selected from our old catalog. It is from the first run of our line as we replace our depleted inventory and prepare for the coming season.

Please accept these cards, properly imprinted, as a gift. Store them in a safe place until next November and avoid the rush. Then, as your staff prepares to mail them, think of us, madly dashing to fill our seasonal orders with temporary help.

Meanwhile, if you need other office stationery or supplies, we would appreciate another opportunity to serve you. I am enclosed a new catalog to invite you to try again.

Sincerely,

EXPLAINING COST DIFFERENCE
DIFF

Dear Mr. Elston:

Your letter, asking why the cost of removing the old sidewalk and replacing it at the Hunter Run location is so much higher per square foot than at the Sycamore location, has been referred to me for reply.

As estimating engineer on both projects, I have the information at hand for comparison, and I can assure you that the added costs are necessary.

The shifting and settling of the sidewalk at Hunter Run and the deterioration of the walk indicate that it needs reinforcements that are not needed at Sycamore. This is due to several factors, not the least of which are the substructure and the drainage problem.

We have, for these reasons, reinforced the Hunter Run walkway. In addition to the ground preparation and two inches of crushed stone base, we have included metal mesh and metal dowel rods sunk into the curbing to prevent the sinking problem that has caused the hazardous condition that exists there. You will remember that you mentioned to me that there have been instances of customers tripping along the north end of the walk where the sidewalk has sunk and is pitched at an angle. In some places, it is four inches below the level of the curb.

I am sure that although the cost per square foot is higher, you will agree that the costs are justified if you join me for a first-hand observation of the conditions at Hunter Run. I will be there all next week as we are working on the repairs of the parking garage.

Please call my office and tell my secretary when you plan to visit the area, and I will arrange to meet you there.

Yours very truly,

INCOMPLETE—IMPROPERLY DONE WORK
INIM

Dear Mr. Stanley:

My partner and I took a tour of the construction site yesterday afternoon. We also talked with Ron Greene, your job foreman, who informed us that they plan to finish within the week,

When we walked through with the foreman more than two weeks ago, we prepared a list of incomplete or improperly done work. You assured us that these matters would all be taken care of without delay. Not one of the jobs on the list was done. We checked them while we were there yesterday.

We are as eager to complete this project and close on the contract as you are. However, we cannot take possession until the building is in shape for us to move into it.

For this reason, my partner and I will meet with you at the site on Monday morning at 10:00 A.M. We can inspect the building addition room by room. This will give us a chance to discuss the problems and set a closing date based on the progress of the work.

Sincerely,

DEFECTIVE WORKMANSHIP
DEWK

Re: Your Invoice #36 4032
    Dated 7/28

Gentlemen:

We have a complaint from our client who is dissatisfied with the draperies she purchased. We placed the order with your firm. The installer hung the draperies and advised her to leave them tied for a few days. When they were untied, they did not hang correctly.

The customer called your workroom and another installer came to retie the draperies. When they were still unsatisfactory, she called our office. We sent a decorator to her home to examine them. There is an error in the construction of the draperies. They will not hang correctly until they are resewed.

We have more than $2,000.00 of our costs involved in this sale. Our client is withholding payment of other money due until an adjustment is made. Please send someone out to take them back to your workroom. We do not know whether they can be reworked or must be replaced. Our only interest is in satisfying our client.

We appreciate the excellent service that we have received from you in the past, and we assure you that we will continue to recommend your firm to our clients.

Sincerely,

WRONG MATERIAL—2
WRFE

Re: Your Invoice #45 67950
    Shipping Date 7/18

Dear Dan:

We placed an order for 800 feet of chain link fencing 4 feet high. It was delivered directly to the site, and when our installers arrived to install it, they discovered that the fencing delivered was 5 feet high. Please pick up this fencing and credit our account.

The customer has changed his mind and will not fence the property for another two months. We do not want to be responsible for the fencing left unprotected until that time. We will reorder 4-foot-high chain-link fencing material when the customer is ready to have it installed.

If the material delivered was as ordered, we would have been able to enforce our sale contract. However, since it was not, and the price was not as quoted, we could not hold the customer to the sale. We both lost out because someone was careless.

Sincerely,

WRONG PART SHIPPED
WRPS

Dear Sirs:

We are returning the gross of 5-inch fan covers that were delivered to us today.

> We ordered: 1 gross Part Number 4097F 4-in. Fan Covers
> You shipped: 1 gross Part Number 5097F 5-in. Fan Covers

We were able to get the needed parts locally. Please credit our account for the returned merchandise.

We have used your company as a supplier for almost five years and have been satisfied with the quality of the materials and the prices. Recently, we have been dissatisfied with the service and increased errors in filling our orders.

The delays caused by the errors have been costly to us. We regret that we will have to start looking for another supplier unless your standards of service return to previous levels.

Won't you see what can be done to eliminate the problems that we have had in our past few orders?

Sincerely,

CARELESS DELIVERY
CADR

Dear Mr. Carpenter:

We are sorry to tell you that we will not accept any more shipments of merchandise until you change carriers. If you do not want to change carriers, we will understand. However, we will then have to cancel any orders that we have outstanding with you and look for another supplier.

Several times in the past, we have told the driver to remain in his cab and sound the horn for the receiving clerk to open the receiving doors. He chooses instead to park the truck unattended in the alley. He then comes into our office to ask the receptionist to call the receiving room.

On Tuesday afternoon, he unloaded six cartons onto the dock. He came into the front office. The receptionist was very busy handling the switchboard and was annoyed at him for not following instructions. By the time she called the receiving room and the clerk opened the door, two of the cartons were missing.

Our receiving clerk refused to sign for the shipment because the shipping invoice clearly stated six cartons. There were only four cartons on the dock. The driver wanted our clerk to sign for the shipment and put in a claim for theft of the two cartons. Our shipping clerk refused. He said we could not file for theft of goods we had never received. I agree. The loss was a problem for the carrier. It was also caused by the carrier.

We refused the delivery of the four cartons, and they were returned to you. The entire incident could have been avoided if the driver had followed instructions.

Sincerely,

RESPONSE TO CLAIM FOR STOLEN MERCHANDISE
RECO

RE: Invoice #902445

Dear Mr. Grantland:

We sincerely regret the inconvenience caused by the theft of merchandise from your dock. We are shocked that the incident was made possible by the carelessness of our driver.

Our drivers have been cautioned repeatedly not to unlock the cargo door of the truck until the receiving room door is opened. Leaving the cartons unattended on the dock while the driver went into the building was inexcusable. We will handle that matter with him.

We are reshipping your order and will file a claim with our insurance company because the merchandise was never delivered to you.

Your policy of instructing drivers to stay in the cab of the truck and sound the horn as a signal for the receiving clerk to raise the doors is excellent. We have posted this instruction on our bulletin board. We will also ask other companies to begin this practice. It should cut down the rate of theft significantly.

Please contact me directly any time that you are not completely satisfied with our carriers or our service. Your satisfaction and our success are goals we are constantly striving to attain.

Yours truly,

RESPONSE TO COMPLAINT—2
REC2

Dear Sirs:

Your complaint regarding the cost of replacement components on the N603867 Motor that was supplied by our company has been taken into consideration. We will make every effort to keep the cost of replacement parts more in line, but I think there are a few points of discussion that would help to alleviate future problems.

Several times in the past, we have informed procurement personnel that it is less costly to order a complete part than to order a specific component of that part. This is because our suppliers charge us more for individual nuts and bolts of a part than they do when the nuts and bolts are assembled into a particular working item. We have never been able to convince one procurement officer to change the method of ordering these replacement parts and we must pass on the charges.

We have also advocated the build-up of small components and a stockpile of replacements through ordering a complete, cheaper replacement part and breaking it down. If this is done, all of the left-over pieces are available when a repair is needed. In view of the time and cost of air freight for each repair part, the savings would be substantial.

Again, I assure you that we will do all that is possible to keep the replacement costs in line. Perhaps you will be able to suggest a change in specifications of reorder procedures.

Sincerely,

RESPONSE TO COMPLAINT—3
REC3

Dear Mr. Eckert:

I am very sorry that you did not get the satisfaction you expected when you talked to our service representative, Karen Smith. She really had your best interests in mind when she suggested that you have a service person look at your oven to see what replacement parts are necessary.

When an appliance malfunctions, the cause can be one of many things from a switch to a burned-out unit. Many times, the appliance is not faulty. The cause may be the wiring anywhere in the building. We could sell many more parts, if we went for the quick fix. However, we want you to be safe as well as satisfied.

Thank you for bringing your dissatisfaction to my attention. It gives me the opportunity to explain to you that Karen felt that the trouble you were describing needed to be serviced by someone who understood wiring.

I sincerely hope that you were able to get a service person to come to your home. If you did not, please feel free to call me and I will give you the names of reputable firms from which to choose.

Cordially,

RESPONSE TO COMPLAINT—4
REC4

I am very sorry that you did not get the satisfaction you expected when you talked to our representative, Randall Smith. He was telling you the truth when he said that patching the surface of the tennis courts was a quick fix that would not hold.

When changes occur such as you have experienced, they can be the result of heaving caused by freezing and thawing. They can also be caused by improper construction or faulty preparation of the subsurface.

Thank you for bringing your dissatisfaction to my attention. It gives me the opportunity to explain to you that Randall felt that the trouble you were describing needed to be serviced by someone who understood the preparation of the subsurface and the drainage problems of tennis courts.

I sincerely hope that you were able to get a service person to come to your complex. If you did not, please feel free to call me and I will give you the names of reputable firms from which to choose.

Cordially,

WRONG SHIPMENT
WRSH

Dear Blake:

Someone must be envious of your reputation of excellent service to your customers. If not, what possible explanation can there be for two fouled-up orders in one month?

We received a shipment today that is obviously someone else's order. The entire shipment has to be sent back. We can only hope that our merchandise has been misdirected. If it is on some dock, we might get it in a reasonable time. We need the goods badly.

Please go into the president's office. Jump up and down and get red in the face. Read him a scene from the riot act and tell him you won't put up with this anymore. If you don't, I'm going to have to go through all that stress and aggravation when you call on me for an order.

This comedy of errors is getting no laughs in my boss's office. Please try to trace our order and redirect it. If it cannot be located, send duplicate merchandise and credit us for the last shipment. We are enclosing a copy of our order in case you do not have your copy.

Good hunting!

APOLOGY AND ADJUSTMENT
APAD

Dear Jack:

In response to your telephone call today, I sent two gross of metal rings to your Peoria plant via Air Express. The package left our dock before 2:00 P.M. It will be delivered before the end of the business day tomorrow.

We are very sorry that our shipment error caused you inconvenience and hope that these parts will arrive in time to allow you to continue production without interruption.

Please accept our apology. The order filler who worked on your order is very conscientious and rarely makes mistakes. We recently changed our stock placement and, as you know, changes cause errors.

Return the merchandise shipped to you instead of the metal rings, and we will credit your account. Also, you will notice that you are not being charged for Special Delivery and Handling. We are absorbing the extra charges because they were made necessary through our error.

Thank you for your understanding. You are a valuable customer, and we would hate to lose your business.

Sincerely,

FOLLOW-UP LETTER OF THANKS
FOLL

Dear Bob:

Thanks very much for sending the metal rings immediately after my call. We are returning the 2 gross of ringbolts that we received by mistake.

You will be glad to know that they were received in time and that we did not have to stop production. (My ulcer thanks you.)

Enclosed with this letter are:

     1.   A copy of the original order.

     2.   A copy of the bill of lading for the ringbolts.

These papers will help you straighten out the charges.

It is my understanding that we will not be billed for Special Delivery and Handling. This should result in a credit for us on this order.

Thanks again, you rode to the rescue like a cavalry officer.

Sincerely,

SECTION 33: COMPUTER PROBLEMS

1. Computer Software Problem   COMP
2. Service Request   SERC
3. Adjustment   INAD
4. System Problem   SYSP

As everyone who works with a computer knows, you need an immediate answer if your system is down. Most computer problems are handled through conversations on the phone. However, when you have a recurring problem that has you stumped, write to your service person and explain the phenomenon.

Points to Remember

- Explain the program.
- Describe the results.
- Indicate what you have done to solve the problem.

COMPUTER SOFTWARE PROBLEM
COMP

Gentlemen:

Six weeks ago, we purchased a Model DM 1117 microcomputer and three software programs for use in our business office. Two of the programs have been working well, but the third one does not load properly. Your service employees have encouraged me to work with it, and they will try to get the bugs out. But I find this too frustrating and time-consuming.

The program that does not work is the Payroll Program that we were expecting would reduce the time and cost of payroll preparation. I have used all of the "quick fix" ideas your service department has given me, and I still have problems. Frankly, I think that I need a new program. If that is not possible, I am going to get a new ballpoint pen and start writing checks.

We have not yet tried a new disc. Please send one Air Express, and I will return the one we are using.

Yours truly,

SERVICE REQUEST
SERV

Dear Glen:

I am sure that you will recall my purchase of a 277A Computer and the customized program to use in my pharmacy. We have been using it with great satisfaction for inventory control. However, it is not perfect as you guaranteed it would be.

It has the nasty habit of spitting garbage all over the screen every time I strike an "X." The messages are meaningless, but I would like to have them exorcised from my computer. There are so many prescription drugs that have an "X" in the name that I cannot avoid using this key.

Please stop in as soon as you can. You will realize how dependent I have grown on the 277A when you see how at home it is in the pharmacy.

Sincerely,

ADJUSTMENT
INAD

Gentlemen:

I have been using a Model 397 word processor for six months with great efficiency. Now, whenever I strike the "r" key, I get a series of three or four "r"s. I have to stop to delete the extra characters. Is there some simple adjustment I can make on my machine to correct this problem?

Thank you.

SYSTEM PROBLEM
SYSP

Dear Sirs:

My computer is excessively noisy. In addition to this, I have been having problems loading the system. There are copies of the system on three discs, and all three present this difficulty. I receive "Error Reading Disc" messages on the screen. More recently, "Bad or Missing Command Interpreter" messages have been coming up.

Usually, after six or more tries, the system will load and run properly. Can you tell me how to correct this problem?

I have been losing much time trying to load the system, and I need your analysis and a solution desperately.

Sincerely,

SECTION 34: REQUESTS FOR INFORMATION AND RESPONSES TO REQUESTS

1.	Request for Catalog Sheets	RQCH
2.	Response to Request	RSRQ
3.	Request for Carpet Prices	RQCP
4.	Response to Request for Carpet Information	RSCP
5.	Request for Information on Brick	RQIN
6.	Response to Request—2	RSR2
7.	Request for Expert to Inspect Paint	RQPA
8.	Request for Engineer to Inspect Building	RQEB
9.	Request for Engineer to Inspect Paving	RQEP
10.	Reply to Request for Samples	RPSA
11.	Notice to Rebid	RBID

There is a vast store of knowledge available to you if you will only ask for it. There are corporate libraries, laboratories, and catalogs of information to help you. Don't send your client or customer elsewhere until you have made every effort to solve the problem or supply the product.

Points to Remember

- State the product type, size, material, color, quantity, or whatever other data will help identify it.
- If there are problems with application of paints, solvents, paving, or whatever materials you use or plan to use, describe them clearly.
- Give a date by which you need an answer to ensure a speedy reply.

REQUEST FOR CATALOG SHEETS
RQCH

Dear Sarah:

We have a client who is interested in purchasing good-quality, tall-back dining room chairs with tie-on seat cushions. We have seen some of your excellent products and believe that you may have something in your line to fill this need.

Please send us catalog sheets and full information on chairs that you think fit this description. We will want to know exact size, finishes available, and the price of each chair. We will also want to know if you make seat cushions or if we will have to find another source.

Our client wants delivery before December 15, 198__; therefore, we will appreciate your prompt reply.

Sincerely,

RESPONSE TO REQUEST
RSRQ

Dear Gwen:

Thank you very much for your recent request for catalog sheets and price information on tall-back dining room chairs. I am sure you will find what you are looking for in the sheets enclosed. They offer a wide choice of top-quality styles.

You mentioned that your client wants delivery by December 15. I sent several pictures of chairs that can be delivered by then. They are stapled together and labeled "In Stock." However, I did send catalog descriptions and pictures of chairs that can be made to order in a wide range of sizes and finishes. It is better to let your client know what is available. He may decide to wait for a design that he likes better.

In answer to your question about the seat cushions, I suggest you contact some of the fabric houses in the Mart in Chicago. You will have a larger selection there. If you want to order from us, we can supply cushions but the selection is limited.

Sincerely,

REQUEST FOR CARPET PRICES
RQCP

Dear Sirs:

We are rehabbing a large building complex that has oak flooring and wooden stairs. We are considering carpeting the whole building foyer, halls, stairs, and mailroom as well as the apartments.

Before we ask for bids, we wanted catalog sheets and price information on industrial quality carpet. Can you furnish this information to us?

Sincerely,

RESPONSE TO REQUEST FOR CARPET INFORMATION
RSCP

Dear Jack:

Thank you very much for your recent request for catalog sheets and price information of carpeting to be installed in the building you are rehabbing. I have given your request to our distributor in your area. He will call on you with several selection cases of industrial carpeting samples.

It will help him to see the building that you are working on before he suggests suitable floor covering. It will also help you to see the variety of colors, patterns, and textures available to you in this grade of carpet. You may want different colors in different areas, depending on the traffic.

I appreciate your consideration of our company to furnish the carpet and assure you that we will work closely with you to install the best-wearing carpet at the best price.

Sincerely,

REQUEST FOR INFORMATION ON BRICK
RQIN

Dear Ed:

One of our local building management companies has approached us for help in painting a wall. It is the brick wall of a five-story building and the bottom part of it has been spray-painted with graffitti to a height of almost fifteen feet.

We want to try to match the brick color as closely as we can. We also want coverage that will restore the appearance enough to make the investment worthwhile. We need all the help and information that you have available. If you have samples we could try on small areas, please send them to us.

Sincerely,

RESPONSE TO REQUEST—2
RSR2

Dear Dan:

Thank you very much for your recent request for samples of paint to be used in your project to clean up a brick building wall covered with graffitti. We are sending you several small cannisters of various formulas and colors that we think will cover and adhere to the surface. They will be shipped via UPS from our factory in Pittsburgh today.

We are enclosing fact sheets that should help you to accomplish the best results possible. The information covers preparation and application instructions. We hope that our response encourages you. We have seen some very good-looking restoration jobs.

If you need further assistance, please feel free to contact me.

Sincerely,

REQUEST FOR EXPERT TO INSPECT PAINT
RQPA

Dear Sirs:

We have a problem with a car that was brought into our shop for repairs. The paint does not adhere properly and the finished job does not look professional. Because it is an expensive sportscar, the owner is climbing all over me. I have done this work over and over. I've sanded, painted, buffed but the finish seems to bubble or creep.

Please send a representative who understands paint and bonding to look at this car. I have heard that the problem is in the metal from the "hot stove" league of engineers. I want to get it finished and out of my garage. I've lost enough time trying to work it out. I need professional advice.

Sincerely,

REQUEST FOR ENGINEER TO INSPECT BUILDING
RQEB

Dear Sirs:

Will you please have an engineer who is knowledgeable with the vagaries of water leaks arrange to inspect our building at 615 Kingery as soon as possible.

We have been having complaints of dampness and wet walls on the 10th, 11th, and 12th floors. The offices having the problems are not directly beneath each other, but they are all in the northeast quadrant of the building. It is possible that all of the complaints can be traced to one source.

We have had our maintenance staff inspect the window casings and roof for signs of leaks. They have not found any. I think it is time for an expert to survey the dampness and determine the cause.

Let me know when to expect your engineer. We want to alert our tenants and staff to the fact that a stranger will be seeking access to various parts of the building. Our building manager will accompany your employee to avoid any conflict.

Thank you very much.

Sincerely,

REQUEST FOR ENGINEER TO INSPECT PAVING
RQEP

Dear Sirs:

Please have an engineer who is acquainted with the effect of freezing and thawing temperatures on pavement visit our premises. We have several areas in our parking lots that have broken patches.

The contractor who installed the parking lots claims that this is caused by our climate and not by inferior materials or workmanship.

Before we become embroiled in a legal dispute, we would like to have an expert inspect the parking lots and take samples of the surface for testing, if necessary.

Let me know when to expect your engineer. We want to have our building maintenance foreman accompany him and apprise him of the drainage and traffic problems we have had.

Sincerely,

REPLY TO REQUEST FOR SAMPLES
RPSA

Dear Matt:

The samples of undercoating and the technical literature you requested will be mailed today from our home office. I am sorry I did not have the materials with me when I called on you.

Thank you for your interest in our new products. We are confident that you will find they outperform any other product you test.

If there is any other way I can be of service to you, do not hesitate to contact me. Just call the office and they will give me the message when I call in.

Best regards,

NOTICE TO REBID
RBID

Dear Mr. Reynolds:

I received your message informing me that you had decided to proceed with the replacement of only that portion of the sidewalk extending from the north end of your building to the main entrance and had deferred the rest of the replacement of the sidewalk until a later date.

Our bid of $2.50 per square foot for the job was based on the premise that you were planning to replace the entire sidewalk, which amounts to more than 3,000 square feet. I am sorry that we cannot do the smaller job at the quoted rate because of the cost of transporting our equipment to the job site.

We will be happy to submit a new bid based on the replacement of the area you mentioned, which amounts to slightly less than 1,200 square feet. However, we ask that you reconsider doing the entire job since it will be proportionately less expensive to do and far more satisfactory when completed.

Yours very truly,

SECTION 35:   SHIPPING AND DELIVERY

1. Careless Handling   CARE
2. Tracing Lost Shipment   TRAC
3. Cancelling Order—Late Delivery   COLD
4. Appreciation for Prompt Delivery   APPD
5. Cancelling Order—2   COR2
6. Merchandise Damaged in Shipment   MERD
7. Shipping Information   SHIN

Points to Remember

- Whenever you have to write about a shipment that is late, lost, or damaged, give all of the information you can in order to identify the order.

- If you know the order number, purchase order number, date of purchase, part number, description of goods, date of shipment, destination or carrier, include all of the information you have in your letter.

- If you do not have the name of a person who will trace the order, write to the president or general manager. The letter will find its way down to someone who will take action . . . but it will never find its way up.

- Keep a copy of all correspondence about shipment to use in case you have to file for damages.

CARELESS HANDLING
CARE

Re: Your Order Number 6083

Dear Mike:

We have received delivery of the above order, which is a replacement fan to be shipped to our customer and installed in the field. I was surprised to find, after all of the discussions we have had this year regarding wheel damage, that you still ship your fans without protecting the opening to prevent objects from lodging in the fan.

May I quote from your letter to me on July 25, 198—, "The surface of the bent fan wheel blade was devoid of any gouges or other marks of abrasion. Such occurrence in a damaged fan wheel merely indicates that the object, or fragment of material (with sufficient mass) that damaged the fan wheel, was, in substance, softer than the metal material of the fan wheel. Usually, in such circumstances of soft foreign object fan wheel damage, a loose piece of 2″ × 4″ or 4″ × 4″ construction lumber, etc., becomes suspect."

When you ship to us, any of these objects can be dropped into the fan at your plant or on the way. If we immediately ship to our customer, as we will in this case, the objects would not be detected. If you feel that you have no responsibility in this matter, you could at least protect the opening during shipment to avoid problems.

Very truly yours,

TRACING LOST SHIPMENT
TRAC

Re: Waybill #59520
    Shipping Date 12/3/

Gentlemen:

Help! Help! Two cartons were shipped from Nollman Manufacturing Company in Lowell, PA via REA to Southloop Freight Company, 401 S. Clark Street, Chicago, Illinois. They were consigned to Whellen Brothers at that address. They were never received. We cannot find out where they went.

Nollman states that they were shipped and Whellen says they were not delivered. You are the only one who can trace these packages. Since they contain a lamp and shade intended to be a Christmas present for our client's wife, I think you will agree that they would be a welcome Valentine. Let's work together and see that they are delivered safely before that date.

Thanks for all the previous times you have come to the rescue of our packages.

- - - - - -

The tracer who supplied the foregoing letter found the packages. He never stopped looking until he did. He says that he is always motivated more by a courteous letter than he is by a ranting, accusing tirade. Try it.

CANCELLING ORDER—LATE DELIVERY
COLD

Re: Our Purchase Order #45322
   Dated

Dear Mr. Hargrave:

This letter confirms my telephone conversation with you today. **We are** cancelling the above order for 6 dozen ceramic statues that were to be delivered on or before November 15. When we placed our order, we were assured that there was plenty of time to guarantee delivery in time for our Thanksgiving Sale. The statues of turkeys and pumpkins are seasonal, and since they did not arrive in time for our sale we do not want them.

If they have not left your warehouse, please cancel the delivery. If they are in transit, we will not accept the delivery but will instruct the carrier to return them to sender.

Sincerely,

APPRECIATION FOR PROMPT DELIVERY
APPD

Re: Our Purchase Order #45322
   Dated

Dear Mr. Hargrave:

Thank you very much for the effort you made to be sure that the statues we ordered were in our warehouse in time for our Thanksgiving Sale. The personal attention you gave to our order resulted in finding out that the goods were misdirected by the carrier. Fortunately, the order came before the deadline for our advertising.

Our order for your Item #6877—as illustrated in your catalog—is enclosed with this letter. Let's hope we do not have the same problems.

Sincerely,

CANCELLING ORDER—2
COR2

Re: Our Purchase Orders #68367 and #68368

Dear Sirs:

On June 10, 198—, we ordered a Displaywriter System on our Purchase Order #68367. It was scheduled to be delivered at a later date, not specified.

At the same time, we rented a Model 6616 Mag Card II on a month-to-month basis. The Purchase Order for the rental is #68368.

This letter is to confirm our cancellation of the purchase of the Displaywriter System. This action was discussed with and accepted by Mr. Ronald Costello yesterday.

We also want to terminate the rental of the Model 6616 Mag Card II. The rental fees for the use of this machine have been paid through December 31, 198—.

Please call 223-4567 and inform our shipping clerk of your date of removal.

Sincerely,

MERCHANDISE DAMAGED IN SHIPMENT
MERD

Re: Our Order Number 97655
    Waybill Number 40376—Dogeway Express Company

Dear Sirs:

The tables that we ordered were delivered on Tuesday, June 5, 198—. This was three weeks after the promised date. Two of the tables were badly damaged in shipment and we are returning them for replacement.

We were aggravated to see how carelessly the express men handled these cases. We are convinced that the damage was due to this carelessness. We strongly suggest that you change carriers. At least, mark our file to indicate that we will not accept merchandise shipped via this carrier.

Sincerely,

SHIPPING INFORMATION
SHIN

Dear Mr. Calder:

Thank you for your recent order for computer parts and supplies. We are shipping the order today. The boards for the terminals have been back ordered and we will send them as soon as they are wired and tested.

You asked us to ship the fastest way. Air freight is the fastest and also costs less than ocean freight. The air freight charges will be about $95.00 for both shipments.

We now have an automated order entry system. It is available to you twenty-four hours a day. You can place your orders during your business day and we will fill them during our next business day. We hope that this improved service will encourage you to call us whenever you need to order materials.

Sincerely,

SECTION 36: LETTER ASKING FOR PAYMENT AND RESPONSES

1.	Asking for Payment of Invoice	ASKP
2.	Sorry for Oversight	SORY
3.	Check Mailed	CKM1
4.	Check Mailed—2	CKM2
5.	Asking for Action	ASAC

Before you mail a letter asking for payment, be sure that the merchandise is not still on your dock or that it has not been returned for credit. These letters of explanation and clarification are important to maintain the goodwill and friendly relationship between the supplier and the consumer.

Points to Remember

- Know your customer. If a client is always on time and the payment is late ... investigate.
- If you are responding to a request for payment, give all of the information you have ... order number, invoice number, date of purchase and whatever other details you know that will identify the proper order. This will help to trace the lost payment.
- If your check was cashed and you have it, send a copy of the front and back of the check without delay. If it was lost, stop payment and issue a new check.

ASKING FOR PAYMENT OF INVOICE
ASKP

Re: Invoice #3456
Date: September 15, 19___

Dear Sirs:

Our records show a balance outstanding of $29.07 for the prepaid transportation charges for one (1) carton of flow meters.

If there is any reason why we should not expect a check for payment of these charges, won't you be kind enough to let us know? Thanks very much.

Please address correspondence regarding this invoice to:

> Loretta Jones
> Accounts Receivable
> Blank Company
> Box 0000
> Smithton, PA 00000

The foregoing letter would elicit several replies depending on whether or not the charges were due. We have cited three answers to give you examples of how to reply to this type of inquiry.

SORRY FOR OVERSIGHT
SORY

Re: Your Invoice #3456
Date:

Dear Ms. Jones:

Thank you for the reminder of the unpaid freight bill. I have brought the invoice to the attention of our Accounts Payable Clerk and a check will be mailed to you promptly.

We are sorry for the oversight.

Very truly yours,

ALTERNATIVE LETTER
CHECK MAILED
CKM1

Re: Your Invoice #3456
Date:

Dear Ms. Jones:

We received your correspondence dated October 17, 198—, regarding the unpaid freight bill in the amount of $29.07 for the prepaid transportation charges for one (1) carton of flow meters.

This bill was paid by our check number 6784, dated October 1, 198—. This check should have been received before the date of your dunning notice. If it has still not been received, please contact our Accounts Payable Department without delay and we will stop payment and issue a new check.

Thank you for your courteous reminder.

Sincerely,

CHECK MAILED—2
CKM2

Re: Your Invoice #3456
Date:

Dear Ms. Jones:

We received your correspondence dated October 17, 198—, regarding the unpaid freight bill from Roadway Express in the amount of $29.07 for the prepaid transportation charges for one (1) carton of flow meters.

The invoice was paid on September 10 by our check 45308. The check issued in the amount of $116.66 covered the following charges:

Date	Invoice #	Amount
7/28/—	3588	$ 36.82
8/19/—	3596	23.68
8/30/—	3601	27.09
8/31/—	3604	29.07
		$116.66

Since we have not received notices of the previously dated invoices being overdue, we assume that the check was received. If there has been a posting error, this information might help you locate it.

Thank you for shipping these badly needed items without delay. We appreciate your service.

Sincerely,

ASKING FOR ACTION
ASAC

Dear Mr. Cavanaugh:

We seem to be having a difficult time getting started on our dialapak contract. I am attaching a list of invoices, billed since the contract was enforced, without the 15% additional discount. To date, you will note, we have received only one credit correcting an invoice. There have been no payments.

In addition, we have not been notified that the AV90s are now available from your stock. Will you please look into this situation and clear it up so that we can continue more smoothly with this arrangement?

Very truly yours,

SECTION 37: COLLECTION, COLLECTION, COLLECTION

These letters are excellent examples of routine correspondence prewritten and available for instant use. You can establish the same bank of instant letters using the letters in this book. The codes given with each letter make it easy to set up a series of collection letters targeted for the type of customer and your previous experience with the account. Section 38 gives you a wide range of letters in series prepared to keep your collection letters fresh and productive.

Points to Remember

- It is safe to assume that most people plan to pay bills.
- When payment is not received, ask for a reason.
- Try to work out an amiable schedule of payment whenever it is possible.

**COCA-COLA COLLECTION LETTER—1
CCC1**

The Coca-Cola Company
Foods Division
HOUSTON, TEXAS

Subject:

                                                    Balance Due $_____

Attached is a copy of invoice(s) #_____
dated _____ open on your account, according to our records. All
invoices dated over 31 days are past due. This has been called to your attention
previously. However, your remittance has not been received.

Your personal attention in expediting payment of this account is requested. Please
forward your remittance by return mail, or inform us of the reason that payment has
been withheld.

                              Yours very truly,

                              THE COCA-COLA COMPANY
                              FOODS DIVISION

                              Credit Department

Attached:
Copy of Invoice

COCA-COLA COLLECTION LETTER—2
CCC2

The Coca-Cola Company
Foods Division
HOUSTON, TEXAS

Subject:

Balance Due $_____

Our recent letter for payment has neither been answered nor has payment of the above balance been received. Please forward your remittance for the balance due now.

Yours very truly,

THE COCA-COLA COMPANY
FOODS DIVISION

Assistant Credit Manager

GB/ac-1

COCA-COLA COLLECTION LETTER—3
CCC3

The Coca-Cola Company
Foods Division
HOUSTON, TEXAS

Subject:

Balance Due $_____

Our requests for payment of the above balance have gone unanswered. We hesitate to take other action to collect your account, but believe you will agree that we have been more than lenient.

Enclosed is a self-addressed envelope for payment. Your file will be updated to
_____.

Very truly yours,

Regional Credit Manager

/ad
Encl.

SNELLING COLLECTION LETTER
SSCL

Employment Service

Fort Snelling

307 NOEL PAGE BUILDING. DALLAS. TEXAS 75206 (214) 369-°'11

Mr. Just A. Applicant
1010 Main Street
Dallas, Texas 75201

Hello, there! I am Snelling and Snelling's computer. As yet, no one but me knows that you have not paid your account. However, if I have not processed a payment from you within five days, I will tell a human, who will resort to other means of collection.

SECTION 38: 27 LETTERS TO COLLECT YOUR MONEY

1. Series No. 1—Five Letters   CL11 to CL15
2. Series No. 2—Four Letters   CL21 to CL24
3. Series No. 3—Five Letters   LC31 to CL35
4. Series No. 4—Four Letters   CL41 to CL44
5. Series No. 5—Four Letters   CL51 to CL54
6. Series No. 6—Five Letters   CL61 to CL65

Collection letters are very important to the financial health of the company. Even more important is the establishment of a good credit system that will develop a firm, fair credit policy that will produce quick action when accounts are delinquent.

Essentially, you are financing your customers; if you do not finance them, your competitors will. You are in jeopardy only when you do not stay on top of your accounts and stay alert to developing problems.

Points to Remember

- Keep a close rein on accounts.
- Set credit limits.
- Set a firm policy for collection and stick to it.
- Remember that you are interested in doing two things: (1) getting the account paid, and (2) keeping the customer.
- Write to the customer promptly.
- Change the letters often.
- Follow the letters with *action*.

MODEL LETTERS

There are times when, despite all your precautions, the collections simply will not come in promptly. The delays will quickly eat into your profits. At this stage, getting your money and keeping the account have you "between a rock and a hard place." The following series of letters is designed to help you increase your receipts and reduce the cost of collection.

Series No. 1
FIRST LETTER
CL11

If the balance shown below agrees with your records, will you please put your check in the mail? If there is a discrepancy, please let us know and we will resolve the problem.

Thanks very much.

<u>(Balance)</u>

SECOND LETTER
CL12

We have not heard of any problems in the receipt of the merchandise you ordered. We made shipment and expected that we would receive payment promptly.

Please send your check so that we can pay our suppliers. We sincerely appreciate your cooperation.

THIRD LETTER
CL13

Our customers are very important to us. We enjoy a friendly relationship with them and work hard to maintain it. But friendship is a two-way street. We need your cooperation to make it work.

Won't you send us your remittance or an explanation of why you have not paid this overdue balance? We hope to hear from you by return mail.

FOURTH LETTER
CL14

What would you do if you had a customer who owed you a balance for merchandise and did not respond to several courteous letters asking for payment?

Frankly, we do not know what to do. We know what courses are open to us, but we do not want to risk embarrassing a customer who is temporarily strapped for funds.

Please send your check or a letter outlining your plans for paying this balance without delay. We will both feel better about handling it this way.

FINAL LETTER
CL15

We have tried as fairly as we know how to give you every consideration in the payment of the balance due as shown on the attached statement.

Apparently, we will have to take more drastic action to clear this account from our books. We ask you once again to send your check without further delay. In the hope that you will do so, we will hold this account in this office until (＿＿＿). If payment is not received by that date, we will have to turn it over to our legal department for collection.

Won't you cooperate and send your payment before this action is necessary?

Series No. 2
FIRST LETTER
CL21

May we hear from you at your earliest convenience regarding the balance of (amount) that is due on your account?

If the shipment was not received or if there is any other reason why we should not expect payment, won't you be kind enough to let us know? Thanks very much.

SECOND LETTER
CL22

We did not receive your check or a response to our letter of (date). Unless we hear from you explaining your reason for not paying the outstanding balance of (amount), we cannot solve the problem that may be causing the delay in completing this transaction.

We appreciate you as a customer and want to continue to serve you. Please make this possible by responding with a check for the balance due.

THIRD LETTER
CL23

In these days of tight money, we cannot leave delinquent accounts on our books indefinitely. Frankly, we need our money to continue to do business.

In the absence of your response to our letter, we have a suggestion that may help both of us. We suggest you send a payment of (amount) by check now. The balance of (amount) can be paid in _____ notes of $_____ each, maturing 30 days apart. The first note will be due on (date).

We sincerely hope that this alternative method of payment gets you out of the temporary difficulty that is causing the delinquency. If you accept this arrangement, please fill in the name of your bank and sign the notes. You can send them to us together with your check.

If this is not satisfactory to you, please send your check for the entire amount without further delay.

FOURTH LETTER
CL24

We feel that we have been more than considerate of you. We have carried your account for _____ months. We have offered to spread the balance over several payments secured by notes. Still you have made no response.

Therefore, it is necessary for us to place the account with our collection agency. We do not have to tell you that it would be better for both of us if we did not have to resort to a third party to collect this bill.

If you send your check promptly, we can settle this amicably. You decide. Will you send your check within ten days or will the account be placed with our collection agency?

Series No. 3
FIRST LETTER
CL31

It has been said that time and tide wait for no man. Evidently, bills do not either.

We are sure you have overlooked the due date on this past-due balance.

We hope that this friendly reminder will encourage you to send your remittance so we can clear your account.

Thank you very much.

SECOND LETTER
CL32

If you have not mailed your check for the amount that is now overdue on your account, will you kindly take a few minutes now to put it in the mail?

We will appreciate your cooperation. We want you to know that we also appreciate having you as a customer and the excellent manner in which you have always handled your acount.

THIRD LETTER
CL33

There has been no response from you to the two letters we sent regarding your overdue account. Because this is unusual for you, we feel that there is some good reason that you have not sent your check or a letter of explanation.

Won't you let us know without further delay if there is any reason you have not mailed your check. We will cooperate with you if we can. However, it is only good business for us to expect payment on this delinquent account . . . and your silence has us baffled.

We hope that you will send your remittance upon receipt of this letter.

FOURTH LETTER
CL34

Our policy for handling delinquent accounts is established by the president of the company with the idea of being fair to our customers and giving them every opportunity to cooperate before we seek a legal solution.

We are sorry that you have not responded to our previous letters, because your inaction leaves us no alternative but to send your account to our attorney for collection.

Please send your check for $____ within the next ten days so we can complete this transaction and continue our business relationship.

FIFTH LETTER
CL35

This letter is sent to you as a courtesy before we forward your account to our Legal Department for collection. We have written you several times regarding the liquidation of this outstanding balance.

Frankly, we would rather receive the payment directly from you and not have to resort to collection procedures. We are sure that you feel the same as we do about credit reference and bad risks.

Your check for the payment of our invoices totaling $____ within 10 days will allow us to settle this matter amicably. Beyond that date, the account will be handled by our Legal Department.

Series No. 4
FIRST LETTER
CL41

Your account is two installments in arrears. The terms of your Conditional Sales Contract provide for payments to be paid as they come due. The terms are listed in the copy of the sales contract for your reference.

We will appreciate receiving your check for the past-due balance that is listed above. This will bring your account up to date.

Thank you very much.

SECOND LETTER
CL42

Your account is still in arrears. We both have been put in a difficult position by this continued delinquency. We want to help you get your account in current status.

Please send a check by return mail. If there is a reason why you cannot bring the account up to date, send us a partial payment and tell us when to expect the balance.

That's reasonable, isn't it?

THIRD LETTER
CL43

It has been more than ____ months since we received a payment on your account. We have written letters that have not been answered and we have offered to take partial payments until you have resolved your problems. You have not responded. Take a minute now and get in touch with our representative, (name), at (phone number).

We have forwarded your account to him because we have not been able to handle it successfully from this office. We hope that you will be able to work out a program for settlement that will be satisfactory to both of you.

A check for a substantial part of the past-due balance and a new schedule of payments can be arranged. Our representative in your area is in a position to assist you in bringing this transaction to a close in a friendly manner.

FOURTH LETTER
CL44

At the suggestion of our representative, (name), we have made several extensions on the schedule of payments of this transaction. He was sure that he would be able to negotiate with you to liquidate this delinquent balance.

We regret that you have not followed through with the remittance as arranged. We have been patient, but we must also consider our obligations. Frankly, we need our money to operate.

For this reason, if your remittance is not in our hands by the last day of this month, we have no choice but to turn this account over to our attorney for collection or repossession of (collateral) in accordance with our contract.

Series No. 5
FIRST LETTER
CL51

The enclosed statement is past due. Will you be kind enough to send us your check today? We will appreciate it very much. If there is a discrepancy, kindly advise us. We will adjust our records to show that your account is current and encourage you to use it again soon.

SECOND LETTER
CL52

Is there a problem with the balance as shown on the enclosed statement? We wrote to you on (date) asking for your check for the past-due portion of the total amount.

If you have overlooked it, won't you send your check today? We need our money for operating capital today more than ever. I'm sure you are aware of the high cost of borrowing.

Thank you very much.

THIRD LETTER
CL53

We were expecting you to pay your account promptly when we gave you the cash discount. However, your balance has been past due for more than 30 days.

During this time, we wrote to you on (date) and (date) but you did not respond. We are disappointed because we dislike losing a customer over so small a balance. You could still put your check in the mail and save your excellent credit rating with us. We understand that a good customer may have a lean month.

Send your payment without delay and get us both off the hook.

FOURTH LETTER
CL54

Your account has been delinquent since (date). We have been patient and understanding, but we are also in business. Good business management dictates that we consider what options are available to collect the balance outstanding.

We are reluctant to turn this account over to collection, but your continued failure to answer our letters leaves us no alternative. We will hold this account for ten more days. During that time, we hope to receive your check and close this transaction.

We are so sure you will want to clear up this balance that we are enclosing a stamped envelope for the check. How's that for having faith?

Series No. 6
FIRST LETTER
CL61

Gentlemen:

We are happy to open an account for you and assure you that we will always feel privileged to have you as a customer.

The terms as negotiated are (amount) to be sent within _____ days. We must adhere to the agreed terms in these days of tight money.

At this time, we have not received your check, which is _____ days overdue. If there are no extenuating circumstances for which we are responsible, please send your check for the balance shown.

Thank you very much.

SECOND LETTER
CL62

Your check for the matured account as listed below has not been received. We hope that this is an oversight and that you will send your remittance promptly.

As we mentioned in our previous letter, we must adhere as closely as possible to the terms of sale. I'm sure you appreciate that we need our cash flow as anticipated to pay our suppliers.

Thank you very much.

THIRD LETTER
CL63

We have received no claim for adjustment on the balance of your past-due account, a copy of which is enclosed.

We can only conclude therefore that the merchandise you ordered was received. The terms of the sales were (amount) to be sent within _____ days. The account is considerably overdue.

We firmly request that you send payment within the next week and let us remove this transaction from our past-due file.

Thank you.

FOURTH LETTER
CL64

When we sent our first reminder of the balance due on your account, we expected that you would send your check promptly or give us a reasonable explanation for the delay.

But this is the fourth letter we have sent in an effort to get you to pay this balance and complete this transaction. Please give this account the consideration we have given you. Put your check in the mail and let us settle the matter in a friendly way. I'm sure this is what we'd both prefer to do.

Thanks very much.

FIFTH LETTER
CL65

There has been no answer to the four previous requests for payment of the past-due balance on your account. We are shocked. We know that problems arise in any firm and we are willing to help. Your past-due account is one thing, but your refusal to answer our letters is hard to understand.

We know what alternatives are open to us for the collection of old bills. We try to avoid such measures. We hope you try to avoid such measures also and will send your check for the amount due within ten days.

If we do not receive payment or a schedule of when we can expect the account to be paid, we will have to refer the matter to our attorney for proper disposition.

SECTION 39:   CLARIFICATION AND EXPLANATION
LETTERS FROM HIGHWIRE

1.	Clarification of Billing	CLAB
2.	Explanation of Subscription Policy	EXSB
3.	Explanation of Subscription Rates	SUBR
4.	Response to Subscription Cancellation	SUBA

When you introduce a new product or a new concept, you will get feedback letters from individuals who are confused. They either do not understand the procedure and need clarification, or they have misunderstood the instructions and given the wrong response.

The publishers of *HIGHWIRE* magazine have given us several letters that they used to handle this problem after introducing the magazine to the market. You can adapt them to your use and your product.

Points to Remember

- Repeat your offer simply and clearly.
- If the fault was in your original statement, say so.
- Making a mistake is a forgivable offense.
- Being arrogant and officious is unforgivable.
- Thank the correspondent for taking the time to write to you.

CLARIFICATION OF BILLING
CLAB

217 JACKSON STREET, P.O. BOX 948, LOWELL, MASS. 01853
(617) 458-6416 ● (617) 459-7181

Dear Sir:

Your confusion about the amount of the bill for your <u>HIGHWIRE</u> subscription is understandable. Please let us explain what happened.

Part of the process of getting a new magazine off the ground is testing different subscription offers and prices. Our subscription cards that are inserted into the magazine itself originally offered a four-issue subscription for $5.97 and then, later, a six-issue subscription for $7.97.

Both of these offers were based on our initial per-copy price of $1.50. As we learned more about the costs of producing and distributing a national magazine, we realized that the per-copy price would have to be increased to $2.00. Our six-issue subscription offer was increased to $9.97 to reflect the higher cover price.

It must seem that we can't make up our minds about the price, but really we're just trying to adjust the price to the constantly changing circumstances of a complicated new venture like <u>HIGHWIRE</u>. We're trying to do what works best and makes the most sense.

We apologize for the confusion and want you to know that we never intended that you pay a higher price than any other subscriber. Our basic subscription price has now been set at $9.97 for six issues, but we are happy to extend our earlier lower-price rates to you if you still wish to take advantage of them.

Please indicate below which term and price you prefer, and return this letter in the envelope provided:

☐   1 year—4 issues @ $5.97 (<u>$1.49</u> per issue)

☐   1½ years—6 issues @ $7.97 (<u>$1.32</u> per issue)

We appreciate your taking the time to write to us about this matter and encourage you to call our toll-free number— (800) 225-7934—if you have any other questions or concerns.

Very truly yours,

EXPLANATION OF SUBSCRIPTION POLICY
EXSB

Dear Mr. Blank:

We appreciate your concern about being billed for a subscription that you think you haven't ordered. Please be assured that we are not trying to trick you or anyone else into paying for something that you don't want.

The <u>HIGHWIRE</u> offer that you responded to clearly stated that you would receive a free issue of the magazine, without obligation, and that a trial subscription would be entered in your name. It noted, several times, that if you didn't like the magazine you could write "Cancel" on the bill that would come, send it back to us, and not owe us anything.

If you don't write "Cancel" on the bill and send it back to us, then we won't know whether you want to subscribe or not—and so we have to send you another bill.

If you have already notified us of your wish to cancel the trial subscription, you need do nothing more. Your cancellation has already been entered in our computer records. Because of the large amount of mail we are receiving, it takes a while for subscription changes to be recorded, and it is possible that you will receive additional bills and/or issues of <u>HIGHWIRE</u> even after you have cancelled your subscription. If this happens, just ignore the bills—and please keep any extra issues of the magazine with our compliments. You don't owe us a penny.

If you decide that you would like to give <u>HIGHWIRE</u> another look, just complete and return the enclosed card.

Thank you for taking the time to write to us about this matter. We hope to hear from you again with happier news.

Very truly yours,

Circulation Manager

EXPLANATION OF SUBSCRIPTION RATES
SUBR

Dear Reader:

Thank you for subscribing to <u>HIGHWIRE</u> magazine.

Recently, we have received many inquiries regarding our subscription prices.

There are several different prices and terms that we are currently testing. They are as follows:

       1 year—4 issues @ $5.97 (offered inside the magazine).

       1½ years—6 issues @ $7.97 (a savings from the $1.50 cover price).

1½ years—6 issues @ $9.97 (this was a test price for which you may have already received an invoice. If you choose to subscribe to <u>HIGHWIRE</u> for 1½ years, we will honor the $7.97 price).

Since I have already received from you a check in the amount of $_____, I will change your subscription to the price/term indicated above.

I am very sorry for the confusion this may have caused. If you have any further questions or problems, you may call me at our toll-free number: 1-800-225-7934.

Very truly yours,

Circulation Dept.

RESPONSE TO SUBSCRIPTION CANCELLATION
SUBA

Dear Mr. Blank:

Thank you for your recent letter regarding the free review copy or copies of HIGHWIRE magazine we've sent you. Our trial subscription offer clearly states that you may cancel this subscription and owe us nothing for any copies of the magazine that you have received.

Your notice of cancellation may not have reached us in time to prevent the mailing of the next issue of HIGHWIRE. Rest assured that you are under no obligation to send us money, as long as you have advised us of your desire to cancel.

If you happen to get any additional issues in the mail, you may keep them without obligation. There is no need to send them back to us.

We appreciate your taking the time to write to us about this matter.

Sincerely,

SECTION 40: BILL ADJUSTMENT LETTERS TO SOOTHE VEXED FEELINGS

Letters of explanation and apology do not have to be long or involved. Simply tell the customer that the error is corrected and the charge is being adjusted. It is rarely necessary to write more than a few sentences.

However, it is generally accepted that errors are reduced when the person who makes them is given the responsibility of sending the letter of explanation and apology. It is not always possible to determine what caused the discrepancy. Whenever it is practical, give the employee who made the error the task of clearing it up.

Points to Remember

- Explain the problem simply and honestly.
- Say you are sorry . . . don't grovel.
- Tell what has been done to correct the error.

COMMONWEALTH EDISON—CORRECTING ERROR
CEEB

Commonwealth Edison
Chicago-North Division
3500 North California Avenue
Chicago, Illinois 60618

Dear Mr. Blank:

An analysis of your current bill shows that an estimated reading was used instead of the actual reading.

In order to bill you accurately, we have cancelled the estimated bill. A correct bill using the actual meter reading will be mailed to you shortly.

Any payment that you may have made will be applied to your account, of course.

We are sorry for any inconvenience this has caused you.

Sincerely,

Customer Service
Representative
267-8181 Ext.

COMMONWEALTH EDISON—CORRECTED BILL
CECB

Commonwealth Edison
Chicago-North Division
3500 North California Avenue
Chicago, Illinois 60618

Dear Sir:

We have reviewed the above electric service account as you requested, and in a few days you will receive a corrected bill.

This correction is being made because it appears as though the meter reading used to compute your current electric service bill was too high. We are basing this correction on a careful review of your previous bills. However, if the current reading is correct, your next bill will reflect the increased usage.

Thank you for calling this to our attention. Please accept our apologies for the inconvenience we have caused you. Should you have any further questions, please contact us.

Sincerely,

Customer Service
Representative
267-8181 Ext.

**COMMONWEALTH EDISON—APOLOGY
CEAP**

 **Commonwealth Edison**
Chicago-North Division
3500 North California Avenue
Chicago, Illinois 60618

Dear Sir:

Thank you for your inquiry regarding your electric service bill.

Our representative called at your address on _____.
We are sorry that you were not there at the time. However, he did gain access to your meter. He found that an incorrect reading had been used on _____. This service bill will be cancelled and a corrected bill will be mailed shortly.

Although efforts are constantly being made to prevent reading errors, they do occur occasionally. We appreciate your calling this to our attention.

Please accept our apology for the error and the inconvenience that this has caused you.

Sincerely,

Customer Service
Representative
267-8131 Ext

THE PEOPLES GAS LIGHT AND COKE COMPANY—APOLOGY
PGAR

THE PEOPLES GAS LIGHT AND COKE COMPANY
122 South Michigan Avenue • Chicago, Illinois 60603 • Telephone (312) 431-4000

Dear Mr. Blank:

I have received your letter concerning termination of your gas service and the unpleasant treatment you received from one of our employees.

Let me begin by offering an apology for any rudeness you may have encountered in talking to our representatives. It is our intent to render the best service possible and to deal with customer inquiries in a helpful, efficient manner. We do not condone rudeness or hostility, and I appreciate your bringing this matter to our attention.

With respect to your gas service, I would also like to apologize for any trauma you may have suffered in the face of an unexpected shutoff. Our records do indicate, however, that a final notice prior to disconnection was mailed to you on June 30. The notice was not returned to us by the Post Office, so we can only assume it was received by someone at your home. It is my understanding that your bill has now been paid and your gas service restored. I hope that this was accomplished in a manner satisfactory to you.

Thank you for writing and bringing these matters to our attention.

                                                Sincerely,

SECTION 41: CUSTOMER RELATIONS LETTERS THAT WILL INCREASE SALES

1.	New Customer	ACNC
2.	Customer Who Has Not Ordered Recently	NOOR
3.	Informing Customers of Change	ICSB
4.	Selling a Service	SESE
5.	Permission to Tour Showroom	PTSR
6.	Preferred Customer Discount Sale	PCDS

Good customer relations pay off in increased sales. Keep your company name in your customer's place of business as you build his/her confidence in you and your product. Welcome new customers. Let those who do not reorder know that they are important and ask for the reason they have stopped ordering. Whatever the reason, write a letter from time to time and remind your customers that you value their business. Keep a friendly line of communication open, and your reward will be personal satisfaction as well as satisfied customers.

Points to Remember

- Send congratulations when a customer opens a new branch or expands his plant.
- If you can accommodate a client through an introduction or service, do so.
- Send a holiday greeting or a personal note from time to time.

NEW CUSTOMER
ACNC

Dear New Customer:

Thank you for your order. Whenever we receive an order from a new customer, we treat it very specially. The order taker stamps "NEW CUSTOMER" on it in red ink. The order filler is alerted to the fact that this is a very important order and fills it carefully. The packer does not waste any time because he knows that this order must be out the door before the end of the day. The glue is hardly dried on the label on the carton before it is on the truck and on its way to you.

Do you want to see us do it again? Send us an order from the catalog of exciting values, which we are attaching to this letter. The order taker will stamp "SATISFIED CUSTOMER" on it in red ink. The order filler is alerted to the fact that this is a very important order ... I think you get the picture. EVERY ORDER IS A VERY IMPORTANT ORDER TO US, AND WE TREAT IT THAT WAY.

We appreciate your business, and we hope you will become a regular customer.

Sincerely,

CUSTOMER WHO HAS NOT ORDERED RECENTLY
NOOR

Dear Mr. Worth:

Some time ago, we installed a new computer that does a lot of things. It keeps track of inventory, does the billing and the payroll, plus a cost analysis. But, Mr. Worth, there is one thing it does not do. It does not worry about customers who stop ordering regularly or whose orders have fallen off in volume. And, Mr. Worth, I still do.

Our company was built one customer at a time and I know and appreciate each one of you. Your orders were always received on a regular basis and the volume was steadily growing and predictable. Lately, however, you have not been ordering regularly and the volume is significantly lower.

Won't you take the time to contact me and let me know if there has been a problem with our product, our service, or our price? Together, we can work it out. If we can't, I'll really have a reason to worry.,

Sincerely,

John R. Downs
President

INFORMING CUSTOMERS OF CHANGE
ICSB

Dear Customers:

In response to the many inquiries we have have been receiving about our new labels, we would like to inform you that we are standardizing our house brands.

Previously, we carried merchandise with brand names that are well known and a second line, supplied by the same manufacturers, but labeled with various tags.

Our decision to adopt a standardized name and label is another step in our effort to bring you the highest quality at the lowest price. When we put our logo on the product, we put our reputation on the line. We will not put our name on any product we cannot guarantee.

We will continue to offer you a choice of national brand names and designer labels. If, however, you buy our house brand, you will be selecting merchandise that has been chosen by experts. It will represent uniform quality, design, and packaging. It will also be priced as low as possible.

It gives us great pleasure to bring this uniformity to you.

Sincerely,

SELLING A SERVICE
SESE

Dear Mr. Crawford:

Allow us to introduce ourselves. We are Judy Smith and Beth Jones, consultants in all phases of business writing and telephone communications techniques. We have experienced the immediacy of news releases, the creativity of public relations, the pressure of deadlines, the accuracy necessary for taking and giving messages and the techniques of successful telephone sales.

As a professional business communications firm serving this community, we would appreciate the opportunity to discuss with you some of the ways we can improve your business correspondence.

We would like to sit down with you and discuss the problems you are having and offer solutions that have been proven successful. Please call and arrange an appointment.

Cordially,

PERMISSION TO TOUR SHOWROOM
PTSR

Dear Mrs. Wells:

We are sending you a courtesy card from Maree Dauphin Interiors in New York.

Please call on them when you are in New York next week, and they will have a representative take you through the furniture galleries and display rooms.

Maree Dauphin Interiors, Ltd., are recognized dealers in furnishings of the quality you are seeking. They will save you time and money and assure you of authenticity of collector's items.

We have placed the orders for the pieces you selected when you were in our showroom in the Merchandise Mart and will advise you of delivery as soon as we get the information from the factory.

Thank you for your patronage. It was a pleasure to serve you. If I can be of further assistance, do not hesitate to call on me.

Cordially,

PREFERRED CUSTOMER DISCOUNT SALE
PCDS

Dear Preferred Customer:

In any endeavor, it is a very few people who are responsible for its success.

And so it is with our business. While we have many people in and out of our store all of the time, we are dependent on a very small percentage of them for our success. It is you, our Preferred Customers, who have been the backbone of our business.

We are celebrating our Tenth Anniversary on June 25. We have ordered exciting new merchandise, rearranged our displays, had meetings with our employees to tell them "what's happening," and placed our ads for the Anniversary Sale.

There is one thing we must do before the big event. We must say "thanks for making it all possible" to you, our Preferred Customers. On June 24, the day before the big event, we invite you to a preview . . . a private sale with special discounts.

Admission will be by invitation only. Your invitation is enclosed so you will not miss this important celebration. The hours are from 6 until 9 P.M. Come and see what we have planned for you!

Besides the special prices on new merchandise, each and every Preferred Customer will be given an additional 10% off on all purchases upon presentation of the "Preferred Customer Special Discount Card," which is also enclosed.

We want to share our success with you who made it possible.

Thank you.

Sincerely,

SECTION 42:   PUBLIC RELATIONS

Have you ever heard that doing business without advertising is like winking in the dark 'cause no one knows what you are doing? That old bromide may be corny, but it is still true. This section will show you the functions of a corporate public relations and public affairs department. It will also give you examples of how to get your message to the public.

Points to Remember

- Use every means to build and project your image.
- Do not wait for a chance to sell your product.
- Create a demand that will sell it for you.

EXPLANATION OF CORPORATE COMMUNICATIONS
EXCC

Dear Jim:

Your letter of May 3, 198—, has come to me for reply.

At R. J. Reynolds, those functions generally included under the heading of "public relations" are administered through the Corporate Public Relations and the Corporate Public Affairs Departments—both headed by vice presidents.

Our company's internal and external communications functions are consolidated under the Corporate Public Relations Department. The head of this department is responsible for advising management in the development of company public relations policies that will build and retain the desired public recognition, goodwill, and support needed to help improve sales and profits and assure future success for R. J. Reynolds Industries and each of its subsidiaries.

Employees are kept informed of individual company interests and developments through a number of internal publications—monthly newspapers, bulletin boards, weekly information summaries, etc.

Below are examples of other activities conducted to carry out this department's responsibilities:

- Preparing and distributing news releases and assisting in the preparation of public statements and speeches by company officials;
- Developing and distributing publicity materials to support the marketing and sales of company products;
- Replying to consumer and general correspondence on matters relating to the company and the various industries of which we are a part.

The Corporate Public Affairs Department is responsible for certain governmental relations and liaison, as well as the company's participation in, and relationship with, public affairs activities of various trade and industry organizations.

R. J. Reynolds Industries, Inc. retains outside public relations counsel in both general and financial areas. For example, The Tobacco Institute, Inc., 1875 I Street, N.W., Washington, D.C. 20006, represents the tobacco industry as a whole on national issues and is responsible for industry-governmental relations.

Good wishes from all of us here at Reynolds. I hope that what we have been able to provide will be sufficient.

Sincerely,

Public Relations Department

Enclosures

EXAMPLE OF CORPORATE COMMUNICATIONS
ECOR

Dear Mr. LeBoeuf:

I understand that an upcoming issue will feature a section on the advantages of word processing for the speechwriter. Wang would be happy to participate and I'd be happy to provide you with product bulletins, press releases, data sheets, application notes, feature articles, brochures, photos, or whatever material you may need. Please contact me at (617) 459-5000, extension 3130, if I can be of any assistance.

Sincerely,

Dick Gauthier
Public Relations
Specialist

cc: Tom Eifler

RESPONSE TO LETTER OF COMPLAINT
RECC

Dear Sir:

I agree with you. There is no doubt that the cost of hospital and medical treatment is, to quote you, "getting ridiculous." You are right again when you say that there does not seem to be any solution.

However, we are working all the time on finding a solution. If we are to continue to pay even minimum wages and provide a staff of competent help, we cannot cut costs in that area. If we continue to provide quality technical equipment for diagnosis and treatment, we cannot cut there.

We are continuing to offer health maintenance and nutritional education to the community. We hope that these efforts will result in cutting down the number of residents of the community who need to be hospitalized.

Thank you for taking the time to write and give us your point of view. We appreciate your comments and have the interest of the general public in our thoughts and goals.

Sincerely,

PUBLICITY FOR CLIENT
PUBC

GROUP ONE ASSOCIATES, INC. □ PUBLIC RELATIONS

Two East Oak Street □ Chicago, Illinois 60611 □ 312/642-0770

Dear Bob:

Here is Sam Savage, 36, former college dropout, grease monkey, sports-car racer, aspiring rock singer, and composer, who is currently a college professor on his way toward fame and fortune with his invention, "The Shmuzzle Puzzle."

Inspired by the drawings of M. C. Escher, Sam devised a mathematical formula based on the principle of tessellation to produce a revolutionary type of puzzle that is turning into a million-dollar business. (I am sending you a complete puzzle under separate cover, Bob.)

I hope you will find Professor Savage an interesting subject for a UPI feature. I hope we can set up an interview when he is in Los Angeles on December 12.

I will call you in a few days.

                                                        Best regards,

                                                        June Rosner

enc.

PUBLICITY FOR CLIENT—2
PUB2

GROUP ONE ASSOCIATES, INC. □ PUBLIC RELATIONS

Two East Oak Street □ Chicago, Illinois 60611 □ 312/642-0770

Dear Larry:

Professor Sam Savage is on a national promotional tour for his remarkable invention: The Shmuzzle Puzzle. He will be in Denver on November 12 and 13.

The offbeat and humorous style of this 36-year-old college professor makes a fascinating interview as he describes how he went from college dropout, sports-car driver, grease monkey, aspiring rock singer, antique car collector, and pilot to college professor and inventor of one of the hottest items in the game industry.

"It's easy to have fun, and it's easy to find a job. What's hard to do is find a job that's fun," says Sam.

I guarantee Sam Savage will be one of the most interesting, funny, and informative guests ever to appear on your program. I will call you in a few days.

Sincerely,

June Rosner

JR/sks
encl.

PUBLICITY FOR CLIENT—3
PUB3

Employment   Service

Fort Snelling

307 NOEL PAGE BUILDING. DALLAS. TEXAS 75206 (214) 369-°'11

dear s.m.u. neighbor,

i am s. mouse of snelling and snelling of university park and the reason i dont use capital letters is because im tired.

a man from s.m.u. asked me about that last night. he called up and said, whos this squeaking and i said s. mouse, night manager, and he said, why dont you write capital letters. it looks terrible.

buddy, i said, you should try standing on the shift key and step on another letter at the same time. every time i try it, i said, this electric typewriter bucks and i am damn tired of getting thrown in the wastebasket.

all right, said the man, i am picking on you because you moused up my s.m.u. order. you mean loused up, dont you, i said, and he said, no you moused it up. i wanted 4 secretaries, 3 typists, 2 bookkeepers, 3 trainees, and 2 accountants. you tell marvin migdol, manager, to straighten it out, pronto.

but you told me 3 secretaries, i said. and he said, see here, are you trying to mouse me up again. i said, no sir. i could squeak my head off.

so now im waiting for his conscience to start hurting him about hanging up on me. in the excitement, i forgot to get his name and department.

sometimes i think i will never learn this business as well as marv and his employment counselors. they know everything about personnel. they will get you the people you need—and fast. snelling and snelling is the worlds largest personnel consultants. and theyre here in the noel page building—near you.

so will you call marv migdol, give him a job order and tell him i tried. call 369-8111 and tell them not to bring that cat back in here.

cordially yours,

s. mouse
signed by hand
snelling and snelling
   of univ. park

enc.

p.s. snelling and snelling will never mouse up anybody.

SECTION 43:   SAYING "NO" NICELY

1.	Cannot Sell Directly	CSWH
2.	Cannot Sponsor	CSTM
3.	Declining Unpatented Idea	DUNI
4.	Declining Advertising Suggestion	READ
5.	Cannot Supply Materials	CESM
6.	Cannot Provide Transportation	CPTR
7.	Declining Invitation to Exhibit Product	DIEP

Regrets are usually hard letters to write. We postpone writing them because we hate to say "no." But it is better to dash off a short note saying "no" nicely than to keep someone waiting for a reply. A polite note declining the request frees the writer to seek help elsewhere.

The letters in this section can be adapted for use in many situations. They are courteous, direct, and final.

Points to Remember

- Write letters of regret promptly.
- Be brief and to the point.
- It is not possible to grant every request and the majority of people know this.

CANNOT SELL DIRECTLY
CSWH

Dear Jim:

Thank you for your friendly letter. Nothing pleases us more than hearing from those who enjoy our products.

From time to time, others have asked about the possibility of buying their products directly from us. Regretfully, we must decline. As a manufacturer, we cannot sell directly to the consumer. We sell only to licensed distributors.

Sincerely,

Public Relations Department

CANNOT SPONSOR
CSTM

Dear Jim:

We appreciate your offering us the opportunity to sponsor _____ and regret we are not in a position to do so. We receive so many requests of a similar nature that we have had to adopt the policy of declining all such requests in order to be fair to everyone.

I might add that, because of Winston's successful experience in sponsoring the NASCAR races, we feel that sponsoring a series is more in line with our marketing strategy than sponsoring an individual or a team.

Sincerely,

Public Relations Department

DECLINING UNPATENTED IDEA
DUNI

Dear Jim:

Thank you for your letter of May 5, 198__.

At the risk of seeming unappreciative, I must explain that we have made it a policy to decline to receive or consider unpatented ideas offered or submitted by other than employees of our company. This has been necessary in order to avoid misunderstandings over the origin of particular ideas, many of which we cannot use until years after they were first conceived. Accordingly, your letter will be held in our Consumer Relations files, where it will not be available to others in the company.

While the above policy will not permit me to pass your suggestion on beyond this department, I do want you to know we appreciate your letter of _____.

Sincerely,

Consumer Relations Department

DECLINING ADVERTISING SUGGESTION
READ

Dear Jim:

Thank you for your letter of May 3, 198_, which has been referred to this department for reply.

So many people have offered to help in the preparation of our advertising that we have had to adopt the policy of declining all unsolicited offers, leaving this preparation to our New York advertising agencies. We regret, therefore, that we will not be able to make use of the idea you submitted for _____.

However, we do appreciate your interest in writing us and assure you of our best wishes.

Sincerely,

Consumer Relations Department

CANNOT SUPPLY MATERIALS
CESM

Dear Jim:

Thank you for your interest in our advertising for _____.

As much as it would please us to comply with your request, I regret we will be unable to do so. A surprising number of individuals, including many who enjoy collecting as a hobby, inquire about obtaining samples of our various advertising materials. Inasmuch as our supplies are not sufficient to fill all such requests, we feel the only way to be fair and impartial is to decline all.

Sincerely,

Public Relations Department

CANNOT PROVIDE TRANSPORTATION
CPTR

Dear Sir:

We are, of course, familiar with the excellent work of Variety International, which has long had our sincere admiration.

I regret, however, that TWA cannot be more directly supportive of your organization by providing transportation in return for public acknowledgement of our role.

As a practical matter, I'm afraid disseminating that information would only serve to compound the distressing problem we already confront, by encouraging even more requests for such assistance than the innumerable ones we already receive, from groups whose aims and activities we wholeheartedly applaud, but which we are unable to aid in the way they suggest.

I hope that you will understand our position, and accept my best wishes for the continued success of your endeavors.

Sincerely,

C. E. Meyer, Jr.

cc.

DECLINING INVITATION TO EXHIBIT PRODUCT
DIEP

Dear Sirs:

We will not be able to exhibit our product line at the Industrial Exposition, which you have scheduled for the week of October 10, 198⸺, because we have made previous arrangements to display our techniques and products in Dallas that week.

Please keep us in mind for the future. We wish you every success in your venture.

Sincerely,

B	O	O	K		5

PLAN YOUR MEETING FOR SUCCESS

SECTION 44:   MEETINGS AND SEMINARS

1.	Preplanning Information	PREA
2.	Response from Convention Bureau	CCBA
3.	Greeting from City	GRFC
4.	Sales Letter—Ambassador East	SALA
5.	Sales Letter—Palmer House	SAPH
6.	Sales Letter—Palmer House—2	SAP2
7.	Preplanning Information—2	IACC
8.	Physical Requirements for a Convention Site	PRCS
9.	Copy of a Convention Schedule	COSC

The ongoing desire to learn, to grow, and to exchange ideas with our peers coupled with our curiosity to know what our competitors are doing has created a complete industry that caters to meetings, seminars, and corporate travelers.

Begin by writing for information. Send the letter to the Chamber of Commerce or the Convention Bureau if you do not have the names of the hotels in the area. You will receive sales letters and brochures to help you plan your meeting.

Points to Remember

- Plan early. Lock in the dates before you make other commitments.
- Make a personal inspection of the site if it is possible.
- Be realistic about your demands and the limitation of the facilities in smaller cities.

PREPLANNING INFORMATION
PREA

Gentlemen:

I have been asked to make arrangements for a regional meeting of the American Society of Opticians in spring 1986. As I have never been involved in the planning of such an event before, I will appreciate any and all help and advice.

The information I was given is incomplete, but it shows that 650 people attended our 1982 convention in this area over a course of a four-day meeting and that the average stay was three days. What dates do you have for us to consider?

We will need several meeting rooms, accommodations for a general introductory meeting and a closing banquet. We will also want a luncheon buffet served in the area of the meeting rooms and coffee service available during the morning break.

We will prepare a brochure to send to our members, and we want to know what special events will be taking place at the time we schedule our meeting so that we can include activities for our spouses and guests.

Please send whatever material you have at this time, and include suggestions for details that I will have to consider in early planning.

Sincerely,

RESPONSE FROM CONVENTION BUREAU
CCBA

Dear Ms. Carroll:

Thank you for considering our city for your upcoming convention. I have taken the liberty of contacting the sales managers at several of our large hotels to notify them of your interest. They will be contacting you soon to let you know what dates they have available to accommodate your group.

When planning your convention, the hotel will need to know the number of rooms you will need for overnight guests, the number of meeting rooms and the equipment needed for each. You will also be asked your preferences for meals and other refreshments. Although there are many details to planning a successful convention, the hotel sales managers have done this type of planning many times and will be able to assist you every step of the way.

If you need help in lining up speakers for your group, feel free to contact me and I will be glad to help you.

Good luck with your assignment!

GREETING FROM CITY
GRFC

Dear Ms. Brown:

Thank you very much for considering Chicago as the site of the 1985 AND 1986 Convention of the American Anthropological Association. We would be very pleased and honored, and offer the following dates and facilities for your consideration:

	1985	1986
Palmer House, Mike Oemet, Sales Manager	11/29–12/3	*
Conrad Hilton, Gary Gregg, Sales Manager	None	11/19–23
Chicago Marriott, Mark Podolski, Sales Manager	11/29–12/3, 2nd Opt.	None
Hyatt Regency Chicago, Bill Leonhardt, Sls. Mgr.	11/16–11/20	*

*These hotels will contact you directly with alternative 1986 dates.

We look forward to Mr. Lehman's visit August 4–6, 198_. Is there a chance that he might be able to meet with me in this regard?

We hope that you will choose Chicago as the site of the 1985 and 1986 conventions. It would truly be our pleasure to have you with us. When you are planning a site inspection trip, could we get together?

Please keep in touch and let me know how I may be of further service to you.

Sincerely,

SALES LETTER—AMBASSADOR EAST
SALA

AN OMNI CLASSIC HOTEL

Dear Mr. Blank:

I was pleased to speak with you today about your 198_ meeting plans. Thank you for the information. I will follow up with you in March when you are planning the June–December agenda.

As I mentioned, a highly successful NRA meeting was recently held at the Ambassador East via the Chicago NRA office. We look forward to accommodating future NRA meetings, including any that might come from your office.

Our location in Chicago's prestigious Gold Coast area is the first stop in on the airport bus. Within close walking distance are Lincoln Park, Lake Michigan, Water Tower Place, and the lively night spots of Rush Street. The entire hotel was renovated over the past few years. Our famous Pump Room Restaurant continues to be a Chicago landmark.

Should you have reason to visit Chicago in the next few months, please drop by for a site inspection. We will gladly extend our hospitality.

Cordially,

Janet C. Hunter
Senior Account Executive

JCH:pk
Enclosure

**SALES LETTER—PALMER HOUSE
SAPH**

*Palmer House
and Towers*

A Hilton Hotel
Chicago, Illinois 60690   Telephone 312/726-7500

Dear Gerry:

It was a pleasure to have met you during my trip to your fine city. I'd like to thank you for the time you afforded me on reviewing all requirements for your future convention activities. As you continue to plan both meetings and social events, we hope you will keep the Palmer House in mind, not only for your annual meeting but also for some of your smaller workshops.

Gerry, enclosed please find our Conference Center 7 brochure. As mentioned, Conference Center 7 consists of 38 meeting rooms on one floor, with the latest in audio/visual equipment and the most modern services available. I know this area would be ideal for your workshops.

Regarding your annual meeting, the City of Chicago would certainly be an ideal site. The major hotels here combined with McCormick Place certainly give you an opportunity to meet your maximum projected needs while providing first-class accommodations for all of your delegates.

Mary Silk, of our Chicago Convention Bureau, and I will be coordinating space for one of your annuals; and we are hoping to provide accommodations as soon as 198_ for you.

We will be in touch soon; in the meantime, if I can be of any help or answer any questions or reserve accommodations for you, please call.

Sincerely,

Gregory L. Rancone
Sales Manager

GLR:rmv
cc: Ms. Betty Smith
    Mr. Richard Noble
    Ms. Mary Silk

SALES LETTER—PALMER HOUSE—2
SAP2

Palmer House
and Towers

A Hilton Hotel
Chicago, Illinois 60690   Telephone 312/726-7500

Dear Ms. Van Goethem:

This is in response to our conversation regarding the 198_ Annual Meeting plans of the Evaluation Research Society. As discussed, we are delighted to learn that the Society is considering Chicago and are most anxious to be of service in the event our fine city is selected for your activities.

The Palmer House has, of course, provided the background for many conferences similar to your own program and there is no question in our minds that we can meet your needs ideally. Enclosed is information which will give you an idea of the quality of the meeting facilities and guest accommodations we have to offer, as well as the many extra services to make your meeting an exceptional one.

At the present time we do have dates available in 198_ that I am sure the Society would consider very desirable and upon receiving more detail on your requirements we would be very pleased to submit a proposal for your review. We realize that cost will be one of the determining factors in making your selection and we are confident that you will find them very attractive in relationship to the quality of our services and facilities.

Should you or Dr. Wortman plan on visiting Chicago, we would be happy to provide accommodations on a complimentary basis during your stay. As soon as your plans materialize in this regard, please let me know and I will be pleased to take care of your reservations.

Again, we are most anxious to be of service to the Society, and I look forward to hearing from you as to how we may be of further assistance along these lines.

Sincerely,

William F. A. Elges
Assistant Director of Sales

WFAE/mp
Enclosure
cc: Dr. Paul Wortman

PREPLANNING INFORMATION—2
IACC

ATTENTION: <u>Sales Representative</u>

REGARDING: <u>National Convention, April 198_</u>

The National Guild of Decoupeurs is looking into the possibility of holding their National Convention and Decoupage exhibition in Chicago during the month of April, 198_, <u>preferably the last part of the month.</u>

The convention usually starts on a Wednesday and terminates on a Saturday. There are also meetings involving about fifteen persons on Tuesday, with their arrivals on Monday.

Luncheons are generally planned for three days of the convention.

Dinners are generally planned for three days of the convention, with the banquet on Saturday evening.

The attached sheet indicates physical requirements and other questions.

Please also advise about available parking facilities.

We are interested in room rates, any meeting room charges, and charges for the exhibit room.

If you have space available during the last two weeks in April, would you kindly answer the questions as quickly as possible? We are contacting eight hotels in the Chicago area and will base our decision on quotations and space available to suit our requirements.

Please direct any questions by phone to:

Please send correspondence to her attention.

Thank you for your early reply.

Ann Standish
Executive Director and National
Convention Coordinator

PHYSICAL REQUIREMENTS FOR A CONVENTION SITE
PRCS

100 Sleeping Rooms
Conference Rooms:

Annual Meeting	(To accommodate approx. 130 persons—theater-style)
Exhibit Room	(40 eight-foot tables with tablecloths) 3,000 sq. ft.
Judging Room	(10 eight-foot tables—helpful if room has 2 entrances)
5 Workshop Rooms	(To accommodate approx. 20–25 persons with eight-foot tables for them to work on in each room.)
Board Meeting	(21 persons—Conference T shape set-up)
Trade Talk	(10 eight-foot tables for exhibitors)

When having planned group meals (luncheons and/or dinners)

Luncheons	(approx. 120 persons)
Dinners	(approx. 130 persons)
Banquet	(approx. 175 persons)

The Guild generally plans three dinners and two luncheons at site.

Customarily, at previous conventions, the Presidential Suite, consisting of the bedroom and parlor, has been complimentary. The parlor has been used for the board meeting on occasion.

We are further interested in a facility's policy for obtaining complimentary meeting and sleeping rooms.

How far in advance is it necessary to confirm for an April convention and is a deposit required? If so, what is the amount of the deposit required?

Naturally, we are concerned with obtaining the lowest room rates possible—what group rates are available? When can room rates and the prices for group meals be confirmed?

We are also concerned that the facility has adequate dining space and efficient service to accommodate our members for meals that are not planned group meals.

We also need to know the proximity of the facility from the airport and available service from airport to facility (cost and frequency back and forth).

Finally, we look for convention sites which are accessible to encourage the surrounding area dwellers to attend our exhibit, which is open for viewing to the general public.

The Exhibit Room is occupied Wednesday through Saturday to 4 P.M. Convention usually spans Wednesday through Saturday evening (banquet) with departures Sunday. Board meeting is held preceding Tuesday, generally in the Presidential Suite. See typical schedule attached.

COPY OF A CONVENTION SCHEDULE
COSC

CONVENTION SCHEDULE
FOR 198_

This schedule is presented to show you how detailed some agendas are. You can decide after reading this sample schedule and the letters in this section what activities to include in your plans.

Monday, April 26:		**Thursday, April 29:**	
5:30 PM	Board Reception and Dinner	8:00 AM to 9:00 AM	Continental Breakfast
		10:00 AM to 9:00 PM	Exhibit open to public
Tuesday, April 27:			
8:00 AM to 5:00 PM	Board meeting	9:00 AM to 11:30 AM	All Workshops
12:30 PM	Board Lunch	12 Noon to 1:15 PM	Lunch
1:00 PM to 4:00 PM	Early Registration	1:30 PM	Bus Tour
		4:30 PM	Bus to Tangiers
Wednesday, April 28:	Members arrival	5:00 PM to 7:00 PM	Cocktails, Dinner, and Entertainment
8:00 AM to 9:00 AM	Judging Setup		
9:00 AM to 5:00 PM	Judging items received	7:00 PM to 8:00 PM	Bus return to Marriott
9:00 AM to 5:00 PM	Registration		
10:00 AM to 4:00 PM	Hospitality Room	8:15 PM to 11:00 PM	Members view Exhibit
11:00 AM to 5:00 PM	Judging Time		
1:30 PM to 4:00 PM	Tour to Fine Arts Museum	**Friday, April 30:**	
6:00 PM to 7:00 PM	Cash Bar	8:00 AM to 9:00 AM	Continental Breakfast
7:00 PM	Dinner		
After Dinner	Chinese Program Finish exhibit setup	9:00 AM to 11:30 AM	Annual Meeting
		9:00 AM to 12 Noon	Guest Tour

Friday (*cont.*)

10:00 AM to 9:00 PM	Exhibit open to public
12 Noon to 1:30 PM	Lunch
1:30 PM	Annual Meeting continues
After Meeting 'til 4:00 PM	Problem Clinic and Show & Tell
6:00 PM to 7:00 PM	Cash Bar
7:00 PM	Dinner
8:30 PM (After Dinner)	Chapter Meeting
9:00 PM to 11:00 PM	Trade Talk
9:00 PM to 11:00 PM	Members view Exhibit

Saturday, May 1:

8:00 AM to 9:00 AM	Continental Breakfast
9:00 AM to 11:30 AM	Workshops

10:00 AM to 4:00 PM	Exhibit open to public
11:30 AM to 1:30 PM	Members: On your own for lunch
12 Noon to 2:00 PM	Board Meeting w/Light lunch
1:30 PM to 4:00 PM	Furniture Repairman
4:00 PM	Dismantle exhibit
6:30 PM	Cash Bar
7:30 PM	Banquet Japanese Parasol Dancers
After Banquet and Entertainment	Chapter Program and Drawing

Sunday, May 2:   Check out time - NOON

SECTION 45: HOUSING AND SERVICE ARRANGEMENTS FOR MEETING

1. Rooming List Worksheet   RLWS
2. Preliminary Room Arrangements   PRAR
3. Response to Preliminary Letter   RPRA
4. Request for Clarification of Arrangements   RCOA
5. Response to Request for Clarification   RRCL
6. Letter Accompanying Meeting Proposal   LAMP
7. Detailed List of Arrangements   DLOA

Each group has individual needs and considerations. When you have decided on your location, work with the staff. They will be a tremendous help in pre-meeting planning.

The letters in this section were contributed by the Chicago Convention and Tourism Bureau, the Ambassador East Hotel, and the Palmer House of Chicago. We know you will agree that their expertise and experience are unique. Use this superb collection of materials to help you plan your meeting.

Points to Remember

- Housing, catering, meeting rooms, hospitality suites, complimentary rooms, setup and dismantling, exhibit space, sightseeing buses.

ROOMING LIST WORKSHEET
RLWS

NAME(S)	DBL. OCC.	SGL. OCC.	SUITE 1 br.—2 br.	APR. DATE	DEP. DATE
Smith, John & Mary M/M	X			11/1	11/3
Jones, Ralph & Green, Leo	X			11/1	11/3
Boyd, Everett		X		11/1	11/2
Lasser, L. M. & Drew, C. R.			2 br.	11/1	11/3
Martin, Ray		X		11/2	11/3
Lee, Brad & Joan M/M			1 br.	11/1	11/3

To prepare rooming list to determine housing needs, be sure to ask:

- Complete name of each individual who will attend
- Kind of accommodations desired
- Date of arrival—date of departure

When this information is complete, inform the hotel of the number of rooms needed and the dates they will be in use.

If you plan to have hospitality suites or any other special-use rooms for exhibits, and so on, be sure the hotel is aware of these room requirements also.

PRELIMINARY ROOM ARRANGEMENTS
PRAR

October 1, 1982

Mr. Bob Bingle
Director of Sales
THE PALMER HOUSE
17 East Monroe
Chicago, IL 60603

Dear Mr. Bingle:

We are in the process of defining the unit block at the Palmer House for the Food Marketing Institute Annual Convention, May 8–11, 198—.

According to our records from last year, our block was as follows:

NUMBER	TYPE	RATE	UNITS
8	P1	$	16
20	P2		60
5	P2		15
4	P2		12
6	P2		18
1	P2		3
5	P2		15
1	P2		3
500	S		500
300	D/D		300
258	T		258
		TOTAL UNITS	1200

Please resubmit a new proposal that includes a similar breakdown for the 198_ Convention, and include the following pick-up pattern:

May

3rd	4th	5th	6th	7th	8th	9th	10th	11th	12th
5%	20%	30%	50%	70%	100%	100%	90%	40%	5%

It is our understanding that the complimentary allotment for our staff at your hotel is one (1) for every fifty (50) units occupied in May 198_.

We will begin assigning space in your hotel as early as January 198_. We would like the cutoff date to be two weeks prior to the convention, approximately April 23, 198_. Of course, we hope to be able to work with you past that date, right through the convention.

FMI will be making ALL ASSIGNMENTS FOR OUR ROOM BLOCK. Please make sure that all new reservations, changes, and cancellations be made ONLY through the FMI office.

All individuals will be responsible for their own room, tax, and incidental charges unless otherwise specified in writing.

We must also have first option on all function space. While we do not plan to use all of your function space, we would appreciate all requests to be cleared by Food Marketing Institute.

Please review carefully the above information. We appreciate your prompt attention to this matter, and we look forward to working with you on a successful convention.

Sincerely,

Diana T. Ohtersen
Hotel Coordinator

DTO/jks

**RESPONSE TO PRELIMINARY LETTER
RPRA**

Palmer House
and Towers

A Hilton Hotel
Chicago, Illinois 60690   Telephone 312/726-7500

December 2, 198—

Mr. Michael S. Brown
Director, Convention Services
FOOD MARKETING INSTITUTE
1750 "K" Street, N.W.
Washington, DC   20006

Dear Michael:

At long last, I have devoted attention to the Food Marketing convention and offer the
following recap of arrangements being held for your May 6–13, 198—, convention.
Please note that we have increased our overall commitment to you to 1,300 rooms,
which includes all one- and two-bedroom suites. Your controls should be set up to
subtract two units when a one-bedroom suite is booked and three units when a
two-bedroom suite is booked.

We have adjusted our anticipated occupancy pattern as follows:

Date	Occupied Rooms
Tuesday, May 3	65
Wednesday, May 4	260
Thursday, May 5	390
Friday, May 6	650
Saturday, May 7	910
Sunday, May 8	1,300
Monday, May 9	1,300
Tuesday, May 10	1,170
Wednesday, May 11	520
Thursday, May 12	65

During your convention in May, 198—, the following room rates will be in effect:

PALMER HOUSE HOTEL

Singles:	\$	\$	\$	\$	\$
Doubles/					
Twins:	\$	\$	\$	\$	\$

PALMER HOUSE TOWERS

Singles:	\$	\$	\$	\$
Doubles/				
Twins:	\$	\$	\$	\$

The room-rate breakdowns for the Palmer House and Towers rooms are as follows:

PALMER HOUSE HOTEL

Room Rate (Sgl/Dbl)	No. of Rooms	Percentage
\$ /\$	115	10%
\$ /\$	230	20%
\$ /\$	460	40%
\$ /\$	230	20%
\$ /\$	115	10%

PALMER HOUSE TOWERS

Room Rate (Sgl/Dbl)	No. of Rooms
\$ /\$	15
\$ /\$	35
\$ /\$	50
\$ /\$	50

With regard to suites, there will be a total of 50 suites available for your use, broken down as follows:

PALMER HOUSE & TOWERS

Room Rate (P&1/P&2)	No. of Rooms
\$ /\$	12
\$ /\$	13
\$ /\$	8
\$ /\$	10
\$ /\$	2
\$ /\$	5

Complimentary rooms will be allocated at the ratio of one (1) room night for every fifty (50) room nights actually utilized by your group during your 198— convention.

The Palmer House agrees to a cutoff date of April 23, 198⸺, and we will honor requests based on availability at that time.

It is understood that all room assignments will be made by Food Marketing and we will channel all reservation changes and cancellations to your office prior to the cutoff date.

It is also understood that all individuals will be responsible for all room, tax, and incidental charges unless specified in writing.

Attached you will find a list of all function space which has been committed to other unrelated groups. We will honor your request to clear all space releases through Food Marketing Institute. This, of course, is an attempt to deter any individuals or companies from bypassing the Food Marketing registration procedure.

Michael, I would appreciate your review of these details, and if they meet with your approval please sign and return the enclosed copy which will act as a confirmation for your 198⸺ convention. Please be aware that the Palmer House is ready to play an integral part in the success of the 198⸺ and all future years' Food Marketing Institute conventions to be held in Chicago. If I can offer you any additional assistance, do not hesitate to contact me.

Sincerely,

Timothy A. Tata
Director of Sales

TAT:hpt

cc: Diana T. Ohtersen, Hotel Coordinator, Food Marketing Institute
David Strahlendorf, Director of Front Office Operations
Ceil Matul, Towers Manager

REQUEST FOR CLARIFICATION OF ARRANGEMENTS
RCOA

Dear Jerry,

I have received the Palmer House packet; however, you have forgotten to provide us with floor plans (preferably to scale). Would you please drop these in the mail to me as soon as possible—I will need these immediately to present my suggested booth layout to the Board on April 21, 198⸺.

The agreement seems to be in order; however, I will need several clarifications made:

1. The 35 AC lines mentioned in exhibit rental portion: How many lines does each outlet accommodate?

2. Dismantling will take place on <u>Saturday</u>, September 24, 198⸺, beginning at 6:00 P.M.

3. I understand there is a drayage service available for those exhibitors wishing to send their materials prior to the show, however, exhibitors who bring their materials with them will be able to handle their own goods for both move-in and set-up operations (i.e., it is not mandatory for exhibitors to use teamster labor, and neither the exhibitors, the association, nor the show management will be forced to assume drayage charges unless they have been individually contracted prior to the event).

4. Also, under drayage: Shipments containing illuminated glass display cases and bookcases will be made to the Palmer House on Wednesday, September 21, 198—, during the exhibition set-up hours. We must be assured that the companies delivering these goods be allowed easy access to the docks and from there to the exhibition hall to deliver these goods to the booths.

6. Labor: The backdrops and side rails are included in the exhibit rental—is the labor (i.e., decorators/draperymen) to erect the booth perimeters also included in the booth package price?

6. The same question as above in regard to the electrical outlets provided in the booth package.

7. Will the Palmer House be directly responsible for placing orders from exhibitors—pegboards, additional tables, spotlight trees, etc.?

8. Most exhibitors will be arriving early Thursday morning, September 22, to set up their booths. As I mentioned, the exhibitors for the most part will be driving to the Palmer House and will have their merchandise in their cars, station wagons, or trucks. We must be assured that the Palmer House will arrange for at least 6–8 additional porters with hand trucks to be available from 8 A.M.–noon on Thursday, and from 6 P.M.–10 P.M. on Saturday, September 24. These porters should be stationed at designated entrances on Thursday—and should be available at the exhibit entrance on Saturday night. The two times mentioned represent the heaviest arrival and departure times for the exhibitors. We must also be assured that our exhibitors will not be subjected to police harassment and ticketing while unloading their vehicles—or waiting to unload their vehicles—at the hotel entrance.

In addition to the floor plans, I would also be most interested in obtaining samples of your equipment rental forms, and copies of Fire and Labor Regulations and Floor Loads. Also, I would like information and prices for a cash refreshment area.

Hoping to hear from you very soon, I am,

Sincerely,

Christine M. Moore
President

CMM/kk

RESPONSE TO REQUEST FOR CLARIFICATION
RRCL

Dear Chris:

Enclosed are the floor plans that are representative of the arrangements we discussed.

To clarify the points raised, we submit the following:

1. The AC lines have a maximum of four outlets per line.

2. We have adjusted the schedule for dismantling and now indicate a 12 midnight closing of the hall.

3. The drayage service is provided as a service to the exhibitors. If they desire to move their exhibits in and out, it is acceptable but they must provide their own manpower.

    The Palmer House does not have the storage facilities to hold the exhibits prior to setup nor do we have facilities to store the empty crates.

    Erection of the booths must be done by skilled labor and an hourly charge will prevail and be charged to the exhibitor.

4. We will assist in clearing the dock for the arrival of the display cases. Elevators are in close proximity to the dock to move them to the exhibit hall.

    Our personnel cannot handle the cases; therefore, the company must supply the labor.

5. The hall will be set with pipes and draped to the specifications you give us and includes the perimeter. The per-booth price is inclusive of the services.

6. As discussed, the 35 AC lines will be placed in the appropriate areas and there will not be an additional charge for the labor.

    If more lines are necessary, a per-line charge of $30.00 will prevail.

    To comply with the electrical and fire codes of the city of Chicago, the cases must meet specifications. If they do not, we cannot illuminate.

7. Our exhibit hall manager will be on duty to provide any additional services to the exhibitors. Charges will be applied to the exhibitor account.

8. For the exhibitors' arrival, we will allow them to pack and unload their display material at either the Monroe or Wabash street entrances. There is traffic that must go through and the police will not permit double parking.

    We can provide bellmen to transport the materials to the hall. Bellmen are not salaried employees and depend upon gratuities for their labor. We will have to discuss this further when we meet to reach an acceptable arrangement.

    Equipment order forms and the fire and electrical codes are enclosed for your perusal as well as the cash bar menus.

I look forward to seeing you on April 29,, 198__, and to finalizing the arrangements.

Sincerely,

Jerry Van Note
Sales Manager

LETTER ACCOMPANYING MEETING PROPOSAL
LAMP

Dear Eleanor,

I thoroughly enjoyed meeting you the other day. I do hope we can work something out with our meeting space that is satisfactory to you and your organization.

Enclosed you will find the proposal, your coffee order, and a credit application for billing. Please look everything over, and if all is in correct order, please sign and return a copy.

One of our catering managers will contact you shortly regarding your luncheon menu.

Please let me know if I can be of further assistance. Have a good day and I will be in touch.

Sincerely,

Marian Pogorski
Conference Center 7
Sales Manager

MP/mr
Enclosure

DETAILED LIST OF ARRANGEMENTS
DLOA

Dear Marian:

The following is a list of the logistical arrangements that we require regarding our Training Meeting at The Palmer House on November 2, 198—.

<u>Schedule</u>

- On Monday, November 1—Meeting Room classroom style 3:30 P.M.–7:30 P.M.
- Our Tuesday schedule will be as follows:

8:00 A.M.	Continental Breakfast
9:00 A.M.	General Meeting
10:30 A.M.	Coffee Break
12:00 Noon	Lunch
1:30 P.M.	General Meeting
2:30 P.M.	Breakout Rooms
4:30 P.M.	Reception (2 hours)

<u>Conference Room(s) - For full day meeting</u>

- We would like to have our main meeting room arranged in a U-shape formation.
- Please set up the main conference room on Monday evening.
- Water, glasses, ashtrays, etc. should be placed on tables.
- Please deliver instructional supply boxes to the room on Monday P.M.

- Extra table will be needed in front of room for instructional supplies, and overhead projector.
- Two (2) breakout rooms available from 1:30 P.M. to 4:30 P.M.

Audio Visual Aids

- We will need one easel board/pad in the main conference room.
- We will need an overhead projector and portable screen (with extra bulb).
- We will need two (2) 19″ color monitors and 3/4″ VCR playback equipped with a network distributor in main room.
- One lavalier mike in main room.

Lodging

- You have already received our rooming list.
- All attendees will pay their own room accounts, <u>EXCEPT</u> those designated as <u>Training Team.</u> (They will be on the master billing.)

Meal Arrangements

- A Continental Breakfast will be set up inside main meeting room by 8:00 A.M.
- Lunch will be held from 12:00 to 1:30 P.M. in a private dining room. Deli buffets are to be served, with a choice of beverages (no liquor).

Refreshments

- Please provide the following refreshments in the <u>rear</u> of the conference rooms.

8:00 A.M.	Coffee, Tea, Sanka, Danish (or choice), juice. (Continental Breakfast)
10:00 A.M.	Coffee, Tea, Sanka
1:30 P.M.	Assortment of sodas and coffee in each of 3 rooms (15 people in each room)

Reception

- A separate room, ready by 4:30 for approximately 50 people (exact number to be supplied on October 29).
- Name-brand liquors and beers will be used.
- One bartender for the two hours.
- Hors d'oeuvres have already been selected (hot and cold).

Billings

- All conference expenditures should be placed on master bill and itemized. That would include conference rooms, audio visual aids, refreshments, luncheons, etc. All lodging and incidentals will be the responsibility of the conferees. Please remind your checkout personnel of this request. Only Jim Martin can authorize expenditures to master bill.
- Please forward itemized statement to my attention:

Messages

- Please remind your telephone operator that our session is not to be interrupted by telephone messages. Please record messages and place them outside conference door.

Instructional Supplies

- Instructional supplies are being delivered to hotel prior to the seminar. They will be addressed to you and marked "Hold for Jim Martin." Please deliver to conference room on Monday evening.

Miscellaneous

- Please list the following on the lobby bulletin board:

General Electric Credit Corporation

Marian, thank you for making the arrangements for us on this seminar. If I have overlooked any additional details, please let me know.

Sincerely,

Richard P. Slowitsky
Mgr.-Education & Training
C & I Financing Division

RPS/mp
cc: G. L. Walters
    D. N. Chichester
    J. P. Martin

SECTION 46:   WHEN THINGS GO WELL

Successful meetings don't just happen. They are the result of a lot of hard work by a few people. When you have a meeting and it goes well, be sure to thank those who are responsible for your triumph. You may need them again.

Points to Remember

- Keep all your records for future use.
- Write notes of appreciation promptly.

WELL-PLANNED MEETING—1
TYM1

Dear Jim:

The visit of the Board of Directors and certain members of our Management Group to Joliet on Tuesday, April 6, 198__, was successful beyond our expectations. Recognizing that the logistical arrangements involved in such an operation would tax the ingenuity and patience of even the best of planners and/or coordinators, I was frankly not prepared for such a smooth operation.

That the individual groups involved had spent hours in preparing for us was quite evident; but I realize that in all such matters it inevitably falls to one individual to coordinate the various phases of the program and make certain that everything fits together perfectly. (Name) assures me that you had that assignment.

Under the circumstances, I felt impelled to drop you this note of appreciation for all of your efforts in our behalf, and to commend you on a job well done.

With kindest personal regards.

Sincerely yours,

WELL-PLANNED MEETING—2
TYM2

Dear John:

This year's annual meeting was not only the largest but also the most challenging that we have experienced in a long, long time. From the moment it was over until today, outsiders have congratulated me on the "success" of the whole occasion. I am sure this praise will continue for weeks to come.

You and I both know that credit is due not to any one person but to all of you who worked harder than usual and under greater pressures than in prior years. It was a job well done and I want to thank you from the bottom of my heart for your tireless and selfless effort.

Sincerely,

WELL-PLANNED MEETING—3
TYM3

Dear Austin:

The sales meeting in New Orleans was a success! Every time you organize a sales meeting, it shows the attention to planning and detail that have become a hallmark of your work.

The participants were able to concentrate on the material presented because the sessions moved along with precision. The speakers were well prepared and the audio visuals were excellent.

These things do not just happen, Austin; you and your staff work hard to make it look easy. I know how hard it is because I tried it. You make the company look good.

I appreciate the effort and will sing your praises in the proper ears.

Cordially,

Jim

THANK YOU FOR EXCELLENT HOTEL SERVICE
TEHS

Mr. Hilary:

How lucky you and I are that Janet Hunter works for the Ambassador East! Janet handled the arrangements for room accommodations for all the relatives and friends coming in for my wedding on 9/11/8—. I had to deal with many different types of suppliers in arranging that weekend and, believe me, Janet outshines them all.

Janet not only professionally handled all the many additions/deletions and other changes without a single mix-up, but her sincere concern that all go well was so impressive. She added a warmth to the excellent quality of service. I don't remember all that much of the actual wedding, but I definitely remember Janet and that personal touch she provided to the weekend.

The rooms were fabulous and everyone raved. You certainly have many new marketers of the Ambassador East and I certainly intend to use you for both my business and personal guests in the future. Janet Hunter deserves the credit, and I wanted you to hear from someone who is extremely pleased and very grateful.

Sincerely,

Holly Bernstein

cc: David Colella
    Resident Manager

REQUESTING PRICE CONSIDERATION FOR ROOMS
RPCR

Attention: General Manager

Dear Sir:

Our agreement for Flight Crew Accommodations will be up for review in April 198—, at which time consideration for extending the agreement will be evaluated.

This is an excellent opportunity for us to thank you for the service and hospitality that you have provided to our flight crews, and, at the same time, to solicit your assistance in investigating means of reducing or maintaining our costs in this area during the next year.

During these times of high inflation and economic recession, the cost of crew accommodations is an area of great concern to United Airlines. We believe that our method of contracting for crew rooms offers you benefits in forecasting and planning your financial outlook for the year. In reviewing your room rate pricing for the next year, please consider the advantages of this "pre-sold" business, and any other suggestions that you may have to permit us to hold-the-line in this cost area.

I'll be contacting you in the next few weeks to discuss our current contract terms, and hope that you will have some concrete cost-reduction ideas for our discussion.

Meanwhile, we appreciate your continued interest in being of service to United Airlines.

Sincerely,

Michael A. Matthews
Purchasing Department

MAM:lr

THANKS TO CLIENT
TYTC

Dear Ms. White:

I wish to express my sincere appreciation and that of the management of the Walton Towers for the privilege of hosting your regional sales meeting and banquet.

It was an honor for all of us that you chose our facilities for this company meeting, and we hope that everyone was thoroughly satisfied with the service rendered by our staff.

Our meeting rooms, banquet and dining room, and our recreational facilities were planned to provide the ultimate in comfort and relaxation to visiting business guests.

I would be very happy to have the pleasure of assisting you on plans for future meetings and hope that you will feel free to call on me whenever I can be of service.

Thank you for your patronage.

Sincerely,

SECTION 47: WHEN THINGS GO WRONG AT MEETINGS

1.	Poor Service	POOR
2.	Apology for Poor Service	APOR
3.	Complaint—Lack of Service	LASE
4.	Lack of Service—Response	LSRE
5.	Beds Not Comfortable	BEDS
6.	Beds Not Comfortable—Response	BERE
7.	Reservations Not Held	RENH
8.	Reservations Not Held—Response	RNHR
9.	Rooms Not Ready	RONR
10.	Rooms Not Ready—Response	RNRR
11.	Room Reservations for Dealers	RRFD
12.	Room Reservations for Dealers—Response	RRES

If things go wrong . . . write. The management of every hotel or motel knows that their success or failure is based on pleasing their customers. They will make every effort to improve their service, but they will not know of your experience unless you tell them. Write to the general manager if you cannot resolve your problems with the hotel personnel. You can be assured that the matter will be investigated.

Points to Remember

- Be sure that you are not asking for the impossible when dealing with hotel employees. They cannot be held responsible for planes that arrive late or guests who linger too long.
- They should be expected to provide you with comfortable, clean accommodations and courteous service.

POOR SERVICE
POOR

Dear Miss Bailey:

Murphy's Law was working overtime on Friday when I arrived for my afternoon seminar.

I came a little early to make sure everything was ready and everything was wrong! Instead of four tables for eight, three tables for ten had been set up. As I explained to you, we wanted to foster small discussion groups and needed four tables. There also was no table for the speakers.

The sign in the lobby as well as the one outside the door had my name on it instead of the company name. Several of the guests had never heard of me, so this was very confusing.

Finally, the refreshments I had ordered were not available.

Since it was your day off, I spoke to the women who had just finished setting the tables, and they tried their best to set things right. Still, we were all left scurrying about when the seminar guests were arriving.

The sign in the lobby never did get changed, and the refreshments arrived noticeably late.

Since I made the arrangements with you months in advance and called two days before to confirm all the details, I was extremely disappointed that everything was handled so poorly.

Gayle Griffin

APOLOGY FOR POOR SERVICE
APOR

Dear Miss Griffin:

I goofed! I have to take full responsibility for all the things that went wrong at your seminar.

When we discussed all the details, I wrote everything down and then simply forgot to pass along the instructions to the set-up crew. The only information they had was your name, the number of guests, and the time of the meeting. So they just set up as best they could.

I am terribly sorry that my error caused such confusion. Please accept my apology and a gift certificate for lunch for two in our Fireside Room. I hope that you will give us another opportunity to serve you.

Sandra Bailey

COMPLAINT—LACK OF SERVICE
LASE

Dear Mr. Goodman:

We were very disappointed with the lack of service and cooperation we received from your sales manager, Mr. Jones, last Thursday evening when we had a sales conference/dinner meeting at your hotel.

For the past two years, Ms. Jane Brown of your sales staff handled our arrangements and our meetings were a success. This year, we asked for her again. However, Mr. Jones told us that he was her superior and he would be our contact and make every effort to give us good service. Unfortunately, he did not do so.

Our biggest problem was his lack of concern and availability. He made it clear that he was very busy and he was not confined to our group. We had to suffer through delay, no microphone, shortage of waiters to serve dinner, and his arrogant attitude.

We think that his cutting in on the clients of other hotel employees is unprofessional and his lack of concern for your guests is detrimental.

Sincerely,

LACK OF SERVICE—RESPONSE
LSRE

Dear Ms. Brennan:

Thank you for taking time to write to me regarding your recent experience at the _____ Inn. Frankly, I am embarrassed to read of the unprofessionalism of our sales manager, Mr. Jones.

Please let me assure you that I will personally meet with the General Manager of this _____ Inn. Steps will be taken to see that the employees will handle their positions properly. In the future, you can be sure that your service at _____ Inn will be up to the high standards that you are accustomed to enjoying.

Your comments are greatly appreciated. Thank you for your continued patronage.

Sincerely,

BEDS NOT COMFORTABLE
BEDS

Dear Mr. Jones,

In all our planning for the Carpet Manufacturers Convention, it never occurred to me to inquire about the comfort of the beds in your hotel. I assumed the mattresses would be satisfactory. I was wrong. I had no fewer than seventeen complaints from our conventioneers. If just one or two had complained, I would not have put much stock in their opinions. With so many, however, I think there must be something to it.

I happen to be one of those people who can sleep on a picket fence, but it seems that your hotel should be able to better accommodate comfort seekers. This matter reflects badly on both of us.

Bob Smythe

BEDS NOT COMFORTABLE—RESPONSE
BERE

Dear Mr. Smythe,

We were very pleased to accommodate your convention. I am sorry that some of your guests found the beds uncomfortable.

All of our rooms are equipped with high-quality, orthopedic mattresses. We buy only the top-of-the-line brand-name merchandise. However, the idea of what is comfortable is always a very personal matter. It is never possible to please everyone with a bed that is just as firm or as soft as the one he or she is accustomed to.

We understand that seventeen complaints certainly are a lot for you to have endured. We hope that you will accept the enclosed gift certificate for dinner for two in our Starlight Room restaurant. Perhaps an evening of fine food and soothing music will help make up for some of the annoyance you experienced.

We hope to be able to serve you again in the near future.

Stanley L. Jones

RESERVATIONS NOT HELD
RENH

Dear Sirs:

Please have a meeting of your employees and explain to them that you are in the hotel business and that without guests in the hotel there will be no jobs for them.

We have just returned from a sales meeting held in the _____ Hotel where the service was poor and the employee attitude was worse.

We booked our reservations six months ago, confirmed the rooms two weeks ago, and yet half of our dealers had to be sent to a nearby hotel because their rooms were not held for them.

The desk clerk admitted that they had oversold reservations expecting no-shows and that since there were no no-shows, rooms were assigned as guests checked in.

Since we are manufacturers who arranged the meeting so that our sales representatives and our dealers could mingle freely when our meetings were not in session, having half of our dealers housed in another hotel was very frustrating.

We are not members of the _____ Association, but we do sell to the members. We planned our meeting in order to see our customers and prospective buyers when they were in town.

I complained to the clerk at the reservation desk, to the manager on duty, and to the sales department. They all acted bored and disinterested. If they continue with this attitude, I am sure they won't be oversold in the future.

Yours truly,

RESERVATIONS NOT HELD—RESPONSE
RNHR

Dear Mr. Green:

Your letter of complaint has been forwarded to me from our corporate headquarters. We are sorry that you were not satisfied with the service you received in our hotel on June 16.

I talked to the assistant manager who was on duty when you checked in and with the reservation clerk who handled your party. They both have told me that the inconvenience was unavoidable because you had not put a deposit on the rooms you reserved and that, without a deposit, they could not hold the rooms for your arrival.

As you stated in your letter, you arranged your meeting to coincide with the convention of the _____ Association, headquartered in the hotel from June 13 through the 17. Our sales representative, who talked to you in March, explained that you could ensure the rooms being available by sending a deposit of one night's charges. You chose not to do so. We had paid reservations at the check-in desk before your arrival. We had to release the rooms we were holding. But our staff did call a nearby hotel and secured accommodations for you.

We hope that you will return to _____ Hotel on your future visits to Phoenix and we hope you will understand our policy of honoring paid reservations as the fairest way to accommodate our guests.

Very truly yours,

ROOMS NOT READY
RONR

Dear Mr. La Beau,

Monday, June 25, when our members began arriving to attend the two-day seminar for which you made the arrangements, our rooms were not available.

As you were not present, I had to deal with Sam Dennis, who, although accommodating, was not at all familiar with our plans. He offered those who were waiting free cocktails in the lounge, but what we all really wanted was to be in our own rooms. What went wrong? How do I make this up to our members, who now think of me as a bungler?

Jack McDonald

ROOMS NOT READY—RESPONSE
RNRR

Dear Mr. McDonald,

We are very sorry about the problem of the rooms not being ready for your group. Sam Dennis tells me that the conventioneers who were to vacate your rooms on the morning of the 25th did not check out on time. He notified them that reservations were being held for those rooms and they did check out. However, as you know, they did not give our maids enough time to prepare the rooms for your arrival.

Occasionally, when all our rooms are booked and guests do not check out when expected, we have this delay problem. To offer complimentary refreshments to the waiting guests is our policy. So Sam did just what I would have done. Except, of course, that he could not extend to you my sincere apology, which I do now.

I hope that you will visit us again, and we will make every effort to see that you and your guests are accommodated promptly and comfortably.

Phillip La Beau

ROOM RESERVATIONS FOR DEALERS
RRFD

Dear Ms. Greene:

Last year, we ordered a block of rooms for our dealers as we have done every year for the Electronic Show. For some reason, there was a lot of confusion at the desk when they checked in. Please help us to avoid problems because our dealers are our guests and we want the meeting to be as congenial and friendly as possible when they are in the city.

We want to reserve:
- 40 double rooms for 2 nights—March 10 and 11
- 20 double rooms for 1 night—March 10
- 20 double rooms for 1 night—March 11

This will be a total of sixty rooms for each night. However, some dealers will be present for one night. This is the reason we want twenty double rooms for each night. The occupants will change, but the rooms will still be charged to our account.

We will send a list of guests' names the week before the show to help you cross-reference the reservations. If the guests ask for rooms in our name or in their own names, you will be able to check them in quickly.

If you need further information, please contact me.

Sincerely,

ROOM RESERVATIONS FOR DEALERS—RESPONSE
RRES

Dear Mr. Jones:

It is a pleasure to know that you will again be the guests of ——————— Hotel. We have enjoyed having you and your dealers in the hotel during the Electronics Show and we are making every effort to ensure that your guests will be well treated.

There was confusion at the check-in last year, but we feel that if you provide a list of your dealers this will not recur. The problem was that some dealers asked for rooms without using your company name and we were not prepared to sign them in. The cross-reference of dealer/company reservation cards will eliminate this.

Thank you again for your continued patronage. We look forward to seeing you in March.

Cordially,

SECTION 48:   INVITING SPEAKERS TO MEETING

1.	To Business Meeting	SPME
2.	To Speak at Seminar	SPSE
3.	To Speak at Luncheon	SPAL

Whether you are putting together a local meeting or an international symposium, you will increase attendance and generate interest if you present guests who are well informed and witty. Those who are well informed make it worthwhile. Those who are witty make it enjoyable. Try to balance the speakers to include the views of the entire membership rather than the views of the committee.

Points to Remember

- Know "what's hot and what's not."
- Invite those who will have something new to say.
- Pique interest through controversy.
- Give speakers plenty of time to arrange their calendars to include your meeting.

TO BUSINESS MEETING
SPME

Dear Glenn:

The Greater Association of Home Builders is having a three day meeting in conjunction with our Festival of Homes Show this Spring. The meeting will begin on April 23, 198__, and close with an awards luncheon on April 25, 198__.

Because everyone in the business community is interested in the plans the city has for development of the expressway corridor, you were the unanimous choice for chairman of the panel that will discuss this subject.

We have not scheduled the other sessions yet because we wanted to give you the first choice of days and time for your appearance. However, we do hope that you will be able to be with us on April 25 for the morning session. This will ensure a larger number of guests for our luncheon meeting on that day.

We will sincerely appreciate an early reply.

Cordially,

TO SPEAK AT SEMINAR
SPSE

Dear Ms. Heim:

Last spring I had the privilege of hearing you speak at a business luncheon in Rock Falls and was impressed by your charm and wit. It is now my task to organize a seminar for the Professional Women of Oswego and you are the first one I thought to invite. I would be honored to have you participate as a speaker.

The meeting will take place on Tuesday, September 21, 198__ at the Emerald Country Club in Oswego from 9:00 A.M. until 3:00 P.M. I would like you to speak at the morning session because your sparkling personality will help set the tone of the meeting.

The enclosed fact sheet will give you all of the information about the meeting and the goals we hope to achieve. There is also a list of suggested topics. The deadline for material to be included in the brochure we are preparing for mailing is June 1, 198__. We look forward to receiving your acceptance in time to include your name in the mailer.

Please don't disappoint me.

Cordially,

**TO SPEAK AT LUNCHEON
SPAL**

Dear John:

Our local chapter of the Jaycees is having a membership luncheon at the Hyatt Regency Hotel on October 23, 198_. The Hyatt Regency is pretty heady for our budget, and we would like to ensure a large attendance.

We would appreciate it if you could regale us with stories of your trip to New Caledonia on a tramp steamer. I'm sure that more than half of the population has dreamed of chucking it all and going to the South Seas. Your trip had all of the adventure and hilarity of a good old movie. Won't you share it with us?

In anticipation of your talk, I'm going to invite everyone I know to attend. Please don't disappoint me.

Cordially,

B O O K 6

SPECIAL SITUATIONS: PERSONAL LETTERS WHEN NO ORDINARY LETTER WILL DO

SECTION 49: LETTERS FOR SPECIAL SITUATIONS

There are many special situations that are so unusual you cannot categorize them. These letters are examples of such situations and how they were handled. We have included them because they are unique and because they are well written.

Points to Remember

- Whenever you are preparing a letter that is not routine, review the circumstances before you write.
- Make a list of the points you want to cover or the message you want to convey.
- To whatever extent you can do so, make the letter an extension of your personality and use the opportunity to express your feelings to the reader.

LETTER ACCOMPANYING REQUESTED INFORMATION
IINF

Dear Mr. Green:

In response to your phone call, please find enclosed information on the incentive program of the Republic of Ireland.

Over 350 North American corporations have set up manufacturing facilities in the Republic of Ireland in recent years. Ireland has continued to be the most profitable location in the world for American investment, giving an average return of over 31% per annum for the last five years.

A summary of the incentives is to be found on page 3 of the booklet, "Industrial Development in Ireland."

If you require any further information, please let me know.

Best wishes,

Yours sincerely,

INDUSTRIAL DEVELOPMENT AUTHORITY
IRELAND

Director/Midwest U.S.A.

FOLLOW-UP LETTER AFTER MEETING
AFTR

Dear Mr. Green:

Thank you for meeting with me during my recent visit to Wisconsin.

I have written to my colleagues in Dublin and have requested the shipping information that we discussed.

Enclosed is a brochure, "The Technical Environment in Ireland for High Technology Industry," which I thought might further underline my statements about the availability of the types of skilled and semiskilled mechanical workers you would require in Ireland.

If you could possibly visit Ireland for a few days to see the situation there at first hand, I can guarantee you that your time will not be misspent.

When we have the information that you requested, I will call you.

Yours sincerely,

INDUSTRIAL DEVELOPMENT AUTHORITY
IRELAND

Director/Midwest U.S.A.

**SUMMARY OF SUPPORT AVAILABLE
AVAL**

Dear Mr. Green:

It was a pleasure meeting with you when I visited Michigan recently. There is definitely some potential for your company to do business in Ireland to service your growing European market. The Industrial Development Authority of Ireland will be very pleased to work with you in pursuing this objective.

In general, Ireland's attractions can be summarized as follows:

1. Ireland is the most profitable location in the world for U.S. manufacturing subsidiaries.

2. Well-established communications and transportation systems provide easy access to mainland Europe tariff free.

3. Irish labor rates are the most competitive in the E.E.C. (approximately $5 per hour including fringe benefits) for semiskilled persons.

4. Industrial relations in manufacturing industry in Ireland are excellent. (Ninety-five percent of U.S. companies in Ireland have never had an industrial dispute.)

5. Ireland offers a business environment unmatched in Europe where "Private Enterprise Is Public Policy."

In particular, Ireland offers the most attractive financial incentive program in Europe. It includes:

1. A maximum corporate tax rate of 10% until the year 2000.

2. Substantial capital grants toward the cost of your fixed asset investment.

3. 100% training grants.

4. Low cost finance availability from the Irish banking system.

If you will send me a brief outline of the potential project—i.e., product, job potential, capital investment, and size of buildings needed—I will draw up a complete financial package for your consideration so that you can assess the idea of manufacturing overseas in a more meaningful manner.

I look forward to hearing from you.

Yours sincerely,

INDUSTRIAL DEVELOPMENT AUTHORITY
IRELAND

Director/Midwest U.S.A.

OFFER OF SUPPORT TO COMPANY
SUPP

Dear Mr. Green:

Thank you very much indeed for the recent opportunity to meet with you and to discuss Ireland's continuing program for industrial development. I have pleasure in summarizing the major elements in my Government's support program for the establishment in Ireland of a Consulting Engineering business such as yours.

1. Ireland is a full member of the European Common Market and this provides for a market place of 270 million people freely accessible to your professional services.

2. Direct Government support includes very generous nonrepayable cash grants on office and equipment expenditure.

3. Maximum Corporation Taxation Rate of 10%, guaranteed until the end of the year 2000.

4. A young, adaptable, and productive labor force.

5. A very well developed educational network, which is currently producing far more business, architectural, engineering and computer science graduates than the current job market requires.

6. Our training grants provide for full 100% reimbursement of salaries and all related expenditures for approved training programs for all your personnel needs.

The Republic of Ireland is enjoying very considerable success from U.S. business investments. Because of our profitability and competitive cost structure, the past five years have seen U.S. investment in Ireland grow by 38% each year. This pace of commitment represents three and a half times the European average for similar investment.

I enclose, as requested, details of some of Ireland's Consulting Engineering Companies, who could be of interest to you as potential joint venture partners. We would be delighted to arrange an itinerary for you to visit Ireland, to meet with some of these companies, and to see at first hand the potential opportunities that await you in an international context.

I will remain in regular contact with you.

Yours sincerely,

INDUSTRIAL DEVELOPMENT AUTHORITY
IRELAND

Director, Midwest/U.S.A.

THANK YOU JEWEL COMPANIES
TYJC

Dear Mr. Beckner:

An oasis in the middle of the desert was never a more welcome sight to a thirsty traveler than one of your stores was to me Wednesday night during the snow storm.

About 11 P.M., after inching along for over six hours from my office near the Loop toward my home in Park Ridge, I had just about run out of gas and out of ideas about how to sustain myself through the cold night. Suddenly I found myself near the Jewel Food Store at 3400 North Western Avenue, lighted up and open. I left my car and went in. Along with about eighty other people, I was made welcome, given hot coffee in the employees' lunch room, and permitted to remain through the night.

Mr. Beckner, I have to admit that, stranded and cold in my car in a strange neighborhood, I had a feeling almost of panic, knowing I could not get home and couldn't even send for help. But once I was inside your store, I felt as though I was back in the real world after waking up from a nightmare.

The manager of that store and some of his staff had been at work since early Wednesday morning and must have been as tired and weary as we stranded motorists were. Yet without exception they responded to our predicament as though it were all part of their day's work. Everyone was gracious and pleasant and helpful. What had started out as a grim night became a heart-warming experience as a friendly camaraderie grew among all of us. It is good to know that there are people who care, people who are willing to get involved.

I resolved that I wouldn't let the occasion slip by without some word of appreciation. Through this letter to you, Mr. Beckner, I want to express my thanks to the manager of that store and to all his staff, who remained on duty throughout the night. I congratulate you on having such fine people to represent your company.

Very truly yours,

Garrett P. Walters
President

YOU'RE WELCOME JEWEL COMPANIES
YWJC

Dear Mr. Walters:

I certainly appreciate your taking the time to drop us your comments on your experience at the Jewel Food Stores at 3400 North Western Avenue during the blizzard last week.

It is very gratifying for me to learn of the help that we were able to provide to you and nearly eighty other people. It is particularly helpful to be able to forward your comments to the Resident Supervisor for the store, Dick Bike, as well as making them available to many thousands of other Jewel Food Store people to reinforce their desire to perform services such as this, which has been a cornerstone of our business for over forty years.

In my association with Jewel in the food business, I am continually amazed at the role the supermarket plays in the well-being and daily life of our metropolitan area. As our people recognize the importance of their business to the well-being of millions of people, which is dramatized by unique situations such as this, it provides the incentive for us to do an even better job.

Thank you for helping us provide that dramatization.

Yours truly,

Harry G. Beckner

HGB/ew

ASKING CUSTOMER TO ASSIST COMPANY IN DISTRESS STRS

Dear SDS Customer:

I hoped that this would never happen, but our company is in trouble. After about a year, we still haven't acquired enough customers in Naperville and the surrounding areas to support this service. I know that most of you have enjoyed this service and want it to continue, so I am asking you for your help.

As you know, the best and most effective form of advertising is a referral from a satisfied customer to a friend, neighbor, or business owner who could use our services. What we need is at least 500 additional customers within the next 60 days. It sounds like a lot, and it is, but if you will help support me, I will always be indebted to you and will try my utmost to give you the very best in service.

I've taken the liberty of enclosing several of our new brochures. Please pass them on to your friends, neighbors, or any business owners who could use our services, and tell them how you've enjoyed our services. If they would prefer, we will call them. Just give Carol their phone numbers.

We believe in the American way of being able to start your own business, but we need your help. Please support us.

Sincerely,

SDS SALT DELIVERY SERVICE

Gary and Carol Crytser

Enclosures

ASKING SUPPLIER TO TRACE INFORMATION LEAK
STIL

Dear Walt:

Take your Sherlock Holmes cap out of your bottom drawer. You and I have a case to solve. Our competition is getting information on our products that gives them an unfair advantage. Is it possible that you can help us trace this source?

We have tried to find the leak in our office and plant without success. Our next step is to check outside. Is it possible that you have an employee who is too familiar with our drawings? Before we change suppliers in our effort to eliminate this piracy, I thought I would alert you to our problem.

It is seriously affecting our business and giving our staff nightmares. Because what affects us affects you, I know you will probe deeply to uncover unauthorized use of our drawings or product information. If you have any information, I will hold it in strictest confidence until you are able to act on it. If you do not find anything, we will look further. I have complete confidence in your judgment and will cooperate with you if you have any suggestions.

Sincerely,

NOTICE OF PLANT CLOSING
PLNT

Dear John:

This letter is a confirmation of the rumors and speculation that have been circulating throughout the company for the past several months. We have decided to close the Kinzie plant.

I am as sorry as you are to see Kinzie close, but there is nothing else that can be done. And, there is no painless way for us to go through it. We have just received the report of the survey taken to determine the feasibility of renovation and modernization of the plant and equipment. As you and I had predicted, it showed that the market is no longer viable in that area. The costs would not be justified in view of the limited return on investment.

Once the decision is announced, I am sure you will agree, the more quickly we phase out the operation, the less anguish the employees will have to endure. For this reason, we will have a team of management personnel assigned to help you in the closing process.

Business is very slow at this time; therefore, we will not be able to absorb many people on your payroll. To whatever extent it is possible, we will consider each employee on an individual basis. Those who are not transferred will be assisted in looking for new jobs. In addition to our company Personnel Department, we are planning to hire consultants who specialize in out-placement, to test, screen, and advise those who will be terminated.

As soon as the details are worked out, I will send a letter to authorize you to make the announcement. Until that time, I will keep you posted as soon as I have any new information.

If there is anything I can be glad about at this time, it is that you and Anne are planning to retire to Arizona and are waiting for the completion of your home before taking your pension. I am sure that we can work out a leave of absence or a temporary transfer to make the dates coincide.

I have only one more thing to ask you at this time. Think about me when you are riding around on your golf cart in all that sunshine. I'll certainly be thinking about you.

Regards.

NEW LINE FOR EUROPEAN MARKET
NEUM

Dear Harry:

Recently when we met for lunch, you expressed an interest in having our sales representative distribute your products to our European market.

We discussed it and see no conflict with our present product lines. On Wednesday, we will be meeting for lunch at the City Club to discuss a sales trip two of our members will be taking next month. Why don't you join us? We will be talking about the itinerary of the representatives and the clients they will be calling on.

We are planning to meet at 1:00 P.M. and hope to see you then.

Cordially,

Warren

INVITATION TO TOUR FACTORY
ITOF

Dear Warren:

Thanks very much for the invitation to lunch with you next Wednesday. I have another engagement that makes it impossible for me to join you.

It would be better for me to have you and your sales staff tour our factory and see how our products are manufactured. I know that this is telescoping the process a little, but I would rather have the people who sell the line know as much as possible about it before we proceed.

Let me know when it would be convenient for you to come to the plant, and I will arrange a tour. It will start with the incoming material and end with the product going out the door. Then, we can talk about the market we are targeting. It should give the sales people the information needed to launch an effective campaign.

I am looking forward to our association and hope that it will be mutually beneficial.

Cordially,

Harry

POWER OF ATTORNEY
PATT

POWER OF ATTORNEY

I, John Carlisle, of Fresno, California, am the sole proprietor of the Acme Furniture Refinishing and Antique Company of Fresno, California (The Company). I am about to leave the United States on an extended buying trip and will be unavailable to conduct my business for two months. For that reason, I appoint my trusted employee Philip More of Fresno, California, as attorney-in-fact for me from _____, 19__, to _____, 19__.

In my name, he shall have the following powers:

1.   To write checks or withdraw sums from the company account at the Greater Savings Bank in order to pay bills and debts that come due during my absence.

2.   To endorse and negotiate or deposit any checks, drafts, notes, or other instruments made payable to the company.

3.   To renegotiate the terms of Certificate of Deposit No. _____ issued by the Greater Savings Bank to me and scheduled to mature on _____, 19__.

4.   To negotiate and sign any and all contracts relating to the conduct of business and to the repair and maintenance of the building, grounds, and trucks of the business.

5.   To have access to any safe deposit box rented by me (including authority to have it drilled) and to remove the contents therefrom.

6.   To do all other acts reasonably necessary to protect my interests and those of the Acme Furniture Refinishing and Antique Company.

Every bank or other financial institution, insurance company, transfer agent, supplier, customer or other person, firm or corporation to which this power of attorney or a photocopy hereof is presented is authorized to receive, honor, and give effect to all instruments signed pursuant to the foregoing authority without inquiring as to the circumstances of their issuance or the disposition of the property delivered pursuant thereto. If permitted by law, this power of attorney shall not be affected by my disability. All acts done hereunder by my attorney-in-fact after revocation of this power of attorney or after my death shall be valid and enforceable in favor of anyone who relies on this power of attorney and has not received prior actual written notice of the revocation or death. All acts done by my attorney-in-fact pursuant to this power shall be binding upon me and my heirs, legatees, and legal representatives.

The following is a specimen of the signature of my attorney-in-fact:

_____
Philip More

IN WITNESS WHEREOF I have signed this power of attorney this _____ day of _____, 19___.

_____
John Carlisle

STATE OF CALIFORNIA
COUNTY OF _____

I, _____, Notary Public, hereby certify that John Carlisle, personally known to me to be the same person whose name is signed to the foregoing instrument, appeared before me this day in person and acknowledged that he signed the instrument as his free and voluntary act, for the uses and purposes therein set forth.

Given under my hand and official seal this _____ day of _____.

_____
NOTARY PUBLIC

My commission expires _____.

SECTION 50:   GOODWILL LETTERS

The theme of this book is "Put It in Writing" and we have tried to address every aspect of your business writing. However, your business and your personal life are so intertwined that we had to include a few of the personal letters you will need for special occasions.

The first two letters of condolence were provided by Rita Joyce Downs, and we are very grateful to her for these beautiful examples of comfort and compassion that dwell on the positive values of life. When you have to send a note of sympathy, express your feelings sincerely and base your letter on your relationship to the deceased. The letter need not be long. In fact, a few sentences of genuine sympathy and understanding are all that is necessary.

The letter referring to divorce is unusual, but divorce is so much a part of the fabric of life that people sometimes forget that it hurts. Be sure that you know the person well before you attempt to write this kind of letter. There are times when it will help a friend and times when it will smooth the road.

Points to Remember

- Do not put off writing a personal note until it loses its effectiveness.
- Let your letter be a personal visit. Do not be afraid to let down your mask and show the warmth of your personality to a friend.
- Be enthusiastic when you write letters of congratulations.

CONDOLENCE—FATHER
COFA

Dear Jack:

I was not surprised to hear of your father's death, but I was deeply grieved. I had known him for many years and considered him one of my dearest friends. One thing that I always admired about him was that he was always quiet and unassuming. He never spoke unless he had something to say; a gentleman in every sense of the word. He was always devoted to your mother and to his family. But, you know all of this, so why waste words telling you. His death to me was like a landmark falling into the sea.

You may rest assured that I will remember him in my poor prayers, but if there is really a heaven, I am sure he is there. If he isn't, the rest of us don't stand a chance.

I cannot wish you a Merry Christmas at this time, but I hope that everything good will come to you in the new year.

Fondest regards to you both.

As always,

CONDOLENCE—FATHER—2
COFA2

Dear Jack:

Permit me to put into writing what I could not express to you verbally when you were in the office. My heart was filled with compassion and sadness over the loss of your father. I could not get the words out to express my sorrow. I know what it means to lose a beloved parent.

I shall always remember your father with admiration and affection. He had the sterling qualities so sadly lacking in some leaders.

Your father left you a fine heritage. It must have been a source of pride to him to know that you are making your own contributions in the same field.

Sincerely,

CONDOLENCE—HUSBAND
CHUS

Dear Mrs. Carroll:

The news of your husband's sudden death shocked all of us. Bill was a terrific man. Not many men have achieved as high a position and remained as charming and understanding.

Everyone who knew Bill knew of his devotion to you and to your children. We know that this love is the strength that will sustain you at this time of sorrow.

We will help in any way that we can. Please feel free to call for information or assistance in filing for his company benefits.

Sincerely,

CONDOLENCE—HUSBAND
CHUS2

Dear Mrs. Smith:

John's death has left us all in a state of shock. He was so healthy and robust looking that his heart attack seems harder to understand.

We do not want to intrude upon your family sorrow at this time, but we do want to offer to help in any way we can. It is possible that there are questions regarding company benefits and insurance that you will need to discuss.

Carl Gordon of the personnel office will be in touch with you shortly. However, if you need information or assistance, please call on anyone in the office. We have all been touched with grief by John's death. Helping his family would give us a way to express our feelings at this time.

Sincerely,

UNDERSTANDING OF DIVORCE
UNVE

Dear Leslie:

When you did not attend the reunion meeting, I understood that perhaps you would rather not answer questions. However, you need not have worried about it. People do not ask questions about divorce anymore.

We have all been ground up by the mill of the gods and there are few who would not admit to a few heartaches along the way.

So please don't think that your friends do not understand. We understand, as you have always understood. Don't make yourself so scarce. We miss seeing you.

Love,

GET WELL WISHES TO FRIEND
GETW

Dear Greg:

If good wishes will help to restore you, you will soon be checking out of that hospital. There are not enough smiling faces like yours in our grumpy day-to-day world. We cannot spare you for even a short time. So take your medicine and get on your feet. We miss you.

Best wishes,

INTRODUCTION
INTF

Dear Claire:

The company has transferred several of our sales reps. One of the nicest fellows in the firm is going to be in your area. He is a skier, plays volley ball, and loves to refinish old furniture. In fact, he is the one who helped me refinish the desk you admired.

His name is Don Jackson and he will probably call you. I hope you don't mind that I have given him your telephone number. He is single and a really great guy. You will have a lot in common.

If you would like to show your appreciation, please ship me one handsome replacement, air freight or best way.

Love,

REGRETS
REGR

Dear Bert:

Thanks very much for your invitation to attend the Open House celebrating the dedication of your new medical building. Unfortunately, Joan and I will be in Atlanta where I have to address a meeting on that day.

I do not want to let the fact that I will not be able to join you on Sunday keep me from telling you how much joy I get from your success. I know the years of work and study you spent preparing for this day.

Please accept my deepest wishes for your personal satisfaction in attaining your goal. It is so typical of you to dedicate the building to your parents. I will be over soon to see the facilities. I might even pass out cards in your waiting room.

Again, I wish you all of the success you so richly deserve.

Cordially,

Paul

CONGRATULATIONS—TALK
CTAK

Dear Gene:

Congratulations! The informative talk you gave to the Executive Club members on Friday was excellently prepared.

You were so surrounded by well wishers, I could not get close to you. I wanted to tell you that I enjoyed your presentation and was impressed by how you handled the controversial subject of foreign trade.

You were right on target. I'm sure you knew from the response of the members that they agreed with your views.

Keep up the good work!